THREE
BLIND
MICE

THREE
BLIND
MICE

HOW TODAY'S FINANCIAL
PLANNING PROCESS LEADS
YOUR MONEY TO A MOUSETRAP

SCOTT S. MCLEAN

ADVISORS' ACADEMY
PRESS

Published by
ADVISOR'S ACADEMY PRESS
Pompano Beach, Florida

ISBN 978-1-7341808-0-0

FIRST EDITION

Book Design by Neuwirth & Associates
Jacket Design by Germancreative

Manufactured in the United States

10 9 8 7 6 5 4 3 2 1

DISCLAIMER

The information contained in this book is for educational purposes only and should not be considered as specific planning advice.

FOREWORD

M oney is the *opposite* of the weather. Nobody talks about it, but everybody does something about it.

This probably applies to everyone, unless you live in sunny Death Valley, California, with 2.36 inches of rain per year. Just a tiny drop makes major headlines. But if you're one of those people who doesn't discuss money, that's about to change.

As we all know, money isn't everything; but it is right up there with really important stuff like breathing. And because the subject of money has both good and bad information being taught and even carried down through generations, you may wish to review these common statements and phrases and see if you are already subjective or biased on the subject of money.

Let's start with a question . . .

Are you Money Savvy or Financially Illiterate?

Consider the following common statements you may have heard or said before:

- Spend it, I'm only young once.
- It's only zero percent interest.
- I work hard and deserve it.
- I'm not sure what's in my bank account; my spouse deals with our finances and I don't know much about investing.
- My parent takes care of it for me.
- Investing is like gambling.
- I'll get to it later, and later never comes.

If you've ever uttered a variation of one of these phrases, this book is for you. If you've decided to take the bull by the horns and learn about your financial health, this book is for you. (The bull reference is not my idea of a financial pun, I promise. And if you don't get that little joke, all the more reason to keep reading.)

I'll show you that diving into your finances doesn't have to be painful. After you're done reading this book, big numbers will no longer scare you—at least, not too much. And you'll know the ins and outs of your personal wealth so well that your financial advisors will wonder as to whether you should start advising them instead.

Thanks for getting my book. As I enter my 37th year as a professional, I'm proud to share with you the common financial blunders, hiccups, screw-ups, and scams we have all done, heard about, or seen on a continual basis when it comes to the Three Blind Mice. As for the Three Blind Mice, well, the beat goes on—it's the same ol', same ol', as a simple shift in their practice could benefit others yet old-school practices continue at your risk.

Feel free to visit www.3Blindmice.com for great information and insight to protect and grow your hard-earned money.

WITH DEDICATION AND WARM APPRECIATION

Thanks, Denise, for your incredible patience and insight. To my best friend, confidante, and wife, truly the Proverbs 31 woman for her wisdom, insight, and understanding, allowing me to do what I love. Thanks to my children as my absence from writing this book has come to an end.

Dad and Mom, thanks for your tough love and guidance as you encouraged me to press on toward the higher calling so others can benefit greatly. Your sound instructions, love, and continued stern and warm prodding were appreciated. As I often think to myself, the older I get, the wiser you become. I can't wait to see you in heaven, but there's no rush, 1 John 5:13.

Sondra, my brilliant and loving sister with more degrees than a thermometer, thanks for your consistent encouragement for me to get better at whatever I tackle.

Now, thanks to all those who have truly shaped my career. Continually learning from you is a jet on the runway of achievement and personal growth. My utmost, sincere appreciation to my mentor, close friend, and "professor," Dave Scranton, and the Advisors Academy members. Dave, thanks for partnering with advisors and me around the country with one higher purpose in mind—to help thousands of families sleep well at night with less financial worry due to your sound retirement income strategies.

Also, thanks for allowing me to work with Michelle O'Halloran and Advisors Academy Press; this book would not exist without her tremendous enthusiasm and encouragement, as she saw a deep need for the

Three Blind Mice to work together and get this book out there for all to benefit from. Special thanks to Bill Johnson, teacher, advisor, writer, and author for your remarkable insight, guidance advice, and friendship during this journey. I cannot wait to barefoot water-ski with you.

Last but surely not least, my awesome staff. I'm so proud of them as they treat each and every client as a family member. They are so conscientious to their needs and concerns, which allows me to continue to serve new and current clients as well as help train others advisors throughout the country.

INTRODUCTION

Heading into my 37th year in professional practice, and going strong with 60 years of life experience, has enabled me to write a book that believes we all deserve and need the best advisors as we head toward retirement. With 75 million baby boomers in the United States alone, and many already in retirement, we *all* need advisors working together. Nothing is more frustrating than paying for three different professionals who are not on the same page. No one really wants their life savings in the hands of the Three Blind Mice.

I've heard "knowledge is power" but I disagree . . . I say "applied knowledge is power."

I trust those reading this will not only enjoy this book as a valuable experience, but will read it at least twice in order to gain deep insight. And the valuable information written inside. Please put into practice as many of the tips and strategic information as possible so you don't easily get entangled. There are many financial traps that are before us, but more importantly, I wrote this book so that you can avoid all the mouse traps that can so easily entangle you.

Now, I know that, as professionals, we are all swamped; so if I can persuade and encourage every lawyer, accountant, and financial professional to make an effort to work together, then this book has done some good. For those who work with their clients, please work harder to communicate with each other and with the other industries that service your client for the betterment of the client so they can sleep well at night knowing their financial and estate affairs hum like Beethoven's Fifth Symphony far exceeding fiduciary responsibility and achieving a beautiful financial masterpiece.

TABLE OF TRAPS

CHAPTER 2
Trap #2: Perceptions And Deceptions Of Risk And Reward; You May Not Want The Biggest Piece Of Cheese **39**

CHAPTER 3
Trap #3: The Destructive Time And Money Illusion: Why One Dollar Doesn't Always Equal One Dollar **49**

CHAPTER 4
Trap #4: The Misunderstood Magic Of Diversification: Free Insurance Against The Mousetraps **62**

CHAPTER 7
Trap #7: The Madness Of Mice Versus Markets: Trying To Profit From Stock Market Patterns 123

CHAPTER 8
Trap #8: Retirement Planning Without Plans: Failing To Plan Is Planning To Fail 145

CHAPTER 9
Trap #9: Tres Ratones Ciegos
(Three Blind Mice): Financial Planning Is
Dangerous, If You Don't Speak The Language 169

CHAPTER 1

WELCOME TO THE RAT RACE

Three blind mice
See how they run
They all ran after the farmer's wife
Who cut off their tails with a carving knife
Did you ever see such a sight in your life
As three blind mice?[1]

You've never seen such a sight in your life. I'm not promoting a nursery rhyme that terrorizes furry critters with a carving knife. It's not a good image to plant in your child's mind at bedtime—unless you're Stephen King.[2] Instead, I'm talking about a similar image that has, unintentionally, been created by the financial planning industry. It doesn't involve wives with knives, but it'll give you nightmares just the same.

My name is Scott McLean; I started in the industry in 1982 and received my licenses in March of 1983. That seems like centuries ago. I was ready to save the world and help as many people as I could. Like most 23-year-olds, I was convinced I knew everything. After meeting so many families, I noticed they all had something in common. They wanted to make money and never took classes teaching them how. Like supply and demand, the need for financial education was overwhelming. All I could think about was how many people I could help and educate in my financial journey. I thought the opportunities were limitless.

Now going on my 37th year in the industry, my clients' financial needs are still the same. Most people seek and need the education, guidance, and coaching to face the unknowns in life—and there are many unknowns. Have you ever told yourself, "I wish I knew then what I know now"? How about, "The older I get, the wiser my parents become?"

So, after many years of working, continuing my education, and guidance from dynamic mentors, McLean Advisory Group[3] was born from the desire to help people grow and protect their wealth. As clients were acquired in the early years, it became clear that most had no idea about their overall financial picture. Most, I found, were seeking a product, a quick fix, not a solution. Failing at finance isn't necessarily the client's fault. The financial education system was broken and remains that way today. In elementary school, high school, and college, students learn everything from the mysteries of the pyramids to the philosophies of Plato,[4] but none learn the value of a dollar, how to balance a checkbook, or how to fund an IRA account. Yet, finance is the one topic that affects everyone's life in the most profound ways. Have you noticed how emotional money is? Yup, that dirty, smelly dollar bill can be very emotional to all. Here's a story you might relate to. Eleven-year-old Charlie had one goal in mind: going to the county fair with his friends—with no parents. Freedom rings.

With that one goal in mind, he decided to earn enough money to have one heck of a fun-filled day. So Charlie mowed lawns, trimmed bushes, picked weeds, and completed many other odd jobs around the neighborhood. In just one week he earned and saved $100. He had never seen so many one-dollar bills. All the excitement he was about to have was well worth the price of his aching muscles, cuts, and blisters. It was the opening day of the county fair and he was ready.

With his entire savings in his pocket, he strutted off to the Freedom Fairgrounds with his buddies. This was the best day of his life. He felt empowered, rich, and proud of himself for all he had achieved. After a few rides, basketball shots, the air rifle concession, and eating the gut-wrenching hot dogs with soda pop, he was off to the most thrilling ride of all—the "Flying Spinner." As he dug into his pocket to pay, he started sweating and looked around frantically as his friends asked, "What's the matter?" He went silent as he tried to recount all his previous steps. Checking his pocket for the fourth time, he realized he must have lost his last $20. He was ready for the best ride in the park but now he had no money. As he searched, the fear of not going on the ride gripped him and he said dejectedly, "I can't afford the ride."

Tell me, how much more emotional can money get for a young child?

Does this sound familiar? Perhaps those of you who encountered retirement just to face not only one death-defying ride of 50 percent or more, but two stock market crashes, one in 2000 and the other in 2008, can relate. Can you recall the feeling of horror? How about not wanting to open the investments statement that reeked with horror? That is the kind of emotional turmoil we all experience. Still not convinced? Another awful scenario—losing your life's savings just to hear a salesman assure you it's not the end of the world and you'll make that money back; just "hang in there" as one's life savings evaporates into thin air, or hang in there, "we're all in this together," or, better yet, "it's time in the market, not timing the market." I'm sure those 60 to 80 years old were not excited at all.

So, as you can see, money is emotional, gut wrenching, and can be devastating. Heck, I think I read somewhere that the number one reason for divorce is money worries. Crows and clowns show up at the funeral. Friends and family ripped apart over money due to simple misunderstandings. Money affects everyone, no matter what their age.

My mission is to help educate, guide, and counsel people—people like Charlie—to make smart decisions with their hard-earned money.

Because of this, people seek advice from financial professionals and what they don't realize is the way the financial planning industry is organized, or perhaps unorganized, which creates the traps, chaos, and trouble, as you'll soon realize, or might be already aware of. Please take these steps so it doesn't happen to you.

I call this the great disconnect. You may have received investment advice from a financial advisor; had your taxes done by an accountant; and your estate plan, such as your wills and trusts, written by the attorney. You took the right steps. You did the adult thing and felt secure. Yet, the trap had been set. The problem is that none of these key consultants, advisors, accountants, and attorneys ever consulted with each other about you. They call it professional client privilege. In the medical world, they call it HIPAA, or the Health Insurance Portability and Accountability Act,[5] which is legislation that outlines the provisions for the safeguarding of personal medical information. My dad called it "passing the buck."[6] Heck, it's easier.

From my competitive water-skiing days I've had many surgeries over the years—knee, shoulder, and elbow, just to name a few. I noticed the professionals who were concerned for my well-being shared their findings with others involved in my care. Brilliant. Let me explain. As they rolled me up to the slab, Dr. Knife arrived at the cutting station as I lay, helpless. In preparation for the procedure, he reviewed all the medical findings from many doctors like Dr. Radio (radiologist), who took X-rays and EKG; Dr. Breath-right (cardiologist), making darn sure my heart and lungs were strong enough to handle the operation; and Dr. Vampire (phlebotomist), who took samples of my blood. Dr. Dreamer arrived the (anesthesiologist) and medicated me for the best nap ever, as I raised my hand like a conductor telling the orchestra to play on when Dr. Knife went to work. When I awoke from my nap, I was greeted by the wonderful staff I call the cleanup crew, who pinched my arm with a needle. Voila: the pain-relief medication eradicated the pain. The cleanup crew followed up immediately after Dr. Knife was done. The nurses whom I call the "Care Crew" were my angels. It was a wonderful harmonization of efforts because they were working off the same sheet of music.

I, like you reading this, desire to be treated with the utmost care and concern when it comes to my health as well as my wealth. The lack of money when you're not feeling well becomes even more emotional.

Does your financial team know what's going on and reading from the same sheet of music?

If not . . . you're working with three blind mice.

For example, you may receive investment advice from a financial advisor, have your taxes done by an accountant, wills and trusts written by an attorney. If it sounds like you're in good hands, the trap has just been set. The problem is that most all key consultants, advisors, accountants, and attorneys don't communicate with each other. In Chapter 11, I'll give you scenarios, ideas, and hints so you will be alerted to traps we are all prone to.

Now, I'm not saying that anyone is being negligent; it's just the nature of the financial planning industry. Everyone trains to become highly specialized, knowing more and more about less and less, until they know everything about nothing. Okay, that may be an exaggeration—specialization means they spend more time sharpening their own skills and knowledge, not each other's. Individually, they may be brilliant, but when they're not working together, they're blind to taxes, blind to investing, and blind to your plan.

Here's how traps are set.

An attorney may have drafted a perfectly valid will, complete with all the asterisks and disclaimers, but that doesn't mean it's a good contract for the client's overall financial picture. Perhaps the client named his wife as beneficiary of all assets in the will, but years ago named his ex-wife as beneficiary on his bank accounts, retirement accounts, and 401(k) plans through his financial advisor. Did you know that beneficiaries will supersede a will? In other words, when his wife finds out she gets nothing, it'll be more than just a bad hair day. If the marriage wasn't dissolved by death, it would have been done in divorce court. Talk about the vultures circling. Believe you me, you've been there, done that, and it can get downright ugly, especially when the corpses rise from the dead, just to get more from you. Now, accountants get blinded, too. Their job is to minimize your taxes, but that's not the goal of long-term financial planning. To achieve financial success, you must maximize after-tax returns. Minimizing income taxes is easy: quit working. You'll do great at tax time but will have nothing to show for it in the future, hardly a good financial plan. The U.S. has a progressive tax system, which means the more you make, the more you pay. Earning more money will never put you in a worse situation, even though you're increasing your tax bill. Higher after-tax returns create the path to overall wealth, even if your tax performance is less than optimal. Concentrating on tax minimization can be hazardous to your wealth.

Here's a good question to consider. If your mom, dad, or spouse passed away and you had financial questions, would you call the financial advisor, lawyer, or accountant?

Does it make sense that the financial advisor should know most of the details? In other words, with one call, you get the concerto with less stress. Hello . . . McFly . . . McFly,[7] can you understand why the concerto needs the conductor to orchestrate the legal, tax, and financial challenges that will appear?

Even financial advisors operating independently can inadvertently create nightmares, too.

Perhaps one certifies a client's accounts are well diversified and that sufficient contributions are being made to retirement accounts. The children's college funds are on track. The bills are all paid. If the advisor doesn't know the client's trust account was drafted in a different state from his current residence, it could separate him from his money quicker than a carving knife.

Now just imagine you or a friend has a special-needs child who is on Medicaid and that same child is a beneficiary on the investments. C'est la vie, goodbye benefits; and the trap could have been avoided because the advisors, lawyer, or perhaps both never asked the simplest critical beneficiary questions to protect the child and estate. We will talk more about that later. Please, avoid this common beneficiary trap.

Now, rather than retiring in luxury, his client may rely on "credit card debt monetization to meet future cash-flow demands." In simpler terms, robbing Peter to pay Paul—just trying to survive this way could be a living nightmare.

You may think I'm exaggerating these issues, but I can assure you that truth is stranger than fiction. These problems are very real and costly. Always remember. The Three Blind Mice never pay the price; you do.

I've always known this three-way blind communication problem existed, and how damaging it can be, which is why I designed my advisory group in-house, with currently two attorneys, three tax preparers, and two financial advisors. I feel it's a necessary arrangement for anyone entrusted with the ultimate fiduciary responsibility—your financial future and legacy. Most of you, however, use separate accountants, attorneys, and advisors to make your financial plans, and that's OK. Yet, they're scrambling in opposite directions, and you must synchronize them.

When have you and your three blind mice (advisor, accountant, and attorney) discussed your financial and estate game plan together? Has your advisor ever offered to call your accountant and attorney to ensure all your documents and goals are aligned? Or is it still just a big disconnect?

That's what inspired me to write this book. My dad, Kenneth L. McLean, Korean War veteran, mentor, friend, and best man at my wedding, spoke six languages fluently and drilled into me that communication is everything. He made it a point to make sure that I should be clear and direct with people; things can get unwieldy. He also made sure if there was a problem that I fix it at once. A problem unattended grows. "If you're not part of the solution, you're part of the problem." So don't complain about it if it's in your power to correct it. Come up with a solution, and then tell others so they can make a course correction to avoid a disaster. As a watchman for my clients' finances, I want to offer sound, strategic solutions to the unforeseen, unanticipated, and unplanned traps that await you as best as I can.

Now, if you're a DIYer (do-it-yourselfer), please read this book carefully to correct any steps you may have overlooked. In my course of meetings with 25-plus families a week, I can assure you the areas described herein are dreadfully overlooked. I'll cover some of the most important financial topics that must be synchronized with your three blind mice. On the other hand, if you're a financial advisor, don't take shortcuts just for the next quick bite of the cheese. Be the leader—you are a vital part of the solution for your clients' care, custody, and ultimate concern. Take the time to make a total impact. If you're an attorney or accountant, why not add to your practice a holistic view so everyone can read the music? This book will highlight many areas of concern to improve and bolster your clients' confidence and avoid the many disconnects that are apparent today. It'll take more time, and your clients will appreciate the extra mile that you take to keep them out of the mousetraps. The financial industry owes it to them, so let's be part of the solution.

My goal is to share with you the key points of financial planning, which I call walking through the valley of the shadow of death. What I mean by that is, like any specialized field, financial planning has its own language, products you've never heard of, and risks you'll never see. Once we shine a spotlight on these important topics, you'll fear no evil and have a better chance for success by knowing the right questions to ask and mousetraps to avoid. It's up to you to keep your three blind mice connected. Your financial future as well as your family's may depend on it, big-time.

Any bad decisions are in the past, but they'll eventually connect to your future, unless you make changes today. However, if your financial plans are disorganized by the Three Blind Mice, they'll make changes that end up being for the worse. We've all seen bull markets, bear markets, crashes, and scandals. Believe me when I say, you've never seen such a sight in your life as the Three Blind Mice. Let's see how to keep them from leading your money into a mousetrap.

TRAP #1:
YOU CAN'T BE BLIND
AS A BAT OR SOMEBODY ELSE WILL
CONTROL YOUR DESTINY

A few years ago, I took my children on a fun trip to the zoo. While we were there, we noticed an ostrich with her head buried in the sand; she was checking on her eggs. Momma ostrich was so focused on the eggs that her vitals were exposed, and she couldn't care less who was watching her. It hit me like a ton of bricks. The ostrich is like many of my clients' spouses. Let me explain. Generally, in life, one spouse is the hunter while the other is the gatherer with their head buried in the sand and with no other concern. Gatherer-spouses are so concerned about the family and the day-to-day duties and tasks, they have no clue or thought of the future. It's normal.

My wife and I both work at different areas as she handles the accounting and payroll for my firm as well as managing the equestrian center. We are in constant communication for the vital areas of concern, but the small day-to-day details we take care of ourselves. Yes, I do get lots of honey-do lists and texts.

Simple, right? Not always. We know we must communicate especially on the critical areas of our businesses so the wheels don't fall off. Working in this energetic, ever-changing industry, in order to get to know the people I meet, I ask them many exploratory fact-finding questions. I often get replies such as, "I don't know," "I'm not sure," "I'll look into that," or, at times, I'll wait to hear a pin drop as one ponders the answer with a quick response—"We need to fix that." These dire questions are vital to one's financial and estate planning. The Three Blind Mice have no clue because they simply don't ask or, just as often, they say the matter in question is not their area of concern. Let me challenge you with just a few basic questions that should be asked whether you're married, divorced, or single.

  A. Do you know how much you're spending? What percentage of the money saved is out of the reach of Wall Street's risk?

B. If your spouse were to die, how much income do you continue to receive from the pension, Social Security, and investments?

C. Do you get to keep the company's health or life insurance benefit? What is the cost and benefit?

D. Have you named beneficiaries on both the primary and contingents on all your investments—401(k), IRAs, bank accounts, and CDs? When the advisor read the will, did they coordinate the assets according to the trust or will? And do they have a current copy of their clients' power of attorney on file?

E. Do you have any disabled or special-needs children or grandchildren? How about wayward children who are on the wrong side of the tracks and who may need the money managed upon your passing?

F. What medications are you currently taking? Are your spouse's lights going dim? Are you or your spouse a veteran and aware of free long-term-care benefits or other service-connected benefits you are entitled to?

These are just a few questions that are basic, yet overlooked, that can easily lead to a chaotic financial nightmare that will stir all three of the blind mice areas of concern, the paying of unnecessary fees, and excessive taxes.

Please address it now. Don't wait. Pull your head out of the sand and visit my website (www.3blindmice.com) for an energetic list of questions you can use to better your overall picture today. The financial process can lead your money to a mousetrap as you'll see as we run through this book.

The financial planning process can leave you in the dark. If you have no idea about the financial products your advisors are talking about, darkness can turn pitch black. Not organizing your three blind mice is bad, but when the blind lead the blind, it's worse. As a client, you can't be blind as a bat. We don't need a fourth blind mouse. As former General Electric CEO Jack Welch [8] said, "Control your destiny, or somebody else will." I say that putting your head in the sand only leaves your vitals exposed. Now let's turn the light on the financial toolbox of investments.

COMMON STOCK

OK, name any big business or product, and chances are it's a publicly traded company. Walmart, Home Depot, Apple Computer, Amazon. com, McDonald's, IBM, and Coca-Cola are all publicly traded. When a company is publicly traded, it's not owned by any one person. Instead, it's owned by the "public," and anyone who wants to buy a piece of the company can do so through regulated exchanges like the New York Stock Exchange (NYSE) or NASDAQ.

Almost all corporations begin as private entities. The advantage of taking a company public, however, is that the founders can quickly generate enormous amounts of cash in exchange for taking on public partners. For instance, Facebook began in a college dorm room by Mark Zuckerberg[9] and a few friends, and while it was probably destined for success regardless of its structure, by taking the company public through an initial public offering (IPO), Zuckerberg raised an instant 104 *billion* dollars to expand the company. That's the power of having publicly traded companies. He no longer owns the company and retains 57 percent of the voting shares, so he still has control over the company's direction. A well-developed stock market is always present in any thriving economy. There's no faster way to create businesses and employment.

Most publicly traded companies have two types of stock: common shares and preferred shares. When you hear investors or advisors talk about shares of stock, they're usually talking about common shares. If you buy shares of Facebook, even just one share, you're technically part owner of the company. Now, don't expect that will get you invited to company picnics or boardroom meetings, but you're still part owner of the company nonetheless. You get several benefits by owning common shares of stock. First, there's no limit on how much money you can make. As the market value rises, so does your investment. Second, you have limited liability, which means you can only lose the amount you have invested. If you buy 100 shares of stock at $30 per share, the most you could ever lose is $3,000. Of course, having a publicly traded company lose 100 percent of its value is extremely rare, but it does happen. For example, in 2000, Enron was one of the largest companies with over 20,000 employees and over $100 billion in revenue. One year later, it was bankrupt. It's not uncommon to see shares of stock lose a significant portion of their value, perhaps 30 percent or more in a short time. Have you ever heard of a restaurant chain called Chipotle? Below is a chart of Chipotle Mexican Grill[10] (ticker symbol, CMG) whose price fell from $490 per share to $302, or about 38.5 percent, over a four-month period between May 12 and August 25, 2017, mostly due to one of many E. coli outbreaks that plagued the restaurant.

Dramatic losses like this are the biggest risk of owning individual shares. No matter how confident you may be in the performance of a company's shares, there are countless factors that nobody can account for—lawsuits, scandals, regulations, competition, and currency valuations just to name a few. Always remember the farmer's plow.

However, in exchange for taking this risk, it's possible you may get dramatic price increases, far larger than the overall market. Like all risk-reward trade-offs, the larger the gains you shoot for, the larger the potential losses.

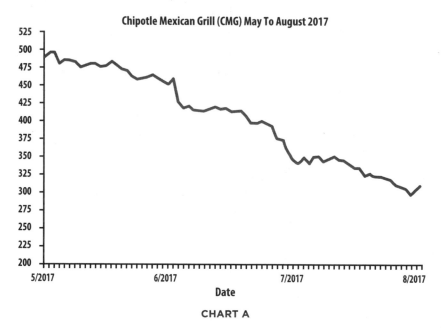

CHART A

Another benefit of common stock is that many pay dividends, which is a cash payment per share, usually made quarterly (although a few stocks pay monthly). For instance, if a stock pays 20 cents per share every quarter and you own 1,000 shares, you'll automatically receive $200 cash deposited to your brokerage account each quarter. However, if a company doesn't pay dividends, it's possible they will begin to pay them in the future. Theoretically, all companies must eventually pay dividends. If a company announced it would never pay a dividend, it would be a financial black hole and be worthless. Still, some companies can go decades before declaring dividends. Is it a bad sign if a company doesn't pay dividends?

Not at all. Most start-up companies or highly profitable companies prefer to take their profits and reinvest it in the business. If the company is doing well, you can make just as much money, if not far more, from the stock price appreciation. Don't discount a stock just because it doesn't pay dividends. For stocks that do pay dividends, however, it's a nice way to generate income without having to sell your shares. For instance, in January 2018, AT&T (ticker: T) was trading for about $37 and pays a 50-cent dividend each quarter. The dividend yield is therefore 5.4 percent, as it pays $2 total during the year or $2 over $37 for a total of 5.4 percent. If you own 1,000 shares, you'll get a nice $500 check every quarter. However, this doesn't mean you're guaranteed to earn 5.4 percent on your money. To make that return, you must buy the shares at the current $37 price and sell them for the same price in one year after you've collected all four dividends. Because it's unlikely that you'll sell your shares for the exact price you bought them, you'll probably make something more than 5.4 percent if the stock price rises, and something less if it falls.

Does the concept of dividends make you wary yet? To add to the uncertainty, dividends may fluctuate based on the company's success. If times get tough, companies may stop paying dividends, or reduce the dividend amount. For instance, General Electric (GE) never missed a dividend payment for more than a century. More impressively, it continuously increased them, until the market crash in 2008. Because of the market uncertainty at that time, GE cut its dividend by 68 percent, from 31 cents per share to only 10 cents per share. Beginning in September 2010, GE increased it to 12 cents and has been steadily increasing it since. In February 2017, it paid 24 cents per share. Just realize that dividends are not guaranteed to continue forever. They may be increased, decreased, or cut at any time, as they depend on the risk of future business.

Sometimes corporations pay *special dividends*, which are onetime payments outside of the ordinary dividends. Special dividends are usually paid after a company has acquired a large cash balance. In 2004, Microsoft paid a $3 special dividend to its shareholders, which amounted to about 10 percent of the stock's value, or $32 billion.

No reason to be completely scared off, though. Despite the risks, common shares have returned about 10 percent per year over the long run. Once you discover the historic returns and potential for dividends, common shares are anything but ordinary. For long-term investors, common shares are necessary to meet nearly all financial goals. Don't let the word "common" make you think they're just average. Common shares are responsible for the majority of wealth created in the stock market. As I've mentioned many times in my radio shows, seminars, and courses, "money is emotional." What is the goal? Is it growth or income you're looking for? Investing in the stock market world can make many folks overdose on Pepto-Bismol just to get through it. So let's put on the scuba gear and slowly make our descent into the world of taxes.

COMMON SHARES AND TAXES

Throughout the book, I hope to explain the basics of how taxation works and how you will be affected. Again, always seek the advice of a tax professional for your situation. Common shares are taxed in two ways: capital gains and dividends. For capital gains, the tax rates depend on your holding period. If you hold your shares for more than one year (366 consecutive days), you'll generally receive more favorable taxation. For 2018, the 22 percent and 35 percent brackets are subdivided into a low and high category for calculating capital gains. The lowest two tax brackets of 10 percent and 12 percent owe zero long-term taxes, none. However, those in the upper end of the 12 percent bracket (those earning $38,601 to $38,700) will actually owe more for long-term capital gains. All other brackets continue to receive much lower capital gains rates as an incentive to hold them long term. Short-term capital gains are taxed as ordinary income, which means they're taxed at your marginal tax rate. For example, if you buy 100 shares of Wacky Widgets for $100 per share and sell them for $110 per share, you'll have a 10 percent return and will owe tax on the $1,000 gain. The taxes depend on your holding period as shown in the table below.

2018 Tax Bracket	Short-Term Taxes	Long-Term Taxes	Percent Savings From Holding Long-Term
10%	$100	$0	100%
12% (low)	$120	$0	100%
12% (high)	$120	$150	-25.0%
22%	$220	$150	31.8%
24%	$240	$150	37.5%
32%	$320	$150	53.1%
35% (low)	$350	$150	57.1%
35% (high)	$350	$200	42.9%
37%	$370	$200	46.0%

TABLE A

The above tax table makes it clear that you must pay attention to taxes, especially if you're close to the one-year holding period. It makes no sense to sell shares after 10 months, for example, when hanging on for two more months can save nearly 40%, or more, in taxes. In fact, since 1957 when the S&P 500[11] took its current form, the index has never returned more than 40 percent in any given year. Yet, by holding shares for just another month or so, you may be able to save that much in taxes. Money saved is money earned.

Investors are often guilty of selling quickly because they're fearful of watching those gains turn into losses. However, most investors take those gains and buy shares of a different company. Who's to say the new purchase is any safer? Continuously jumping in and out of stocks to preserve profits is like switching to a different-colored car every few miles on your way to work believing you'll be safer. You're still in a car in the same traffic. Switching to different stocks through the year keeps you in the same market, exposed to the same overall risks. If your retirement goals can be met with 10 percent or 15 percent market returns, you must question the motive of advisors who suggest lots of buying and selling through the year. Just a couple more months may add an extra 40 percent or more to your nest egg.

If a stock pays dividends, they're usually taxed as ordinary income. However, certain dividend payments may be "qualified dividends," which means they're taxed as long-term capital gains. To qualify, it must be an American corporation or qualified foreign corporation. Second, there's a tricky holding period requirement that you must meet. The IRS usually requires investors to hold preferred shares for more than 60 days during a 121-day period that begins 60 days before the next dividend date. Sound confusing? Just ask any of your three blind mice, and you'll likely get a number of different answers. Financial planning isn't just about finances. It's about understanding the legalities of it.

MUTUAL FUNDS

The long-term benefits of common stocks are hard to beat, but that's assuming you're buying low and selling when they are high. But what if you're close to retirement and bought Chipotle Mexican Grill just before the large drop? At the other extreme, what if the stocks you bought had lackluster performances, but you missed all the stocks that were Wall Street's home runs? Stepping into traps and overlooking the winners is the price you pay for choosing individual stocks.

However, those regrettable outcomes can be greatly reduced by purchasing mutual funds. A mutual fund is a professionally managed investment that owns many different stocks at the same time. In a sense, you're buying into another investor's portfolio. Mutual funds[12] are created for nearly every opportunity you can think of. You can buy the S&P 500 index or specific sectors such as oil, technology, health care, or banking. There's also real estate, emerging markets, solar energy, commodities, and more. If you can imagine it, there's probably a mutual fund for it. Regardless of your choice, one small investment instantly allows you to hold a large, well-diversified portfolio.

Another benefit of mutual funds is that they have low minimum requirements. Depending on the fund, you may be able to start a position with as little as $500 and subsequent purchases of $100. Most allow you to have money automatically deducted from your checking account and invested each week, month, and quarter. It's a great way to ensure you stick with your plan.

LEVERAGED FUNDS

Some mutual fund companies offer *leveraged funds*[13] that create double or triple the returns of a particular index, which are called 2X and 3X funds, respectively. For example, if you buy an S&P 500 2X fund and the index is up 10 percent, you'll earn twice that, or 20 percent. If you bought the 3X fund, you'd be up 30 percent. Leverage, of course, is a double-edged sword. It magnifies your gains and your losses. If the index is down 10 percent, you'd be down 20 percent or 30 percent, respectively, in the leveraged funds.

INVERSE FUNDS

If a company offers leveraged funds, they'll also create *inverse funds*,[14] which move in the opposite direction of the stocks held in the fund. For instance, if you have an S&P 500 inverse fund, you'll be up 10 percent if the index is down 10 percent. Inverse funds allow you to take bearish exposures on the market. In other words, you can make money if market prices are falling. Inverse funds are a great tool for some types of accounts, such as many retirement accounts that may not allow you to take bearish positions. Even though there's a long-term upward bias to the market, bearish positions can be an important hedge for long-term investors. Inverse funds are an easy way to hedge price risk.

In case you're wondering why the falling market is described as bearish, it's because bears attack by swiping *downward,* and a rising market is described as bullish because a bull charges ahead with its razor-sharp horns thrusting upward. Keep that in mind if you're on their menu.

OPEN-END FUNDS

Mutual funds come in two basic flavors: open-end and closed-end.[15] Most of the mutual funds you'll be introduced to will be open-end funds. If you buy funds from any of the well-known companies such as Fidelity, Janus, John Hancock, Vanguard, and T. Rowe Price, you can be sure they're open-end funds. With open-ends, it means the fund doesn't have a fixed number of shares floating around the open market like shares of stock. Instead, the fund creates or destroys shares as needed to mathematically reflect the fund's full net asset value. Because there's not a fixed number of shares, open-end funds are always liquid; you'll always have a buyer if you want to sell. You can think of open-end funds as private funds. They don't trade on an exchange. In other words, if you wish to buy shares of a Vanguard fund, you must buy it through Vanguard rather than through the New York Stock Exchange.

A caller from my radio show called in at around 8:30 a.m. and saw the Dow Jones futures was down around 450+ points and plummeting. He did not want to lose any more money. I had to say that unfortunately he was stuck and had to ride it out till 4:00 p.m. Most open-end funds only trade one time per day, which is when the market closes at 4:00 p.m. ET. At that time, the Net Asset Value (NAV)[16] is calculated, which is just the fund's assets (value of all the shares at the closing bell) minus liabilities (such as expenses, salaries, and other operational expenses) divided by the outstanding shares. Everyone who wants to buy or sell shares of the fund on that day gets the same price, the NAV. A few funds calculate the NAV twice per day, so they will have an afternoon NAV and an evening NAV. This just allows for a little more flexibility if you wish to sell your shares in the afternoon. Because investors never know the NAV until it's calculated later that evening, they must always buy in dollars and sell in shares. For example, you might place an order to buy $1,000 worth of the fund, but you won't know how many shares you purchased until the NAV is calculated that evening. However, if you wish to sell, your order must be for a certain number of shares—let's say 75 shares, for example—and you won't know how many dollars you received until the new NAV is calculated that evening.

It may sound like it's a risky proposition to buy or sell open-ended mutual funds since you're not 100 percent sure of the prices at the time you're placing orders. However, because they hold shares of many different companies, mutual fund prices generally don't rise or fall too much from day to day. Investors are concerned with long-term results and not the small day-to-day fluctuations, so the small discrepancies aren't a big concern.

LOAD FUNDS

Most open-end mutual funds today are no-load funds. However, in the 1920s when mutual funds were on the cutting edge of investing, all companies would charge hefty fees, called loads, for buying shares. This fee was to compensate the brokers for their time and expertise. The clients, in other words, were paying their commissions. Load funds come in two varieties: front load and back load.[17]

With a front-load fund, also called Class A shares, you must pay to acquire shares. For instance, if the fund charges a 5 percent front load, it means you're paying $500 per $10,000 invested. If you deposit a $10,000 check to invest in the fund, only $9,500 gets invested, which means the fund must rise over 5 percent before you'll break even. The maximum front-load charge is 8.5 percent.

Back-load funds, or Class B shares, are just the opposite. Here, you don't pay a fee up front to acquire shares, but you'll pay a fee to sell your shares and may not even be made aware of it. As Gomer Pyle would say, "Surprise, surprise, surprise." When it comes to load funds, you either pay now or pay later. Some load funds charge the back load based on the value of your initial investment. For example, let's say the fund charges a 5 percent back load and you invest $10,000. You'll pay $500 when you sell your shares regardless of their value. However, most charge a fee based on the current market value of your position. This can be especially troubling over decades of investing. For instance, you may invest $10,000, but find it's worth over a million dollars when you sell. That same 5 percent back-load fund will now charge you $50,000 to sell.

Some back-load funds use a sliding scale over 5 to 10 years, also called a contingent deferred sales charge (CDSC)[18]. They may charge a 5 percent back load after the first year, 4 percent after the second, and so on until they charge no fee after five years. Today, you can almost always find no-load funds that accomplish the same goals as load funds. Many investors feel that load funds must be better because of the premium charges. It's not true. They're really dinosaurs left over from the early days of mutual fund trading, and with very few exceptions, there's never a reason to buy a load fund.

NO-LOAD FUNDS

By now, you've probably guessed that no-load funds have no charges up front or on the back end. However, all mutual funds, even load funds, have annual operating expenses (AOEs), which are built into the fund's

WELCOME TO THE RAT RACE ■ 21

performance. I'll talk more about the significance and dangers of these in Chapter 6. For now, just understand that all mutual funds have some type of expenses associated with them, even if your advisor says they're no-loads and commission free. No fund operates for free, but unless you know where to look, it can be nearly impossible to determine just how much you're being charged.

CLOSED-END FUNDS

Closed-end funds are more like shares of stock than mutual funds. They trade on an exchange, and their prices will fluctuate continuously throughout the trading day, just like shares of stock. With the same speed and ease of buying shares of IBM, you can buy a closed-end fund.[19] The main difference with these funds, compared to open-end funds, is that they have a fixed number of shares outstanding issued during an IPO, again, just like shares of stock. After that initial cash is raised, the fund generally no longer accepts new investors; it's closed. However, a closed-end fund may offer new shares, but usually requires shareholder approval.

The advantage of closed-end funds is that the fund manager doesn't need to keep a lot of cash on hand or sell many shares unexpectedly to meet redemptions. Instead, once the fund raises money from the IPO, that's all it ever sees. If you wish to buy or sell shares of the fund, you can only do so on the secondary market, or stock exchange, so the fund's value is determined by the forces of supply and demand, not by the NAV. If there are more sellers than buyers, you'll see the fund trade at a discount from its NAV. For instance, perhaps the fund holds shares worth $30 per share, but you can buy it for $27. On the other hand, if there are more buyers than sellers, it will trade at a premium. That $30 fund may trade for $32. In other words, unlike open-end funds, closed-end funds don't create or destroy shares to keep the NAV where it mathematically belongs, so its value can fluctuate above and below the NAV.

Many times, closed-end funds trade at a discount, sometimes a substantial one. This leads many advisors to think clients are better off with discounted closed-end funds because it seems like they're getting a bargain. On the surface, it appears that way. If the fund's NAV is $30 and you can buy it for $25, you have two ways to profit. First, the fund can appreciate. Second, its discount can shrink. However, many closed-end funds use leverage (borrowed money to make investments) and they can also have high fees. Because the fund never receives new money from investors, the high fees can keep them trading at deep discounts for a long time. There is no free money in the markets. Make your mutual fund purchases based on your outlook and needs, not because it's a closed-end fund trading at a discount.

MUTUAL FUNDS AND TAXES

Mutual funds are a completely different animal when it comes to taxes. If you recall that buying a mutual fund is like buying into a private investor's portfolio, it'll make more sense. During the year, the fund managers buy and sell securities based on the fund's objectives, stock price valuations, and other criteria. However, because all shareholders are in the fund together, the capital gains and dividends are passed through to investors, usually at the end of the year. That means you'll most likely end up paying some type of tax on your mutual funds. That's true even if you never sell your shares, or if you're having capital gains and dividends reinvested, or even if the fund reports losses for the year. If distributions are made, you'll owe taxes. As an investor, it's not a good idea to buy a fund just before distributions are made, which is usually in December.

In a sense, the fund manager is acting on your behalf, and you're responsible for your portion of the taxes on any capital gains or dividends. So, one of the drawbacks to mutual funds is that you lose control over when to trigger capital gains[20] and losses. The good news is that the calculations are easy. The fund reports capital gains and dividends to you at year-end on IRS Form 1099-DIV. However, just because there will likely be some type of capital gains tax owed at the end of each year doesn't necessarily mean they'll be short term. Most mutual funds strive for long-term capital gains, so most of the sales will be long term. In addition to these internal distributions by the fund, there's another way you can incur taxes.

Investors often move money from one fund to another. For example, perhaps you invested $10,000 into the Mutant Money Fund, which is now worth $15,000. You decide to transfer the entire amount to the Prodigious Profits Fund. The mutual fund company offers to "switch" the money from one fund to another at no cost. However, technically speaking, you sold Mutant Money for a $5,000 capital gain, on which you'd owe taxes, and purchased Prodigious Profits on a new cost basis. This catches many investors off guard as they may switch prior to holding for one year and not realize they just triggered a short-term capital gain. Holding for long-term capital gains is essential for long-term financial planning.

Mutual fund dividends are taxed much like other investments. Most of the dividends will be classified as ordinary income, so you'll be taxed at your marginal tax rate. However, some dividends will be "qualified," which means they're taxed at the lower capital gains rates. To qualify, the fund must have held the shares for at least 60 days within a 121-day period beginning 60 days prior to the ex-dividend date. Bear in mind it's how long the fund has held the shares, and not how long you've held the fund. If you're ever in doubt about any financial transaction, even something as simple as switching to a different mutual fund, it pays to speak to a financial advisor.

EXCHANGE-TRADED FUNDS (ETFS)

As investors' needs change, so do investments. In 1993, the mutual fund world was transformed when the first exchange-traded fund (ETF) began trading. An ETF[21] is similar to a mutual fund, regular or closed-end, because it holds shares of different companies and can cover many indexes and sectors. Key differences exist, however.

First, ETFs are also not allowed to issue debt or preferred shares to create leverage. Second, ETFs are more transparent, which means investors always know which shares the fund holds. ETFs must publish the full portfolio on their website every single day. Mutual funds, on the other hand, disclose their portfolios quarterly, but even then, it's for the previous 30 days. The danger is that mutual fund managers can stray from the fund's intended goals, which is called "style drift," so if you happen to purchase shares in between reporting periods, you're never 100 percent sure of the shares it's holding.

The most popular ETF is the SPDR (pronounced "spider"), which stands for S&P Depositary Receipt[22] and trades under the ticker SPY. It began trading in 1993 and now has volumes ranging between 100 million and 400 million per day, making it one of the most liquid assets in the world. With one single purchase of SPY, you instantly own the 500 different companies in the S&P 500 index.

Another benefit of ETFs is the expense ratio, which is the fee deducted from the fund's assets to help with running and managing the fund. It's not a fee that you physically pay to the fund, but it comes out of the fund's performance, which means you're indirectly paying for it. The expense ratios are usually a fraction of those charged by mutual funds. The SPY expense ratio is 0.0945 percent, so a $10,000 investment will cost $9.45 per year, which is significantly less than the 0.74 percent rate charged by most indexed mutual funds. It all adds up.

ETFS AND TAXES

As with any investment, you'll pay taxes on capital gains. If you buy the shares for $30 and sell for $35, you'll owe taxes on the $5 capital gain. Perhaps the biggest benefit with ETFs is the way internal capital gains are distributed. ETFs are more tax efficient than other mutual funds, partly because about 90 percent of all ETFs are index funds, which means they're passively managed. In other words, you're not paying for the expertise of a money manager to buy and sell securities in an attempt to beat the market. However, there's a bigger reason ETFs are more tax efficient.

Regular mutual funds and closed-end funds distribute capital gains to investors at year-end, which means you lose control over triggering capital gains or losses. ETFs are different. They're set up as trusts and have a unique redemption process. When you sell shares of an ETF, the fund can swap assets. By exchanging assets, it's not a taxable event. It's rare for an ETF to distribute capital gains. However, any dividends or interest paid by the funds will get passed to investors just as with mutual funds, and the tax treatment is the same. If you like the idea of a mutual fund that trades on an exchange but is far more tax efficient, ETFs are a hard choice to beat.

BONDS

Bonds are on the opposite end of the investment spectrum from shares of stock or mutual funds. Common shares have price risk, which means you may end up with less money than what you invested. Bonds work the opposite way. They're contractual agreements between the issuer and investor, and you'll receive a steady stream of fixed payments, usually every six months, plus your initial investment back at maturity. When you buy common shares, you're buying equity in the company. When you buy a bond, you're making a loan to the company. You can think of a bond as an IOU issued by the government or a corporation. You give them money today, and they guarantee the return of that money, plus interest, in the future.

Like most financial assets, bonds come in a variety of flavors. Government bonds are truly guaranteed since Uncle Sam has the power to raise taxes, or, at the very least, print money to make good on its obligations. Technically, government bonds are classified as bills, notes, or bonds depending on the time to maturity. Bills mature in 1 year, notes mature in 2 to 10 years, and bonds mature between 10 and 30 years. Aside from the time to maturity, the basic idea is the same.

However, you can also buy corporate bonds, such as those issued by Microsoft or General Electric. Because corporations cannot tax people or print money, they're usually not guaranteed, but still considered highly secure. However, corporate bonds may also be insured by an outside insurance company, which would then make them guaranteed. You can also buy non-investment-grade bonds, called junk bonds, which are bonds in default, or close to default. If the company makes good on these bonds, the payoffs can be tremendous, but most of the time you're just throwing your money away, so they have little room for long-term financial planning.

Ratings agencies[23] such as Standard & Poor's, Moody's,[24] and Fitch[25] Ratings provide bond rating tiers to let investors know the degree of a company's creditworthiness. Conceptually, these are like FICO scores for consumer credit ratings.

Because all investment-grade bonds are either guaranteed or near-guaranteed, you won't get large returns on your money. That's just part of the risk-reward trade-off. In early 2018, one-year government bonds were paying a paltry 2 percent, hardly enough to cover the cost of inflation. Bonds are therefore usually used in the latter years of financial planning when it's more important to secure the money you have rather than trying to increase the portfolio's value and possibly lose a lot.

Bonds are issued with different due dates, called the *maturity*, which can range anywhere between 10 and 30 years, although in mid-2017, the U.S. government was mulling over the idea of issuing 50- and 100-year bonds to take advantage of today's low interest rates. However, that doesn't mean you must invest for a minimum of 10 years. As time passes, the maturity date gets closer. For example, one year later, the 10-year bond will only have nine years to maturity, then eight, then seven, and so on. In an active market with many bond issuers, you can always find a bond with a short-term maturity date.

Bond payments, called the coupons and the interest rate, are bound by a contract, called the bond's indenture. If a bond is issued as a 4 percent bond, that rate never changes. Whether market interest rates move up or down, the bond's interest rate won't change; much like a home's fixed-rate mortgage won't change with changes in interest rates. It's locked in according to the contract. As a general rule, the longer the time to maturity, the greater the bond's interest rate.

Bonds are usually sold in $1,000 increments, which are called the *face value*, *par value*, or *maturity value*. If you hold the bond all the way to maturity, you're guaranteed to receive all the interest payments plus the face value back at maturity. For example, let's say you buy $10,000 worth of a 10-year, 4 percent bond. You'll receive $400 per year, or $200 every six months. At the end of 10 years, you'll receive your final coupon payment along with your $10,000 investment.

However, even though bonds are sold as highly secure investments, understand that comes with one big caveat—you must hold the bond all the way to maturity. If you sell your bond prior to maturity, you're subject to price risk, just as you are with shares of stock. If you buy a 10-year, 4 percent bond today for $10,000, its price will change between today and the maturity date. Why?

As interest rates change in the market, so will bond prices. Specifically, bond prices move inversely to interest rates, which means as interest rates rise, bond prices fall; when interest rates fall, bond prices rise. To see why, let's say that after you buy this 10-year, 4 percent bond, interest rates rise to 5 percent at the end of the first year. All new bonds will now be paying 5 percent. No investor wants your 4 percent bond when 5 percent bonds are available. How can you make your 4 percent bond more attractive to potential buyers?

You must lower the price.

As the bond's price drops, it will trade at a discount to the $10,000 par value.

I'll run through some examples, but don't worry about the math. Any financial calculator or advisor can show what your bond's value would be under certain interest rates. The concept is what's important. For instance, if interest rates rise to 5 percent after one year, your bond's price falls to $9,282. If you hold your bond to maturity (another nine years), you're guaranteed to receive the $10,000 face value. If you must sell it today, you're only going to get $9,282, which is a 7 percent capital loss on your investment. Again, even though the bond is "guaranteed" to return your $10,000 investment, that's assuming you're holding it to maturity. By selling the bond at a discount, it mathematically makes your 4 percent bond trade at an effective 5 percent interest rate, which is called the *yield to maturity*. If another investor buys your bond for $9,282, it's mathematically the same as buying a new 5 percent bond selling for $10,000. Now you can see why bond prices fall when interest rates rise. By selling your bond at a lower price, it compensates the new buyer for the smaller coupon payments. In the financial markets, price equalizes all bonds (of the same investment grade) to trade at the same effective interest rate.

Of course, interest rates could fall. If rates fall to 3 percent after one year, your bond's market price rises to about $10,784, and is trading for an 8 percent premium over par. As before, if you hold your bond to maturity, you'll only receive $10,000. It sounds like you're better off selling the bond to capture the nice gain, but that's not necessarily true. If you still want to invest in bonds, you're only going to receive 3 percent coupon payments with new bonds, not the 4 percent payments you're receiving now.

If another investor pays $10,784 for your bond, he's effectively receiving 3 percent on his money, even though he's receiving 4 percent coupon payments. The higher bond price has equalized the 4 percent bond to behave like a 3 percent bond. When shopping for bonds, don't worry about the interest rate it pays, as they're all the same once the market price is factored in. Instead, focus on the investment grade and time to maturity that suits your needs.

BONDS AND TAXES

As a general rule, bond taxation is fairly straightforward. Any interest is taxed as ordinary income in the year received, so it is subject to being taxed at your marginal tax rate. You may also have capital gains or losses, depending on whether you sold your bond for a profit or a loss in the open market.

ZERO-COUPON BONDS

There's one more type of bond we need to cover, as it belongs in a category all its own, zero-coupon bonds,[26] or "zeros" for short. You guessed it. They make no periodic coupon payments. Instead, they trade at a deep discount to the face value, and you receive the full value at maturity. The difference between your purchase price and face value is effectively your interest. For example, if interest rates are 4 percent, you could buy a $10,000 face, 10-year, zero-coupon for about $6,756. You won't receive a single penny in interest payments for 10 years, but will collect the $10,000 face value at maturity, effectively receiving the $3,244 difference as interest. Over 10 years, that return on your money turns out to be exactly 4 percent. One of the benefits of zero-coupon bonds is that your money compounds at the coupon rate, which is 4 percent in this example. If you bought regular bonds, you may not be able to invest your proceeds each year at 4 percent, which creates an interest-rate risk. If you know that 4 percent allows you to reach your goals, zero-coupon bonds not only guarantee the return of your money, but they guarantee it to be returned at that stated rate.

However, some investors are drawn to zeros because they seem like they're making a lot of money. Something just feels good about paying $6,756 today and receiving a guaranteed $10,000 in 10 years. Remember, though, the bond's price factors in all benefits. It's still a 4 percent return on your money no matter how good it looks.

Zeros are primarily issued by the government, but they can also be issued by corporations. Most government zeros are issued with maturities of 10 to 15 years. Zeros are nice investments for many situations. First, if you have a set goal in mind—saving for your daughter's or son's college fund, for instance—zeros allow you to put a relatively small amount of money down today, but realize a guaranteed amount in the future.

Second, they can be great tools for gifting money to children. You can gift a much smaller amount today, but ensure it grows to a much larger value in the future and avoid the associated tax.

The two biggest risks with zeros are default risk (except for government zeros) and price risk. Corporate zeros usually pay higher interest rates, which can also be a positive attribute. However, it's also a reflection of the greater risk since the company gets the money today and never makes a single interest payment, possibly for decades. If the company isn't financially responsible and setting money aside to pay these future obligations, it's easier for zeros to go into default. As a result, corporations usually pay higher interest rates to entice investors to accept the risk.

ZERO-COUPON BONDS AND TAXES

Even though you'll never receive interest payments while holding your zero-coupon bond, the IRS says you're "earning" that interest each year, which is called phantom interest. Of course, that means Uncle Sam wants his share every year, and you may be subjected to federal, state, and local income taxes, even though you never received any money. Here are the basics of how it works. If you paid $6,756 for your 10-year zero at 4 percent, you're earning at the rate of 4 percent per year. Therefore, after the first year, you'll be taxed on 4 percent of $6,756, or $270.24. However, your cost basis increases by the amount of taxes you paid. Therefore, in the second year, your new cost basis rises to $6,756 + $270.24, or $7,026.24. Therefore, the following year, you'll be taxed on 4 percent of $7,026.24, or $281.05. Each year, your "interest" gets tacked onto the previous cost basis, a new cost basis is created, and so is a new tax. The good news is that, at maturity, you'll owe no taxes when you collect the money.

Naturally, these taxes can be avoided when zeros are placed in an IRA or other tax-advantaged account. There are also some tax-exempt zero-coupon bonds, which will also avoid the phantom income tax.

PREFERRED STOCK

All publicly traded companies have a pecking order in which they must pay investors in case of bankruptcy. The first to get paid are the bond-holders, but also included are debts such as office mortgages, company leases, and other direct expenses. If any money remains, preferred share-holders are paid next. The last to get their money are the common stock holders.

It may seem that preferred shares,[27] or preferreds, are better than common shares, since you'll have priority should a bankruptcy result. However, preferred shares are a hybrid of common shares and bonds. With preferreds, you don't participate in the corporate earnings, so when you hear Wall Street saying things like, "Shares of Apple Computer have doubled over the past year," they're talking about the common shares, never the preferred shares. With preferred shares, you'll get dividends, which are usually paid quarterly, but that's it. Dividend payments on preferreds aren't required like they are for the bondholders. Instead, they just have a priority over the common shares. But if the company makes a dividend payment, it must pay dividends to all preferred shareholders first before making them to the common shareholders. It's only in this sense that these shares are "preferred" to the common shares.

Bonds are normally issued at $1,000 face values, but preferreds are normally issued at $25. If the company pays a $2 dividend, the yield is $2 divided by $25, which equals 8 percent. Remember, however, that the dividend is always listed at the annual rate. If it pays $2 in dividends, it means 50 cents per quarter. If you own 1,000 shares, you'll receive 1,000 shares multiplied by 50 cents, or $500 each quarter. Just as with bonds, this $2 annual payment never changes, as it's part of the preferred stock's contract. Instead, if market interest rates change, you'll see the preferred stock's price change in response. For example, if rates fall to 7 percent, you'd see the preferred stock's price rise from $25 to $28.57 since $2 divided by $28.57 equals 7 percent.

If rates rise to 9 percent, the preferred stock's price will fall to $22.22 since $2 divided by $22.22 gives investors a return of 9 percent. Just as for bonds and zero-coupon bonds, preferred share prices are sensitive to interest rates and move in the opposite direction: when rates are up, prices go down, and when rates are down, the prices go up.

CUMULATIVE VERSUS NON-CUMULATIVE

Investors can buy two different types of preferred shares, *cumulative* and *non-cumulative*. Cumulative preferreds have priority over non-cumulative. If the company misses any cumulative dividends, it must make up all past payments before any payments can be made to non-cumulative holders.

As an example, your best friend went to broker A and bought $100,000 worth of XYZ preferred, with an 8 percent dividend or a potential $2,000 every three months or $8,000 a year, but you went to broker B and bought $100,000 worth of XYZ at 6 percent, so you realized $1,500 per quarter or a total of $6,000 a year. Yep, the same company. The first three quarters, *neither* of you received a dividend, yet in the fourth quarter your friend received $2,000 for the year and you received $6,000. Confused? At first glance, you're ticked off and ready to fire your advisor. I mean, you were getting $2,000 less a year than your friend. So why the difference? Because your friend's preferred was a non-cumulative, meaning he does not get all the missed quarters as you did. Yours was a cumulative preferred. So getting a second opinion is helpful for many, as having a keen eye for details may help improve your income.

However, all preferred shares, cumulative or non-cumulative, always take a back seat to bonds. If you're comparing yields on preferred shares, be sure you're comparing apples to apples.

CONVERTIBLE PREFERRED STOCK

Preferred shares are like a hybrid between common stock and bonds. They are shares of stock, but their prices act more like a bond. However, you can also get more exposure to common shares of stock by using *convertible preferred*[28] stocks. With these, you can exchange your preferred shares after a specific date for a predetermined number of common shares.

For example, assume the conversion ratio is four. This simply means the investor can exchange the preferred shares for four shares of common. Assume you purchase preferred shares for $100 and the common stock is trading for $20. If you wish to convert to common shares, you would receive four shares worth $20 each, for a total value of $80. In this case, it would not be beneficial to convert since you paid $100 for the preferred stock and exchanged it for something worth $80.

There is a price at which it would be advantageous to convert, which is called the *conversion price*. Just divide your preferred purchase price by the conversion ratio. In this example, $100 divided by 4 equals $25. If the common shares are trading for any price greater than $25, it's advantageous to convert. Otherwise, continue to hold the convertible preferred and enjoy the dividends. However, even if the stock's price hasn't reached the conversion price, as long as it's moving close, the convertible preferred stock's price will climb, too. Convertible preferreds are a way to earn steady dividends, but also participate in company earnings. However, as with all financial assets, nothing comes for free, and you must pay for any advantage. The drawback to convertible preferreds is they'll be far more expensive than regular preferred shares. If you're ever looking for the steady income of bonds along with the ability to participate in the company's earnings, convertible preferreds are a great solution.

PREFERRED STOCK AND TAXES

The dividends on preferred shares act like bond interest payments. However, these dividends are considered "qualified dividends," which means they're taxed at long-term capital gains rates, far lower than ordinary income tax rates. For 2018, the bottom two tax brackets (10 percent and lower 12 percent) pay no tax. The next five brackets (upper 12 percent, 22 percent, 24 percent, 32 percent, and 35 percent) pay 15 percent, and the highest 35 percent and 37 percent pay 20 percent. Recall that regular bond dividend payments are taxed as ordinary income and don't receive the same favorable treatment.

However, to receive the favorable tax rates, the IRS usually requires investors to hold preferred shares for more than 90 days during a 181-day period that begins 90 days before the next dividend date. Sound confusing? Just ask any of your three blind mice, and you'll likely get three different answers. Financial planning isn't just about finances. It's about understanding the legalities of it. If you're looking for an asset that behaves like a bond and gets favorable tax treatment, preferred shares may be your answer.

REAL ESTATE INVESTMENT TRUSTS (REITS)[29]

What portfolio would be complete without real estate? For decades, it's been responsible for much of the wealth created around the world. Can you remember when you bought your first home? Do you remember the feeling and worries? I sure can. Like anything new, it has a package of unknowns. I purchased my first house in 1984 at the age of 25. It was a charming small duplex in Ocean Gate, New Jersey, a cute little town. My $41,500 became a reality from many sleepless nights as I went to bed before we closed asking myself if I could do it, if I could afford it, and wondering what I would do if the rates kept going up or if my business did poorly. All kinds of doubts and fears were dancing around in my head. Though excited and scared at the same time, I'm glad my dad was there to coach me. I created a pacifier mantra, which for me was a godsend as I sang to myself *The Wizard of Oz* theme ("Lions, Tigers, and Bears, O my"). My version was, "Mortgage, Taxes, and Insurance $528, add a renter ($225), and I won't be late. Only $303 and that's for me." As I fell asleep, yes, many times I awoke thinking: "What if they don't pay?" As I put the pacifier back in, I fell asleep.

This was the start of my wonderful real estate venture. Purchasing many houses, apartment buildings, and, yes, designing my own subdivision development—today it's called Todd Road Estates in Toms River, New Jersey. OK, I was a little vain at 28; I really wanted my own family street name, McLean Court, and one for Pop-Pop I named "Winston Court." But I can say every venture my wife and I did was calculated and I sought advice. Yes, apprehensive—OK, scared—but excited as well.

There was a problem—not only was it a ton of work and time consuming, but it could be risky and expensive. And we did make lots of mistakes, I can promise you that. So unless you have an iron stomach and high risk tolerance at your age then perhaps go for it!

However, the financial markets created a solution with Real Estate Investment Trusts, or REITs (pronounced REETS). The idea is the same as a mutual fund, but rather than holding shares of stock, the fund holds real estate. REITs fall into three basic categories: equity, mortgage, and hybrids. Equity REITs, sometimes called EREITs, buy actual properties such as homes, office complexes, apartment buildings, hotels, resort properties, and other similar investments. Mortgage REITs, or MREITs, make money by purchasing and selling mortgages and earning interest much as a bank would. If you want a combination of the two, you can buy hybrid REITs.

Like mutual funds, REITs can be open-end or closed-end. Like all closed-end funds, more shares may be issued but generally require shareholder approval. REITs offer investors the benefit of a diversified portfolio of real estate. They also offer high yields, mostly due to special tax considerations.

However, it's not easy to qualify as a REIT, as it must pass many strict tests:

1. Must be structured as a corporation with fully transferable shares.
2. Must have at least 100 shareholders and must have less than 50 percent of the outstanding shares concentrated in the hands of five or fewer shareholders during the last half of each taxable year.

3. Must distribute at least 90 percent of its annual taxable income, excluding capital gains, as dividends to its shareholders.
4. Must have at least 75 percent of its assets invested in real estate, mortgage loans, and shares in other REITs, cash, or government securities.
5. Must derive at least 75 percent of its gross income from rents, mortgage interest, or gains from the sale of real property. And at least 95 percent must come from these sources, together with dividends, interest, and gains from securities sales.
6. Cannot have more than 20 percent of its assets consist of stocks in taxable REIT subsidiaries.
7. Less than 30 percent of the gross income can come from the sale of real property held for less than four years.

Many investment advisors say that home ownership gives most people adequate exposure to real estate. However, it's undiversified. Your home is one type of real estate in one specific area. To get proper exposure and diversification, you need to own homes, rental complexes, office space, warehouses, and hotels across the country. What is the current real estate market like in your city? Almost every major city has experienced real estate booms and busts, but rarely has the entire nation gone bust. To get adequate returns from real estate, you must be adequately diversified, and REITS are a simple yet effective way to do that. In one second, you can own multimillion-dollar properties across the United States. However, expense ratios can vary dramatically for REITs, so be sure you understand just how much you're paying to participate in the fund.

REITS AND TAXES

As with most investments, you'll be taxed on any capital gains when you sell your shares. As for dividends, REITs distribute at least 90 percent of their income as dividends to investors. Like most dividends, they may be qualified or non-qualified. If qualified, investors are taxed at the more favorable capital gains rates. If non-qualified, they're taxed at their marginal tax rate. In some cases, the REIT may pay some portions that qualify as a nontaxable return of capital, which can reduce your taxable income. However, because REITs distribute gains from real estate properties, the dividends tend to be high, so be careful about using REITs in taxable accounts, as the income tax rates for dividends are usually higher than those for capital gains.

MOUSETRAP #1:
YOU CAN'T BE BLIND AS A BAT

Many investment advisors are paid commissions based on the products they sell, and this can create a conflict of interest. Stock commissions pay well, load funds pay better, and variable annuities pay among the best. It shouldn't be a surprise that you're going to be led to the most expensive products, even if they're not the best for your needs. You must understand the various types of investment choices, and if there are cheaper alternatives. For instance, you can find load funds that track the S&P 500 index, but some, such as the Vanguard S&P 500 ETF, charge a fee of just 0.04 percent. That's only $4 per year for every $10,000 invested. On the other hand, there are about 17 mutual funds that track the same index, but charge loads as much as 5.75 percent, just to buy the shares. That's $575 just to get in. Then they'll hit you with expense ratios topping 0.6 percent every year. It's the same index, so there's no reason to pay a higher fee to track the same index. In Chapter 6, you'll see just how dramatic of an effect this has over years of investing.

Using a load fund with high expenses is like trying to drive your car uphill with the parking brake on. It's a huge drag on your performance, and there's no reason in the world to use a fund like this. But you'd need to know what to look for, or ask about it, as the broker isn't going to point out cheaper versions. That 5.75 percent is his commission.

One of the best ways to avoid these conflicts is to use a fee-only advisor with fixed assets under management[30] (AUM). It's a relatively low price to pay for sound advice, and the advisor will offer no-load funds and other low-cost alternatives.

Product complexity and commissions aren't the only problems. The bigger issue is with the Three Blind Mice. Few financial advisors fully understand how these products affect taxes or legal issues with trust accounts, wills, and estate planning. There's far too much for one person to know, which is why advisors, accountants, and attorneys act independently. Unless they're sharing this information, however, you're going to end up with less-than-optimal planning. Remember, three blind mice never pay the price.

The investments outlined in this chapter are intended to give you an overview of the various choices you'll most likely be using and the tax implications that may result. There's a lot to consider. Most financial advisors are only interested in getting you to buy and sell without regard to taxes. Few tax advisors understand financial planning, and accountants won't understand the legal issues. To get the most from your investments, you must have experts in each field working for you, and that means your advisor, accountant, and attorney must communicate. A financial plan without this three-way communication is a long-term trap.

TIP: Review your goals yearly.

CHAPTER 2

TRAP #2

Perceptions And Deceptions Of Risk And Reward; You May Not Want The Biggest Piece Of Cheese

Journalist Frank Scully[31] said, "Why not go out on a limb? Isn't that where the fruit is?" To get the best fruit, you must venture out onto small, unstable branches. Anyone walking by an orange tree can grab the low-hanging fruit; there's no risk in it, and so it's easily snapped up. That leaves the fruit at the top more time to grow bigger, ripen, and become better quality, but it comes at a price. You must go out on a limb to get it.

Financial products work the same way and for the same reason. However, for those who don't understand the risk-reward relationship, the perception of what's at risk and what's a reward gets clouded. If there's one topic that causes more confusion, more errors, and more bad investment choices than anything else, it's the risk-reward relationship. Even seasoned professionals struggle with the concept, so you can imagine the problems that could occur when dealing with three blind mice. At the end of this chapter, I'll even show you a case that caused a $330 billion bond collapse that many investors could have avoided had they understood the interaction between risk and reward. Understanding this section may not save you that kind of money, but it will save you a lot of headaches and provide a safer path for your financial future.

THE OBSCURE RISK-REWARD RELATIONSHIP

For any financial transaction you make, whether an investment or a gamble, risk is always defined by the probability of losing money. A high-risk deal means there's a good chance for you to lose some, or possibly all, of your money. A lottery ticket, for instance, is a high-risk proposition, as you're virtually guaranteed to lose your dollar.

At the other extreme, a riskless investment means there's no chance of losing any money—it's guaranteed. If you hold a government bond to maturity, you're guaranteed to receive the face value. Naturally, there are many shades of risk between these two extremes, which is what makes investing so complex.

However, risk is easy to misinterpret. Many investors, and even some advisors, think risk is defined by the amount of money you have invested. If that were true, a lottery ticket would be low risk because you can only lose a dollar, and a Treasury bill would be high risk because you've got a lot invested. Believing that risk is defined by the amount of money invested is a surefire way to spring a trap.

If that weren't bad enough, there's another easy trap to fall into. Risk is never defined as missing out on some reward. Investors often make the mistake of saying things like the risk of keeping money in cash is that you'll miss out on market gains, or the risk of selling a stock is that the price continues to rise. You can call it a missed opportunity, a regret, or even Murphy's Law. Just don't call it risk.

It sounds like you should only buy low-risk investments, since having a high probability for losing money defeats the purpose of investing. There's another side to the story. Low-risk investments don't provide much of a return. Don't expect to make much money. On the other hand, while high-risk investments have the potential to lose a lot of money, they can also generate large returns. Some of the greatest wealth in the world was created by those who took extremely high risks, such as Marian Ilitch, Bill Gates, Zhou Qunfei, Henry Ford, and John D. Rockefeller.[32] Unfortunately, you never hear about the countless people who tried to do the same and went bust. There's always risk in going for the big rewards.

The risk-reward relationship is simple. As risk rises, the reward rises, too. Conversely, as risk falls, so does the reward. It's easy to memorize, but also easy to misinterpret. To avoid the traps, you must understand what causes this relationship to always hold in the financial markets.

GOING ONCE, GOING TWICE, SOLD

The financial markets are a live, continuous auction like eBay, with investors buying and selling stocks and bonds rather than used iPhones and sporting equipment. The process is the same: goods go to the highest bidder. All things being equal, investors don't like risk, so they're willing to pay more for investments with low risk. By bidding higher, it leaves a smaller reward. Alternatively, if there's risk, investors bid lower; this could lead to a bigger reward.

When financial assets have no risk, such as government bonds, investors respond by bidding the price higher. For example, a Treasury bill, or T-bill for short, is a type of zero-coupon bond, so a $1,000 face bond is guaranteed to pay that amount at maturity. These are sold periodically to investors by auction, and because investors don't like risk, they're willing to bid high. In early 2018, investors paid about $980 for a one-year Treasury bill, which left a measly $20 reward. The return on their investment, or yield, was $20/$980, or just over 2 percent. It's not a big reward and that's because the $1,000 future value was guaranteed.

However, let's say another one-year $1,000 bond was being offered by a corporation whose business is on shaky ground. Their credit rating was downgraded.

Investors sense risk, so they respond by bidding lower. Perhaps the high bidders pay only $840, thus leaving a $160 return, which is $160/$840, or about 19 percent. Even though it's the same $1,000 maturity value being auctioned, the price investors are willing to pay is much lower due to the risk of loss. The lower price creates a larger potential reward. If the bond does pay off at maturity, it's a nice payday for those investors, as they'll earn 19 percent versus 2 percent, but it comes at the risk of possibly losing some or all of their $840 investment.

The main point to see is that, as risk increases, the market price falls, and that creates a higher return. As risk falls, the market price rises, which creates a lower return.

Sometimes, new investors think a risky asset is like a trip to the casino, so it has no investment value, but that's not true. If someone offered you this risky bond for free, there's no reason to turn it down. The worst that can happen is its price falls to zero. Instead, the price must get lowered enough to make it worth an investor's while. In the financial markets, lower prices eventually equalize the risk. You can always make any risky investment a fair deal, if given the right price.

PRICE IS THE EQUALIZER

No matter how much risk may be present, there's a price at which investors will accept it. For instance, regardless of mileage on a used car, someone will buy it for the right price. No matter how run-down a home may look, lower the price enough and someone will buy it. Are you trying to sell shoddy-looking homes? They will be snatched up for the right price. Risk and reward are like two children balancing on a seesaw, risk on the left side,

CartoonStock.com

reward on the right. The bar on which the seesaw balances is the market price. If the risk or reward gets bigger, the seesaw gets out of balance, but it can always be brought back into balance by adjusting the price. If risk gets bigger, the price gets lowered. If the rewards get bigger, price is increased, but the seesaw always remains in balance. Price is the reason.

All financial assets are priced according to risk, so it's wrong to say that one investment is "better" than another. Instead, your investment decisions come down to how much risk you're willing to take. Once the market determines a price, risk and reward are equalized. No matter how you alter the risks or the rewards, investors respond by altering price. At that price, the risk is worth the reward.

No matter what type of financial asset you're talking about, this risk-reward connection always applies. For instance, are auto insurance companies better off insuring adults with perfect driving records, or teenagers who just got their license? If you said adults with perfect records, you forgot the risk-reward connection. Teenagers are riskier and that means they'll pay higher premiums. With higher premiums, the insurance company is properly compensated for taking the additional risk. From the insurance company's perspective, neither group is better, but instead, each provides different sets of risks and rewards. Price equalizes risk. My advice? Don't allow your teenager to drive.

The risk-reward relationship also explains why stocks outperform bonds in the long run. If stocks and bonds were expected to yield the same amount each year, investors would flock to bonds since they're guaranteed. In doing so, their price rises and yields fall when compared to shares of stock. Bonds always underperform stocks in the long run. Risk, or lack of risk, is the reason. Once you understand why the risk-reward relationship must hold, it should seem simple, but let's now see how risky things get when dealing with the Three Blind Mice.

MOUSETRAP #2:
PERCEPTIONS AND DECEPTIONS
OF RISK AND REWARD

Investors and many professionals often misinterpret the risk-reward connection, and it's easy to do. Rather than trying to understand that financial assets are priced according to risk, the probability for losing money is thinking risk is measured by the price. Again, if that logic were correct, lottery tickets would be low risk while Treasury bills would be high risk. When viewed in the eyes of probability, however, the answer is exactly the opposite. If you want to know what will cause more financial wrecks, it's having a perception that's exactly the opposite of reality. Try driving north in the southbound lane.

So when an advisor suggests you buy 100 shares rather than 200 because it's less risky, it's wrong. The risk is the same; it's the same stock. The stock doesn't know how many shares you own or how much you paid for it, so a 10 percent, 20 percent, or other price decrease is identical for all investors. Yes, you may have a smaller amount to lose, so be sure you're willing to risk that money. You can't turn a risky stock into a Treasury bill by purchasing fewer shares.

Perceptions get worse than that.

You'll hear many advisors talk about using investments with high *reward-to-risk ratios*,[33] which is a way to compare how much money your investment could make (reward) compared to the amount you could lose (risk). Already you should get a hint at where the trap lies, as risk isn't defined by the amount of money invested.

For instance, if you pay $1,000 for an investment that allows you to possibly make $5,000, the reward-to-risk ratio is 5:1. That is, you have the potential for making five times the amount of money you're "risking." These advisors suggest making investments where you can make more than you can lose, such as ratios of 2:1, 3:1, or more. In their view, the higher the ratio, the better. It implies that the odds are in your favor, as you have far more to gain than to lose, and that makes it seem like low risk. However, if you can buy a bond for $333 that may pay off $1,000, your reward-to-risk ratio is 3:1. The only reason the market priced the bond that way is because of the high risk. If you could buy that bond for $200, your reward-to-risk ratio rises to 5:1. It's not safer—it's even riskier. On the other hand, if you paid $980 for the T-bill that matures to $1,000, your reward-to-risk ratio is $20/$980, or .02:1, which means you're making two cents for every dollar invested. It's easy to misinterpret this to equate to high risk since you're "risking" one dollar to only earn two cents. The misperception comes from not understanding that there's no risk, and that's why it comes with a low return.

However, you'll hear many advisors boast that they work hard for you to find "high" reward-to-risk ratios, implying that the probabilities are in your favor. It's usually not an intentional error, but instead, a common misperception. That's what makes it such a dangerous trap. As humorist Artemus Ward[34] said, "It ain't so much the things we don't know that get us into trouble. It's the things we know that just ain't so." Any time you can make far more money than you can lose, it's only because of high risk. The higher the ratio, the greater the chance for you to lose.

MAXIMIZE AND MINIMIZE

It's not hard to find financial advisors with web pages that say their investment style allows clients to maximize returns and minimize risk. In other words, you'll get big returns for taking very little risk. What more could one want?

For starters, a better understanding of risk and reward is necessary.

If you could minimize risk and maximize returns, you could invest in T-bills but get the payoffs of a lottery ticket. If that sounds too good to be true, well, you know the rest. There's no way to minimize risk *and* maximize returns. Instead, you get one or the other. You can choose to minimize risk, in which case you must accept a low reward. Or you can choose to shoot for high returns, but that means there's a good chance you'll end up with large losses. Telling clients they can minimize risk and maximize returns is a common reckless claim made by many advisors.

If your advisor is searching for investments like this, find a new advisor before he finds another investment for you.

AUCTION-RATE SECURITIES: THE DAY BANKS DIDN'T SHOW

Attorneys and accountants can easily miss these risks, too. Wall Street is always creating new products to meet different needs. The more complex the financial system gets, the more complex the products will become. In 2008, many investors lost a ton of money in the auction-rate securities (ARS)[35] debacle. Auction-rate securities are long-term bonds, usually 20 or 30 years, but have their interest rate reset at auction every 7, 14, 28, or 35 days. Because of these short-term resets, brokers marketed them as short-term cash equivalents. They told clients, "They are very liquid investments, and you can always get your money back by just waiting until the next auction. There's always a long line of banks just waiting to buy these bonds."

The first clue is to think back to third grade when your teacher warned you about using the word *always*. Who knew that would be a great investing tip decades later?

Auction-rate securities seemed like a great alternative to broker's money market rates, which were close to zero at the time, and the market boomed with over $330 billion in ARS notes. But then the credit crisis hit and the banks got skittish about buying bonds. In February 2008, many banks decided not to show up for auctions, and there were more sellers than buyers. Eighty percent of the auctions failed. Investors couldn't convert bonds to cash and were now stuck holding long-term illiquid securities.

As a result, many investors resorted to selling stocks and mutual funds at all-time lows to generate the cash they were counting on. The crash led to billion-dollar class-action lawsuits, but investors could have avoided the turmoil by asking a simple question. Why were the ARS bonds priced at 4 percent when Treasury bills, the truly risk-free rate, were yielding 2 percent? ARS rates were *double* that of Treasuries and there's only one reason that happened. It's a footprint of risk. Even if you don't know why the rates are higher, the overall market does. The smart money wasn't willing to bid higher for these bonds, which would have pushed the yields lower. It doesn't matter how safe a broker, financial advisor, or glossy marketing brochure says the bonds may be. When you understand the risk-reward connection, the difference in yields is an instant giveaway that auction-rate securities cannot be cash equivalents.

Why didn't the attorneys or accountants catch it? The issuers' attorneys just made sure the bond contracts were legally binding. Their job wasn't to identify risks to investors, or to make opinions on the bonds' quality. Even if an in-house attorney felt there were serious risks to investors, they were employed by the issuer, not the investors. Don't expect one to send out alerts on Facebook and Twitter in exchange for a pink slip.

Accountants, on the other hand, were concerned with how to record market values when rates were reset at auction. They figured out how to handle the taxes and coupon payments. They're not experts in bond mechanics, the intricacies of auction-rate markets, or financial risks to investors. If they're not looking for risk, they'll never see it.

And the brokers who sold the bonds? They're salesmen who were instructed by their firms that the bonds are just as good as cash equivalents. To make the miscommunications worse, all investments must be registered with the Securities and Exchange Commission (SEC), which investors often believe makes them "approved" for investing. It's critical to understand that while all publicly traded investments are registered with the SEC, the agency doesn't pass on the merits of any security, or the adequacy of the information in the *prospectus*, which is a formal legal document that must be filed with the SEC before offering securities for sale to the public. Instead, the SEC just ensures that all legal filings are properly done. That's hardly the government's seal of approval.

If advisors, accountants, and attorneys communicated, many investors would have been spared years of legal battles trying to get their money back. A good advisor would have known something was strange with the bonds priced at 4 percent when the Treasury's risk-free rate was half that.

They could have passed that information to the attorneys who would have found the auction buyers amounted to a handful of banks. Accountants would have seen that the supply of bonds may not have been equal to the demand. And everyone knows accountants lose sleep if they can't balance debits and credits. But none of these professionals could see all the problems and that left investors holding the risk.

As legendary investor Warren Buffet[36] said, "Risk comes from not knowing what you're doing." If you're working with three blind mice, be sure you understand the risk-reward relationship. You'll never see an instance where it doesn't hold. If you at least know the right questions to ask, it's the first step in knowing what you're doing and reducing your risk.

CHAPTER 3

TRAP #3
THE DESTRUCTIVE TIME AND MONEY ILLUSION: WHY ONE DOLLAR DOESN'T ALWAYS EQUAL ONE DOLLAR

Comedian Steven Wright[37] tells a story, about being in the middle of the desert when a UFO lands. Three one-inch-tall aliens get out and he asks, "Are you really one inch tall?" They reply, "No, we're really very far away."

Distance changes perspective, whether you're talking about Martians or money. For any type of financial planning, you must understand how time changes the way money looks. Otherwise, you may be on track for a large sum of money at retirement, but when that day arrives, it looks very small. The joke won't be so funny then.

Financial professionals call this changing perspective the *time value of money*. It's a concept that says one dollar payable today is worth more than one dollar paid in the future. In other words, if you receive one dollar today, you can invest it, earn interest, and have more than one dollar in the future. If given the choice between receiving a dollar today and a dollar in one year, take the dollar today.

As Warren Buffett puts it, "It isn't how many dollars you have, but how many cheeseburgers you can buy."[38]

In other words, if stocks double but so does the price of milk, gas, and cornflakes, you haven't actually gained anything in real net worth.

For example, if you have $100 today, that's called the *present value*—it's the value at the present. However, if the risk-free interest rate is 5 percent, you could invest the money, earn interest, and have $105 in one year. That's called the *future value*. It's the value you'd receive in the future assuming a given risk-free interest rate.

As with any math problem, we can work it backwards and find out what money due in the future is worth today. If someone owes you $105 in one year, you should be willing to accept $100 today to settle the debt. By taking the cash today, you can invest it and have $105 in one year, so both deals are the same. Financially speaking, if the risk-free interest rate is 5 percent, $100 today equals $105 in one year. You won't pass a basic math class saying $100 equals $105, but you'll get an "F" in financial planning if you don't understand that they're the same. We're just viewing money at different points in time, and that changes the perspective.

By increasing the time, the perspective gets more distorted. If you invest $100 for two years, it's worth $110.25. In 10 years, it's worth $162.89. But in both cases, it's worth $100 today.

Changing the interest rate changes the perspective. If the risk-free rate is 10 percent, $100 today is worth $110 in a year. Because money is earning a higher return at 10 percent, it will grow to a bigger future value. However, higher rates have the opposite effect on the present value—it becomes smaller. If someone owes you $100 in one year, it's worth $95.24 today at 5 percent interest, or $90.90 at 10 percent. In other words, because money has more earning power at 10 percent, you don't need as much money today to reach the same future goal.

If it sounds complicated, that's what causes money illusions. It causes investors to think things are cheap when they're not, and it makes them think they're financially ahead when they're really behind. If there's one trap that causes financial goals to fail, it's a plan that makes your money look big when it's really very small.

For investors, the time value of money is critical, as most financial planning isn't for short periods of time. It usually spans decades, and the distortions will cause you to think the math is wrong. For example, at 5 percent interest, a 30-year $10,000 zero-coupon bond is worth $2,314 today. At 10 percent interest, today's price falls to just $573. If we push the maturity date out far enough, or raise the interest rates high enough, you can make any future cash payment look incredibly small today. If there were such a thing, a 100-year zero $10,000 face bond priced at 20 percent would be worth 42 cents today. Steven Wright may ask, "Are you really that small?" The financial planner would say, "No, it's just really far away."

In December 1989, I took my wife for a very romantic candlelit dinner and a movie. It was my birthday: hamburgers, fries, soda, and, yes, a chocolate milkshake. (As everyone knows, birthday dinners are fat-free.) I ordered two hamburgers, for $0.67 each. We spent a whopping $4.15 with $0.85 to spare.[39] Today, 30 years later, that same delicious meal would cost over $14.52. Man, those were the days . . . *or were they*? This means I needed to plan for retirement 25 to 30 years ahead. Especially if I want to afford a luscious hamburger date at the same restaurant. Is it possible it would cost $50.82? It's much easier to put blinders on and say it won't happen. This is a real concern for those on a fixed income. They say to themselves, "I don't want to run out of money with so much life ahead of me." The thief is at your door and needs to be dealt with. Don't worry. I'll show you a solution to the inflation problem.

INFLATION:
A THIEF IN THE NIGHT

Ronald Reagan once said, "Inflation is as violent as a mugger, as frightening as an armed robber, and as deadly as a hit man."[40] Discussing inflation in your Economics 101 class will put you to sleep faster than the strongest sleeping pill. Inflation, however, causes even bigger distortions.

Inflation is the modest rise in prices each year. Most people know the effect and understand that the $30,000 car they were eyeing this year will probably cost $31,000 next year. The cause, however, is misunderstood.

It's usually attributed to greedy businesses competing for extra profits by simply marking up prices each year. As producers increase prices, it gets passed onto suppliers, who in turn must raise prices, and the cycle continues. Competition, however, has the opposite effect and keeps prices down. Competition is a counterbalance to inflation.

Inflation is caused when governments print money to pay off debts. Rather than raising taxes or issuing bonds, it's easier to print money. Imagine if you could get out of debt by printing money off your office Xerox machine. It beats working, right? That's the way the government sees it, and it can't resist the urge to print off a few extra dollars or a few extra billion to get out of debt. From its perspective, it beats raising taxes and losing votes.

However, those extra dollars influence the value of the dollars currently in circulation. If you managed to stay awake in your basic economics course, you may remember that when the supply of something increases, its value must fall. Increase the amount of oil in the market, and gas prices will fall. Increase the number of cows in the market, and the price of beef will fall. Money is no different. With more money circulating, the dollar's value must fall. The illusion is that most people think of inflation as an increase in prices, but it's caused by the dollar's value falling. When the dollar falls, it appears that prices are rising.

Regardless of the cause, inflation creates distortions for financial planning. The only reason for investing is to set money aside today in exchange for being better off tomorrow. However, "better off" doesn't necessarily mean having more dollars. It means having more *purchasing power*. To be better off, you must be able to buy more things, not just have more pieces of paper. Focusing on purchasing power is the key for financial planning. Fort Knox could take one of its 440-ounce gold bars and stamp "one dollar" on it, but that doesn't mean it'll spend like one dollar. The purchasing power will be closer to $500,000. On the other hand, you could take $500,000 in Monopoly money, but it won't buy a thing except a lot of small plastic homes on Boardwalk and Park Place. Don't get caught up into the number of zeros in your net worth. Focus on the purchasing power.

To make sure you're focusing on the right numbers, economists put returns into two categories: nominal and real. The nominal return is the stated return. If a bond pays 5 percent interest, that's the nominal return. The real return, on the other hand, accounts for inflation. Just subtract the inflation rate from the nominal rate to find the real return. If you invest in a bond paying 5 percent, but the inflation rate is 3 percent, the real return is 2 percent. In other words, your purchasing power is only increasing by 2 percent and not 5 percent as you may think. The real return shows that, mathematically, you're investing at 2 percent with no inflation. Always focus on the real returns.

To understand how inflation eats away at your money, let's say you have $100 today. Wine costs $100 and cheese costs $5. If you buy wine, you'll have no cheese. However, if you can invest that money at 5 percent interest, you'll have $105 in one year and can buy both assuming prices stay the same. Your incentive to loan the money is that you'll be better off in the future by having both wine and cheese. However, if prices rise 8 percent next year, wine costs $108 and cheese costs $5.40. Although you planned to buy both with $105, you can't even buy wine. You have more money but you're worse off in terms of purchasing power. How can you be worse off with more money? Your nominal return was 5 percent, but your real return was 5 percent to 8 percent, or minus 3 percent. In other words, your $100 lost 3 percent of its purchasing power and will spend like $97. That's why you can't afford the wine even though you have more money. Inflation's eroding effects must be considered, as it becomes more pronounced for long-term financial planning. You may be on target to amass one million dollars at retirement in 30 years, but if you think it's the same as having the same amount today, you'll realize you've been mugged. At 3 percent inflation over 30 years, it'll spend like $412,000 today. It's another risk of long-term financial planning, and why you can't overlook inflation's effects.

Inflation not only reduces the value of your future nest egg, it also eats away at your current savings. If you have $10,000 in savings that's not earning interest, but inflation is 3 percent, it'll spend at about $9,700 next year. Ten years later, it'll spend like $7,440. Even though you may shy away from taking investing risks and want to keep your money in cash, you're silently being robbed by a thief over time.

Inflation is a true problem for bond investors. Because of the low returns, inflation eats into your earnings far more than stock investments, which usually have higher returns. If your bond pays 2 percent but inflation is 3 percent, you're losing purchasing power. Your real return is negative 1 percent. For instance, perhaps you invest in 30-year zeros at 2 percent and buy a million-dollar face bond for $552,000. Yes, you'll have a million dollars at retirement, but in 30 years, it'll spend like $408,000 today. Even though you have more pieces of paper, you have less purchasing power. For financial planning, don't get lured by large numbers far into the future. Today they'll look big. At retirement, they'll look small if you're not counting for the effects of inflation.

For the U.S., the average annual inflation rate is about 2.5 percent to 3 percent per year, although there have been periods when it's been above and below this range. The highest 30-year period experienced inflation rates near 5.5 percent while the lowest was 0.78 percent. The two highest years were 1778 with nearly 30 percent inflation and 1913 with almost 20 percent. When financial planners talk about an average inflation rate, no matter which number they want to assume, understand that it will fluctuate above and below that level. If you plan for 2 percent inflation, but it turns out to be 3.5 percent, it can have devastating effects on your retirement plans, so you must account for inflation, even if seemingly modest levels. At 3 percent inflation, prices double every 24 years and triple every 38 years.

While inflation is bad for investors, governments like modest levels of inflation for three key reasons. First, when prices rise, it encourages a person to buy today, which means greater current tax revenue. Second, your assets are taxed at inflationary rates. If you buy a home for $500,000 and inflation is 3 percent per year, its value will rise to $515,000 next year, all else being equal. If you sell your home, you'll be taxed on the $15,000 gain even though you're not any better off in terms of purchasing power. In fact, you're worse off after paying the tax. In the words of economist Milton Friedman, "Inflation is taxation without legislation." Third, the government issues debt in nominal terms, but pays it back in real terms. The money is cheaper to borrow.

Inflation is fairly low in the U.S., although not desirable; it's not a big problem. That's not always true worldwide, which is why the U.S. dollar becomes the world's currency in times of financial crises. How bad can inflation get? Enter the hit man.

Right before our eyes, a much-loved and respected South American country, Venezuela,[41] with the richest oil reserves in the world, is currently in shambles. The once fourth-richest country in the world is under siege with hyperinflation. Imagine going for a cup of coffee and the following week the price doubles. As of January 14, 2019, a new 300 percent pay raise was ordered by President Nicolas Maduro.[42] Just imagine your new monthly paycheck up from $2.23 to $6.70. It's still not time to break out the bubbly. It's a shame.

Some governments can't resist the urge to print. Many times, it's a result of political turmoil or the lingering effects of war. Governments lose their taxing ability and resort to printing money. Once inflation begins to show, the government must print more and more money—just to keep up. If acceleration is more than 50 percent, it's called *hyperinflation*. There's a long history of hyperinflations, and in every case, the currency ultimately collapsed. Beginning in 1989, Yugoslavia[43] had one of the worst bouts of inflation in history, causing the government to print the 500-billion dinar note in 1993. If you think you'd be wealthy holding one of these notes, you're falling victim to money illusion. You're not considering the purchasing power. Yugoslavia's inflation rate peaked at *313 million* percent per month. That's not a typo, that's hyperinflation. The currency was worthless.

After World War I, Germany[44] had inflation rates pushing 30,000 percent *per month*, with prices doubling every two days. Some journalists reported that bar patrons would order two beers at a time to avoid the price hikes between the first and second.

Hyperinflations aren't just a thing of the distant past. In 1990, Brazil suffered hyperinflation rates of 30,000 percent per year, or 300-fold per year. To put it in perspective, if a television cost $1,000 today, it will be $300,000 next year. Hyper-inflations wreak havoc on an economy because nobody knows what money will be worth in the future. For example, with 30,000 percent inflation, you wouldn't want to sign a three-year employment contract for $50,000 per year. Instead, you'd need $50,000 in the first year, $15 million in year two, and $4.5 billion in year three. It sounds like you're signing an NFL contract, but with those inflation rates, the real rate of return is $50,000 in each of the three years. However, if inflation turns out to be higher, you'll end up on the losing end of the deal. If it turns out lower, the employer ends up losing. Because the currency is so unstable, it's safer for both parties not to sign the contract. The result is that nobody wants to work, nobody wants to hire. The economy collapses.

Zimbabwe[45] is the first country to hyper-inflate in the 21st century and certainly won't be the last. Around 2008, prices were doubling each day, an inflation rate of *80 billion* percent per month. As a result, the government had to print larger and larger denominations just to give the notes any value at all. In 2009, Zimbabwe's government resorted to printing the *100-trillion-dollar* note—that's a 1 followed by 14 zeros, the largest ever printed in history. With this bill in your wallet, you may think your wealth surpassed Bill Gates' fortune. But having a note with a lot of zeros doesn't mean it has a lot of value. In 2009, just before the currency collapsed, it was only worth about five U.S. dollars. Looks can be deceiving, and that's the ravages of inflation. At that time, many Zimbabweans retired with wealth measured in trillions of dollars, but they could forget about buying a Rolls-Royce. They couldn't even afford to take the bus. It's unlikely the U.S. will ever see rates like these, but you may have part of your portfolio invested internationally, so your financial plan could be indirectly affected by future hyperinflations. While international investing is an important component of a well-diversified portfolio, you must be aware of the risks. Just because a country's production appears to be on the rise and looks like a good investment, you still face the risk of the government inflating its currency.

MEASURING INFLATION:
THE CONSUMER PRICE INDEX (CPI)

The most used measure of inflation is the Consumer Price Index (CPI),[46] which is published each month by the Bureau of Labor Statistics. The CPI measures the percentage change in price for a set basket of goods such as food and beverages, housing, clothing, transportation, medical care, education, and other goods and services that people buy for day-to-day living. The basket of goods changes periodically to reflect changes in consumer habits. For instance, in the past few years, the use of landline phones has dropped dramatically, so the spending for that service isn't as important in today's world, and the CPI takes that into account. Prices are recorded from month to month. The CPI is an index with the base period starting between 1982 and 1984, a neutral time when the economy wasn't in a recession or an expansionary period. At that time, the index began at 100. If the index was 103 at the end of the following year, prices rose 103/100, or by a factor of 1.03, or 3 percent for the year. In early 2018, the CPI stood at nearly 248, which means prices have risen 248/100, a factor of 2.48 times, which is an inflation rate of 148 percent since the base period. Something priced at $100 in the base period costs $248 today, on average.

One of the biggest drawbacks to the CPI is that it only accounts for price changes, not quality. For instance, say a car that is tracked by the index sells for $30,000 one year and comes with a four-cylinder engine, AM radio, and no air bags. The following year, the same model has a turbocharged V-6 engine, MP3 player, GPS, driver and side air bags, and sells for $31,000. Most people would agree the car price has dropped, but the CPI measures a price increase simply because the sticker price rose from $30,000 to $31,000. For accurate financial planning, you must not only understand inflation's effects, but also the measurement's limitations.

That's everything about inflation that you slept through in college. This time it's not about a grade, it's about your financial future. Let's see how three blind mice get trapped by money illusions.

MOUSETRAP #3:
THE DESTRUCTIVE TIME AND MONEY ILLUSION

The illusions created by time, money, and inflation are perhaps the financial industry's best mousetraps. You can't touch them, you can't see them. And it's always easy to overlook the things you can't see. But these traps are always set and ready to spring. If you're working with three blind mice individual advisors, attorneys, and accountants, be sure you understand how time and inflation affect your investments. Individually, these professionals may be giving sound advice from their perspective, but it's the collective opinion that counts. Because they remain hidden from each other, there's a big price to pay and it's you who's going to pay it.

For instance, say an attorney creates a trust account where you stipulate it can only hold low-risk investments. He suggests using zero-coupon bonds since, after all, they're risk free. In legal terms, he's correct. What could go wrong?

SNNAAAP. That's the sound of your money in the mousetrap.

Good financial planners understand that when people say a bond is risk free, it means it has no *default risk*—you're guaranteed to get your money back. The only true default-free bonds are issued by the government, since it can always raise taxes or print money to pay them off. You may also find insured corporate bonds, which would also qualify. All others can possibly default if the company goes under.

Just because you hear the word "bonds" doesn't mean there's no risk. All bonds, including Treasuries, face inflation risk and interest rate risk. Inflation risk is quite easy to understand. You may be earning a guaranteed 2 percent on your money, but if inflation is greater, you're only guaranteeing a loss in purchasing power. You can always protect Treasury bills from inflation by purchasing Treasury Inflation-Protected Securities, or TIPS. With these bonds, your principal increases with inflation and decreases with deflation, as measured by the Consumer Price Index.

Interest rate risk is a little more difficult to see. To get your money back with any bond, it comes with a stipulation: you must hold the bond all the way to maturity. While waiting for that day to arrive, however, there's plenty of price risk. In fact, the variation in prices, called the price volatility, can be far greater for bonds than stocks, especially over longer periods of time. The longer the time to maturity, the more sensitive bond prices become. Even if you own U.S. Treasuries, you can end up with negative returns in any given year. The chart below compares a 30-year zero bond (dark line) to a 5-year zero bond (shaded line) both purchased at 6 percent. As the market interest rate changes (horizontal axis), the bond's price changes, as shown in percentages (vertical axis).

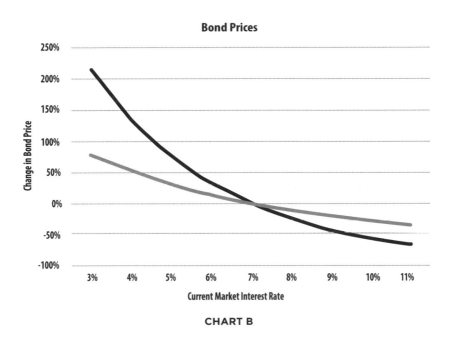

CHART B

The five-year bond (shaded line) is relatively flat, which shows if interest rates fall to 2 percent or rise to 10 percent you won't see big changes in the bond's price. In fact, it will only rise or fall by about 15 percent. The 30-year zero (dark line) sits on a much steeper curve and that's the risk. Small changes in interest rates can mean big changes in your bond's price. If rates fall to 2 percent, the 30-year's price rises 217 percent, and if rates rise to 10 percent, the bond's price falls 67 percent. It may be a risk-free bond, but it's not safe to say it has no risk.

Let's say you buy a $100,000 face, 30-year zero priced at 4 percent in your trust account. It costs about $31,000 today. However, five years later, you unexpectedly must sell your bond to raise some cash. You're thinking it must be worth at least the price you paid, as five years have passed, so the bond's price must have appreciated at least a little bit, right?

That would be true if interest rates stayed the same or had fallen. However, if interest rates have risen, say from 4 percent to 6 percent, your bond's price is $23,300, a 25 percent loss even though it's a guaranteed asset. If rates increased to 7 percent, you'd have a 40 percent loss. Now you can see how sensitive long-term zero-coupon bonds are to rising interest rates. If your financial advisor and attorney never talk, you may never uncover the true risk of a risk-free bond until it's too late. Does this mean you should never invest in zero-coupon bonds?

Not at all. It just means you must understand the price mechanics of all bonds, and those forces can be used offensively as well as defensively. The same forces that can create losses can also be used to generate profits. For example, on the right-hand side of the above chart, notice that the bond's price can only fall by a maximum of 100 percent, which is why the dark line begins to flatten as interest rates rise. If interest rates fall, however, you'll get explosive gains on longer-term zero-coupon bonds compared to shorter term. In the 1980s, I put many clients into 30-year zeros for this very reason when interest rates were approaching 14 percent. It was only a matter of time before rates would fall back to their long-term average of about 4.5 percent. About six years later, rates plummeted to 7 percent, and the 14 percent expected returns turned out to be over 800 percent. All financial instruments are tools, and you must select the right tool for the job. To do so, you must understand the market mechanics of bond prices, not just the legal obligation to return the face value at maturity.

Accountants create their own distortions, too. Accountants, by the nature of their business, are conservative. If they're helping you with financial planning, they may know the average inflation rate is 3 percent, but may suggest using 5 percent to be safe. However, to preserve the same purchasing power, you must now take more risk. If 10 percent returns will accomplish your goals but you're assuming 3 percent inflation, you'll need to shoot for 13 percent returns, on average. But if you assume 5 percent inflation, you'll need to aim for 15 percent. The higher the required rate of return, the greater the risk you're taking. It's ironic that by being conservative in your inflation assumptions, you'll end up with a riskier portfolio. In the financial markets, risk can lie in unusual places. If you know where to look, you'll be on your way to financial success. When working with three blind mice, however, they may never see the traps.

Inflation is like a thief in the night. Make sure your long-term projections are protected by always considering inflation's effects. There's no worse financial nightmare than reaching retirement and finding your large nest egg looks small or cracked. The illusion turned into reality.

A PLANNING IDEA

If you have a spouse or children who spend money frivolously, perhaps you should consider adding a spendthrift clause in your will. This way the recipient can get a steady monthly check with an increase in payments tied to the CPI.

CHAPTER 4

TRAP #4

The Misunderstood Magic Of Diversification: Free Insurance Against The Mousetraps

Every activity has secrets for success. No matter what you're doing, whether it's starting a business, building a home, or just playing a simple game of tic-tac-toe, there are certain things you do and certain things you don't. They're the pearls of wisdom collected from decades of experience that allow you to succeed and with less effort. As I told my children when they were dating, treat everyone with the highest respect and kindness because, attractive or not, the word spreads. You never know who you'll meet.

Financial planning is no different. Some plans are better than others, as they make use of financial principles that allow you to increase your nest egg with less effort. There's no reason to take a more difficult path and end up with less money. That's what happens to most individual investors who create their own financial plans and build their own portfolios. Imagine working with three blind mice.

Of all the financial principles that should be followed, diversification is the least understood and the least used. Diversification is the simple idea of not putting all your eggs in one basket. Drop that basket, and you'll lose all your eggs. But if you spread half your eggs across two baskets, it's less likely that you'll drop both baskets and at least have something to take to market. That's the idea behind portfolio diversification. By purchasing many different stocks, you'll reduce the chances for large failures. Okay, sounds simple enough, so why don't more people do it?

Many financial advisors say buying a diversified basket of stocks is a loser's game, as it moves your expected returns toward the long-term market averages, perhaps around 10 percent or so. They argue the only reason for investing in the market is to do better than average. But if you're not willing to pick next year's Wall Street winner, you'll have no chance of beating the overall market.

If you ask about the benefits of diversification, they'll mockingly say, "Oh, you mean *di-worse-ification*?" "How can you possibly expect to do well," they'll ask, "when you're just increasing your chances for selecting stocks that will perform poorly?"

The logic should be clear. If you have a dozen eggs, and one is rotten, you have a better chance for a good breakfast by choosing one to eat and not choosing three or four to make an omelet. The more you pick, the better the chances for failure. For similar reasons, some financial advisors who charge high fees for picking stocks will convince you that you're worse off by selecting a large basket of stocks. Doing so only increases the chances that some will be rotten, and you'll reduce the returns of your high-performing stocks. It can be a convincing argument.

However, it's only half the story. Whether we're talking about eggs or stocks, by choosing more, you do have a better chance of picking some duds and you also have a better chance of hitting some home runs. When advisors tell you that diversification is bad because you'll reduce the value of your big gains, they're missing the entire point. Remember, risk is not defined as missing out on some reward. Instead, it's defined as the probability for loss. No stock-picking advisor in the world is going to choose 100 percent winners. However, by selecting a small handful of stocks, it's quite possible they'd choose nothing but losers. By selecting a large basket of stocks, diversifying the home runs will cancel out the failures, on average. Does this mean you're left with no returns at all?

Not at all. Diversification just cancels out the extreme observations. On average, there's a long-term upward drift to stock prices. Much of this is due to a growing population, increasing productivity of the country, and more companies selling more goods and services. It's this consistent, upward drift that you need to capture your long-term financial goals. But if you choose just a handful of stocks, it's very possible you're going to pick some big losers and destroy your plans in the process. The benefit of diversification isn't about increasing your returns. It's about meeting your goals while reducing the chance for disaster.

THE MAGIC OF DIVERSIFICATION

To see diversification in action, let's look at a simple example. Let's say that your financial plan requires you to earn $1,000 per month, on average. If you meet that mark, you'll reach your goal. The more you fall short, the more you'll miss your target.

Don't lose track of the $1,000 target, as staying with your plan is always a key for successful financial planning.

To make the benefits of diversification clear, let's use a simple example. Rather than investing in complex stocks or bonds, let's assume you can invest in coin flips. Each month, you can play a game where you toss a coin one time. If you call the outcome correctly, heads or tails, you win $2,000. Otherwise, you get nothing. There's a 50-50 chance for either outcome, so if you played this game hundreds of times, you'd expect to win $1,000 per flip, on average, exactly what you need to accomplish your goal. By taking only one toss, the following chart shows your possible outcomes.

Notice that even though you'd expect to win $1,000 per flip over many tries, there's *no possible way* to do it with just one toss. That's an important observation. You're faced with extreme outcomes of winning $2,000 or nothing at all. One of the fundamental principles of financial risk management is to avoid extreme outcomes, and winning it all or losing it all

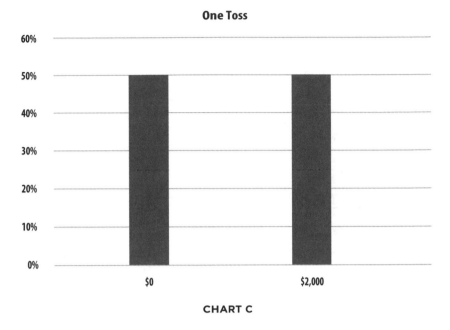

One Toss

CHART C

is as extreme as it gets. If your long-term goal is to win $1,000, you can't even accomplish it with one flip. You have no choice but to either double your target and possibly win $2,000 or lose it all. That's exactly what happens when people buy one stock thinking they can predict Wall Street's next winner. It's either a winner or a loser. Be wary of financial advisors who have such a plan. It may seem like an impossibility, but is there a way to increase your chances to win $1,000 per flip and simultaneously reduce the chances for losing it all?

Enter the magic of diversification.

What if you could diversify by flipping *two coins* to determine your result, and collect the average winnings? By taking two tosses, some interesting things happen. First, you'll reduce your chances for a total loss. Second, you'll greatly increase your chances for accomplishing your goal. The following chart shows your possibilities by taking two tosses.

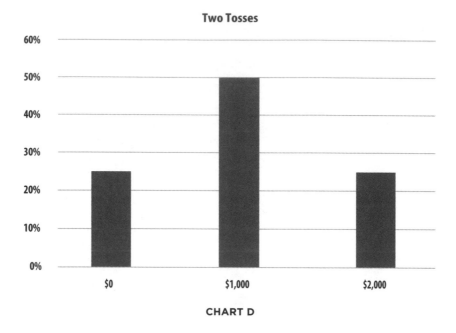

CHART D

By taking two tosses, you have a 50 percent chance to win $1,000 plus a 25 percent chance to win $2,000. *Overall, you have a 75 percent chance to win at least $1,000.*

If your goal is to earn $1,000, doesn't a 75 percent chance of success sound better than a 0 percent chance, which is what you have with only one toss? It gets even better. By greatly improving your chances for success, you must also be decreasing your chances for a loss. By taking two tosses, you've cut your chance for a total loss from 50 percent to 25 percent.

Of course, we could look at this with a negative perspective. By taking two tosses you've also reduced your chance of winning $2,000 from 50 percent to 25 percent. That's the angle taken by advisors who tell you not to diversify, which is what leads them to call it di-worse-ification. Remember, though, missing out on some rewards isn't risk. You're trying to reduce the chance for total loss and increase the chance for accomplishing your goal. Diversification accomplishes both. It works because you're increasing the chances to see the average outcome, while reducing the chances for extreme outcomes.

The more tosses you take, the more you improve the chances for success, and the smaller the chances for big losses. For instance, if you could toss eight coins each month, the results become even more dramatic. You have a 64 percent chance to win *at least* $1,000 per flip. There's also an 86 percent chance you'll win at least $750, and a 99.6 percent chance to win at least $250. There's virtually no chance to lose it all.

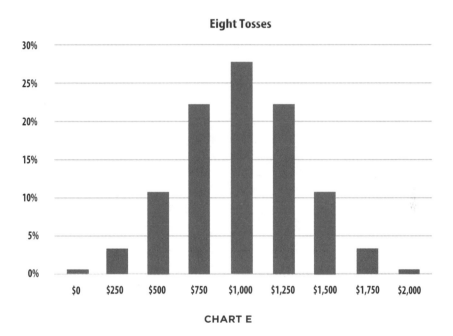

CHART E

In all three of the above charts, as you increase the number of tosses, you're expected $1,000 winning remains the same—it's always the center value in the chart. However, as you increase the number of tosses, you greatly reduce the chance for total loss. Notice how the probability for getting nothing continues to shrink. That's the big benefit.

Diversification allows you to increase your chances for accomplishing your goal—winning $1,000 per flip—and reduces your chances for a total washout. If you lose sight of these goals, diversification does make things look worse since you have virtually no chance for winning the big money. Now you should see that's a misperception caused by forgetting the risk-reward relationship and why so many people fail with financial planning.

Interestingly, if you want to maximize the chances for winning it all, there's no question you should take one toss, and you'll have a 50 percent chance for success. However, you must also accept the 50 percent chance to go bust. That may be an acceptable strategy to use in Vegas, but it has no place for your long-term financial planning. By diversifying your holdings, you make it easier to accomplish your goals. When it comes to financial planning, there's nothing wrong with using diversification to make the long road a lot easier.

HOW MANY STOCKS IS ENOUGH?

Diversification works on a simple principle. When some stocks are up, others will be down, and the effects tend to cancel. That's what makes the coin-tossing game so easy to see. You should expect that half the time you'll guess the outcome right, and half the time you'll be wrong. The same thing happens when you hold a large basket of stocks. They won't all go up, but they won't all go down either.

Well, how many stocks do you need in a portfolio to make it work?[47] It's a tricky answer, but without getting into the details, with as few as 18 stocks, you can achieve reasonably good diversification. For most people, upwards of 30 stocks will do the trick. However, no matter how many stocks you choose, you must make sure that you don't buy them in the same industry. That's not diversification.

Purchasing all tech stocks, for instance, is equivalent to putting your eggs in different baskets and loading them onto the same truck. If that sector hits a bump in the road, all your stocks may suffer losses even though the overall market is rising. Diversification works because when one stock or sector's value rises, another one may fall. Those extreme effects cancel out, leaving you with the long-term stock returns, on average. Okay, diversification sounds like a good idea, but who wants to take the time to research and select so many stocks to manage?

SPIDERS TO THE RESCUE

Fortunately, diversification is easy. By holding a broad-based market index, such as the S&P 500, you'll instantly own 500 of the largest, most highly capitalized companies in the world representing every sector. Almost all mutual fund companies have an S&P 500 fund. However, the choice preferred by many investors is to use an exchange-traded fund that tracks the index. Probably the most popular are the Standard & Poor's Depositary Receipts,[48] abbreviated as SPDR and pronounced "spiders." It's an entire family of over 130 ETFs managed by State Street. Recall from Chapter 1 that ETFs are like mutual funds, except they trade on an exchange like a stock. There's an entire family of spiders you can buy to get great diversification in sectors like financials, pharmaceuticals, biotech, health care, oil and gas, and emerging markets, just to name a few.

The most popular is the SPDR S&P 500 ETF, which trades under the ticker SPY. Rather than taking your chances with buying a single stock like Amazon, Apple, IBM, Home Depot, or any other big-name stock you can think of, by simply buying SPY, the individual stock you had targeted is most likely part of the index. Why do most fee-based advisors have arachnophobia and not advise investing in a broad-based index such as the S&P 500?

They're not fearful of spiders. They're fearful of not getting paid.

Index funds, like SPY, are passively managed, which means investors aren't paying for the manager's stock-picking skills, so the expenses are at rock bottom. That means there's no money for the fund to distribute as commissions. Consequently, advisors often bash the notion of diversification and talk investors into buying the stocks or mutual funds they want to sell. You can see how easy it is to spin a story. Your fee-based advisor may say, "Mr. Client, the reason index funds don't charge a high fee is that there's no skill involved. Our company, on the other hand, uses a proprietary, highly sophisticated computerized program to pick the best stocks. And, with only a 2 percent fee, it's a steal. You tip your waitress more than that, right?" That's usually all it takes to be sold. You'll find out in Chapter 6 just how big that fee is once you consider how it compounds over time. But for those who work with three blind mice, buying a broad-based index, such as the S&P 500, is the easiest and cheapest way to get instant diversification

WHEN RISK ISN'T RISKY

Diversification works because extreme values tend to cancel out. That same idea can be used when selecting different assets for investments. One choice may be risky if used by itself, but when combined with another, it may not be as risky. In fact, if combined in the right ways, all risks may be removed. It's ironic that you could have a portfolio of assets that are each quite risky, but when held together, they behave like a T-bill. There is no price risk.

For example, using the previous coin-tossing game, there was a lot of risk because you had to choose between heads and tails. You had a 50 percent chance to win or lose. Diversification helped to greatly reduce those chances, but it didn't eliminate all risk. However, what if the rules allowed you to choose both heads *and* tails per flip?

The market realizes both choices can be combined, which means you're guaranteed to win. Recall from Chapter 2 that if interest rates are 2 percent, a one-year $1,000 Treasury bill is priced at $980. If this coin-tossing game was a financial asset, the "heads" bet and "tails" bet would each be priced at $980. You could pay $980 to bet on heads and another $980 to bet on tails. In total, you've spent $1,960 to be guaranteed to win $2,000, exactly a 2 percent return on your money. Even though the coin flip bets are riskier individually, the market will price them like Treasury bills since it's easy to diversify away the unwanted risk. The most important point is that when you embark on a financial plan that encourages you to hold a few hand-selected stocks, you're taking excess risk for which you're not going to earn a single return. That doesn't make a bit of sense, yet many advisors suggest it. However, when a portfolio is properly diversified, it allows you to earn additional rewards for which there is no additional risk—a pretty neat trick since the risk-reward relationship suggests it can't be done. But now that you understand diversification, we can clarify that relationship. Risk is only rewarded if it can't be diversified away. By using proper diversification, it's the closest you'll get to money for nothing. And if you're going to meet your long-term financial goals, you must pick up all the free money you can get.

TAKING RISK FOR NO REWARD

In the stock market, there are two basic types of risk. There's *company-specific risk*, and overall *market risk*. The market risk is present just by being invested in the market. It doesn't matter which stocks you buy, but just by being in the market, you're faced with certain risks that you can't control. Think of market risk like driving on a busy highway. It doesn't matter what you're driving or how safely you drive, there are risks just from being on the road.

However, company-specific risks are those related to a specific stock. Company-specific risk is like driving an unsafe car at high speeds on the highway. It's a risk that's unique to that driver and car—not the overall highway. Risks range from things like a bad earnings report, new competitors, legal issues, or just plain fraud. For example, even though General Electric (GE)[49] is a highly respected and well-run company, its stock price fell 45 percent in 2017, even though the S&P 500 rose nearly 20 percent. That loss is obviously due to unique risks in GE, not the overall market.

The most insightful thing to learn about diversification is that you'll only get rewarded for risks that *cannot* be diversified away in the market. In other words, if you choose to buy one or two stocks, you're taking additional risk (company-specific risk) for which you'll never be rewarded. Why?

The market knows that risk could be eliminated by diversification. The fact that you're choosing not to diversify is of no consequence. You're not going to get rewarded for it. The real irony of not diversifying is eye-opening. Any advisor who suggests you don't diversify is suggesting that you take additional risk for which you'll get no reward. Taking that advice is hardly a good idea for long-term financial planning.

MOUSETRAP #4:
THE MISUNDERSTOOD MAGIC OF DIVERSIFICATION

A mousetrap isn't dangerous if it's not set, and risk works the same way. Some investments appear risky, but if you know how to disarm them, they're less risky and may not be risky at all. It depends on how they're combined with others.

As this chapter shows, diversification isn't an easy concept, and the benefits are far deeper reaching than most people realize. Because of the complexities, you can run into trouble with three blind mice.

Your trust account, for instance, may stipulate the use of conservative investments. You wish to buy 100 shares of Walmart, but your attorney says that shares of stock violate the trust account agreement because they're too risky. However, if he doesn't know you own a Walmart bond through your advisor, he won't see that much of the potential risk is shielded by the bond. The shares won't be nearly as risky as if purchased alone. Had he known you held the bond, or had you known to tell him, the overall picture would show there's little risk with that decision.

As another example, a popular strategy is to buy a long-term discount bond, and invest the difference in a broad-based index, such as the S&P 500. Because bond prices get cheaper when interest rates are high, the strategy works best during periods of high interest rates. For example, say interest rates are 8 percent, and you have $500,000 cash in your brokerage account. You could buy a five-year, zero-coupon bond for about $463,000. Take the remaining $37,000 and invest in the S&P 500. If market prices rise during that time, you'll make money on the $37,000 invested. But if the market unravels and you lose some or all of your $37,000, at least your bond will mature to $500,000 in five years. In other words, you're guaranteed to get your $500,000 back in five years.

Even though it appears to be risky to drop $37,000 into the market, when combined with the discount bond, you're only investing the future interest that would have been earned on the bond. However, if you deposited $37,000 to the trust account to invest in the S&P 500, it may be viewed as too risky.

Short sales present a new element of traps. With short sales, you borrow shares from the broker with the requirement to return 100 shares of the same stock in the future. The hope is that the share price falls and you pocket the difference. As a simple example, say you short 100 shares of IBM[50] at $150 per share, which means you'll collect the $15,000 cash just as if you sold actual shares. At a later date, you buy the shares back for $130 per share, or $13,000, so you pocket the $2,000 difference. When buying, you hope to buy low and sell high. When you short shares, you want to sell high and buy low. You're still buying low and selling high, just in the opposite order.

Shorting shares can be risky, but again, it depends on how it's used. Many times, you'll see corporate managers shorting shares to secure profits against their employee stock options. Say someone shorts 100 shares of IBM, but now wants to fund a trust account by purchasing 100 shares of IBM. Again, the attorney may say it violates the trust agreement, even though when combined with the short shares, there's absolutely zero risk. That's the danger of working with three blind mice. None can see your entire financial picture, so they act accordingly from their isolated perspectives. Each may believe they're doing what's best for you, but because they don't communicate with each other, the result is that you may end up holding more risk. To properly measure risk, you must look at the entire financial picture.

Accountants are notorious for being blind to diversification, too. If you show a list of assets on a spreadsheet, say for taxes, accountants love to put numbers into boxes and look at financial ratios—this number divided by that one is too big; that number divided by this one is too small, and so on. They may see a *red flag* because you have far too much invested in the stock market and suggest diversifying it. However, they don't see that you have the discount bond in the trust, or short shares in your brokerage account. They don't understand that your overall financial picture is well diversified because they're only seeing a small portion; they're blind to the rest. If you take their suggestion and reduce your exposure to the stock market, the trap is sprung, and you just increased your overall risk even though the accountant's intentions were good and designed to help you reduce risk.

The biggest risk is too little diversification. All too often, financial advisors select a small basket of handpicked stocks. They'll give great spiels on why these stocks give you the best chance to make the most money, but they're probably just the ones where they'll earn the biggest commissions. Chances are, those same stocks are already in the S&P 500, but you're now just pressing your bets on a select few. Just like the coin-tossing examples in this chapter, the more you take, the more likely you are to receive the long-term average. By not diversifying, you're taking too much risk for no additional reward.

Understand that diversification is a powerful, but highly misunderstood, financial tool. If you're working with three blind mice, it's your job to make sure they see the full financial picture. In the world of financial planning, the biggest risks are always the ones you can't see.

Solomon, the richest man who ever lived, said, "Divide your portion to seven, or even to eight, for you do not know what misfortune may occur on the earth."

CHAPTER 5

TRAP #5

The Best-Laid Plans Of Mice and Men: Average Traps That Will Foil Your Financial Plan

The best-laid plans of mice and men often go awry. That's a line from an 18th-century poem[51] about a mouse that carefully builds its winter nest in a wheat field only to have it destroyed by a farmer's plow. So much for being careful. The irony is that while the mouse was trying to find a secluded, safe place to make its nest, it inadvertently exposed itself to greater risks.

Financial planning has similar risks. No matter how carefully you build your nest eggs, there are always factors you'll never see coming—the unknowns that can make you fall short. Or worse yet, put them in line of a farmer's plow that destroys them. For investors, the risks you can't see are bigger than those you can. Some are mathematical. Some are psychological. But none are commonsensical. If your financial plans are handled by three blind mice, you must understand the traps to keep them out of the wheat fields. The best-laid plans often go awry.

AN AVERAGE TRAP THAT'S
NOT SO AVERAGE

Financial planners have a difficult job, as they must make projections far into the future. How much will the market return each year? What will the inflation rate be? What will health care cost? All of these are important factors, but we don't know the answers until after the fact, so all we can do is estimate them. As Yogi Berra said, "It's tough to make predictions, especially about the future."[52]

To make things easy, why not use average growth rates?

Averages have tremendous predictive powers, and they're used by practitioners in every field from actuaries setting insurance rates to gamblers predicting the turn of a card at Black Jack tables. If they work so well for other fields, why not use them for financial planning? Rather than trying to predict how the market will perform over the next 20 years, just use the long-term average, plug that number into your financial calculator, and presto, you've got your answer. If it sounds like a great idea, your three blind mice just put you in the middle of the wheat field. Hold on a minute, what's wrong with using the average? Isn't it the closest thing to a crystal ball?

Ask any statistician, and you'll hear the past is the best predictor of the future. If there's a long history of information, just take the average, and you'll have a good estimate to use for all future expectations. How tall will your son be? Probably five feet ten inches. How much rain will the Sahara Desert get next year? About four inches. In many cases, you'll get reasonably accurate forecasts just by using the average, so people love to use them to make estimations easier. Which golf score will win the Masters Tournament[53] in 2017? Since 1935, the average score has been 279.6, and Sergio Garcia's winning score for 2017 was 279, right on the average. Amazing, right?

Well, not so fast.

Using averages to make predictions works well if there's not a lot of variation, or what market practitioners call volatility, in the data. Since 1935, the lowest winning golf score at the Masters was 270 and the highest was 289, so for 82 years, all scores were reasonably close. Because each year's winning score is not too far from the average, it makes sense that using the average to predict next year's score works well and probably always will. Market returns, however, aren't like that at all. Instead, markets have dramatic variations in returns, or volatility, and that's where the trap not only lies; it just begins.

The first trap is that advisors usually use simple averages. You know the kind you learned in high school where you add up all the numbers and divide by the number in the set? For example, if a stock rose 5 percent in one year, 10 percent in the second, and 15 percent in the third, they'd say the average return is 10 percent. There's nothing mathematically wrong about adding up the numbers and dividing by 3, as it's one way to describe the average. The trouble for you is that this simple average normally doesn't reflect the returns you're going to experience. It sounds like a small, nitpicky thing. But once you see the damage it can do, you'll see why you must keep your three blind mice connected. This is far from your average trap.

THE AVERAGE IS MOST LIKELY WRONG

The first problem with averages is that they're most likely to be wrong. The average is deceptively simple. It's the single number that best represents all the data. Just add up all the numbers and divide by the number in the set, and that's the average.

Averages are useful in many cases, as they can create mathematical shortcuts. If you want to add up the numbers from 1 to 100, you can take the long way and add them up one by one. It's slow, and there's lots of room for mistakes.

Averages, however, make it simple. The average is 50.5, the number that lies exactly in the middle[54] of 1 and 100. Therefore, the sum must be 50.5 * 100, or 5,050, attained much faster using the average, and with 100 percent precision. Averages can be powerful when efficient, accurate calculations are needed, and that's what makes them tempting for financial advisors to use. However, there's a side to averages that most advisors never consider. While the average number is your best estimate, it doesn't mean it's good. If there's a lot of variation in the numbers, it's more likely to be wrong.

For example, if you toss a coin 20 times, the average number of heads that will show is 10, so by guessing that number, you'll be correct more often than by choosing any other number. It's a powerful statement and leads people to believe the result must always be close to 10. After all, how else could it be the best guess, unless it's right the vast majority of the time? It's like the math joke of the statistician who drowned in a river with an average depth of three feet. It sounds impossible until you realize the average depth is quite different from the shallowest and deepest parts of the river.

If you did this experiment thousands of times and tallied the results, you'd see that, just like a river, there can be a lot of variation, and you'd get a bell curve representing the wide range of possibilities.

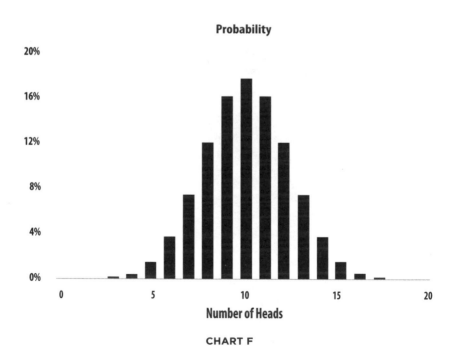

CHART F

The center of the curve lines up on 10, which is why it's the average and the best guess. However, notice there's a lot of variation around that guess, and observing 10 heads only occurs 18 percent of the time.

Even though 10 is the best guess, you'll be wrong 82 percent of the time.

The more variation, the wider the curve gets. If you think this curve is wide, wait until you see what market returns look like. It's ironic that everyone's best estimate is often wrong and no one's average is ever the same. Market returns work in a similar way. Over the past 100 years, the market return is about 10 percent. However, rarely will you ever see 10 percent. Instead, you'll see a wide range of gains or losses, possibly more than 25 percent in any given year. The chances of getting 10 percent in any one year are slim, even though it's the long-term average. Of course, half the time, the observed number of heads will be above 10 and half the time it'll fall below. Isn't this the very reason for using the average in your financial calculations? If your market returns are 10 percent, on average, then using 10 percent should get you the same answer in the long run, right? It's an easy belief, but it sets a complex trap.

THE CAGR TRAP

When explaining financial plans, I try not to get too much into the math because it can be easily misunderstood and quite overwhelming. Numbers can scare people. But hey, if you want to earn a million dollars, that's a number, and a big one at that. Sometimes, we must talk numbers, but I'll keep them as simple as I can. When calculating your market returns, there's a big difference between the simple average—the one you learned in high school—and what's called the compounded annual growth rate, or CAGR,[55] the one your money's going to earn.

For instance, let's say you invest $1,000 into Monster Mousetrap Fund and expect to earn 10 percent per year over four years. That means your ending balance should be $1,464.10. The math is easy. Just multiply your initial deposit by 1.10 for four years:

$$\$1,000 * (1.10) * (1.10) * (1.10) * (1.10) = \$1,464.10$$

But let's say the fund's actual numbers were 5 percent, 25 percent, -8 percent, and 18 percent over the four-year period. The simple average return is 10 percent, so there shouldn't be a problem. It's exactly what you were expecting, on average, so your balance should be exactly what you were expecting—$1,464.10.

However, if you checked your broker's statement, not counting fees, you'd see your balance is slightly less at $1,424.85. It's not a big difference, and you need to understand why there's a difference at all. It's the key to the trap. When you invest, you don't get the average. Instead, you get the compounded growth rate. Rather than multiplying by 1.10 for four years, you add "1" to each return, so 5 percent becomes 1.05, and a loss of 8 percent becomes 0.92 (keeping 92 percent is the same as losing 8 percent). If you multiply your $1,000 investment to each of these returns, you'd get a different answer:

$$\$1,000 * (1.05) * (1.25) * (0.92) * (1.18) = \$1,424.85$$

Mathematically, your compounded annual growth rate, or CAGR, is 9.3 percent per year. You were expecting 10 percent but you came up a little short, so that's why the balances are different. The small difference, however, is magnified even more if the discrepancies in market returns are larger or as time is increased.

For example, let's say you had found a more volatile fund, Radical Rodent Fund, which returned 90 percent in the first year, 15 percent in the second, *lost* 70 percent in the third, and then gained 5 percent in the fourth. If you take the simple average, you'll get the same 10 percent average, which makes it sound like you should expect the same $1,464.10 after four years. After all, the average is the average, and it either works or it doesn't. However, if you invested $1,000 in this fund, your ending balance would be $688. You lost 31 percent, or almost 10 percent per year. Wait a minute—what's that sound?

Yep. That's the farmer's plow. It's like a mousetrap, only bigger. How could the simple average return be a 10 percent gain, but the actual result is a 10 percent loss?

When you calculate a simple average, all returns get equal weight, but when returns compound, the average can get pulled far higher than what's truly representative of the data. It would be like saying the average net worth of Microsoft employees is 10 million dollars. But if you actually checked, you'd find that's far from true. It was Bill Gates'[56] $90 billion net worth that skewed the numbers. Even though it's technically "the average," it's not representative of any of the employees. Extreme values, higher or lower, artificially influence the simple average.

That means large balances get increasingly big during good years—but can take dramatic drops during bad years, too. Likewise, high returns don't bolster small balances much, whereas high balances are greatly affected by small declines. A 30 percent return isn't going to make much of a difference on a $100 deposit, but a 5 percent drop makes a big difference on a million dollars. Just a simple tweet from Donald Trump caused havoc for Amazon. In May 2018, Amazon's stock price dropped 4.2 percent in a day, causing Jeff Bezos,[57] Amazon's founder, to lose $5.2 billion. Don't be too concerned. With a net worth of $120 billion, he's still managing to make ends meet, but the point is that the sequence of returns can make a dramatic difference between the simple average and the compound growth rate if the variations are large enough.

Most advisors use simple averages to project your expected returns, and show the performance of their stock selections or mutual funds. At best, it's a misleading figure, but if there's been a lot of volatility, it's borderline criminal and on the wrong side of the border. It's not necessarily their fault. Many are just shown the returns from their company's research department and simply don't know how the numbers were calculated. Regardless of how the numbers became part of your plan, the problem is bigger; three blind mice never pay the price you do.

Let's say an advisor tries to sell you on his stock-picking prowess and says one of his picks earned his clients an average of 73 percent for the past 10 years. He thinks it's going to have the same performance over the next 10 years and wants to know if you want a piece of the action—for a hefty fee, of course. A quick calculation shows a $10,000 investment would be worth over $2.4 million. What's the first thing that comes to your mind?

If you say, "Wait. I need to take out a second mortgage," you need to go back to the beginning of the chapter. Hold off on signing the mortgage papers until you ask how the numbers were calculated. Otherwise, you can end up in a trap that defies logic.

LOSE MONEY BY EARNING AN AVERAGE OF 73 PERCENT PER YEAR

If you can earn an average of 73 percent per year, it's tempting to base your decisions on that average. Even if you don't get exactly 73 percent, you must be earning something close because it is, after all, the average. You ask for the data and can't believe your eyes. You check the calcula-

Viavi Solutions (VIAV)	
Year	Return
1997	48.0%
1998	74.0%
1999	820.0%
2000	-51%
2001	-80%
2002	-72%
2003	42.0%
2004	-13%
2005	-25%
2006	-12%
	Average = 73.0%

TABLE B

tions again, and, lo and behold, the advisor's right. The stock did earn an average of 73 percent per year.

Now, however, let's check the compounded annual growth rate—the rate your money actually earned during the 10-year period. Investors lost 50 percent of their money at the end of 10 years. That's a compounded annual growth rate of negative 7 percent per year.

If you're wondering how that's possible, it helps to prove my point that you must be careful with averages. Here's how it happened. From 1997 to 2006, Viavi Solutions (VIAV)[58], formerly JDS Uniphase, had one of the most astonishing rises and falls in stock market history, giving it a profile that looked more like a Hawaiian volcano rather than a stock price chart.

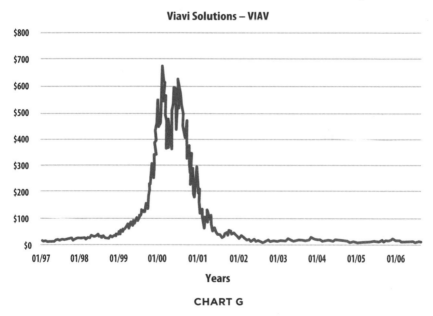

Viavi Solutions – VIAV

CHART G

Its price was about $15 at the beginning of 1997 and peaked at $666 in March 2000, just before the tech wreck. It closed near $10 at the end of 2006. If you paid $15 in 1997 and sold for $10 in 2006, you don't need a finance degree to see that's an overall loss. You don't even need a calculator. However, it's easy to mask with simple averages. Because of the large prices that occurred during that 10-year period, the average return wasn't negative at all—it was 73 percent.

To further see the effects of compounding on the results, notice that if you paid $15 per share in 1997 and sold for $10 in 2006, you didn't lose one-third of your money as it may appear. Overall, the math shows you lost 50 percent. Simple averages are deceptive when large deviations occur. That's what happened with Viavi, especially with the 820 percent return posted in 1999. It pulled the simple average returns very high; your balance, as you might imagine, was most damaged by the following three years, with *losses* of 51 percent, 80 percent, and 72 percent. These aren't holes in the boat. It's the *Titanic* striking the iceberg. Calculating an average return of 73 percent per year but actually losing half your money sounds impossible, until you understand that the simple average may not reflect an accurate picture of extreme values.

I recently held a lunch and learn workshop for clients and friends on the false/positive returns in the stock market. In the seminar, I asked the group, "Imagine you're the advisor and you've invested your friend's retirement monies in the S&P for 10 months, from January 2019 to October 2019. How would you feel if their account went up over 17 percent?" (in other

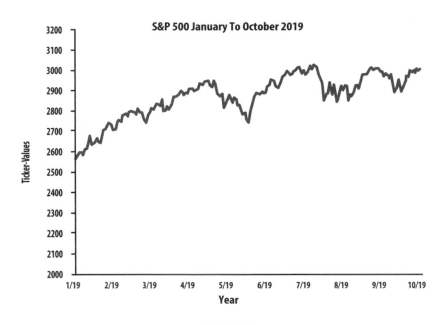

CHART H

words, $100,000 is now $117,000!) Smiles lit up on everyone's face as one guest shouted out, "My friends would say I'm the man! They would love me and I'd want to tell everyone what I did and get more business."

Another woman perked up and said, "Well, I've been in the market two years and haven't made any money!"

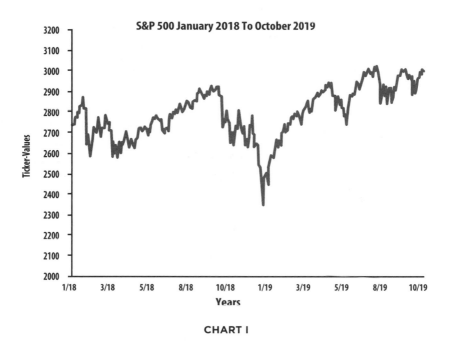

CHART I

I showed a graph from January 2018 to October 2019 where the return averaged 1.6 percent over that period of time before fees! I then asked the excited gentlemen, "How do you feel if you invested your friend's money during THAT time?" I heard the client grumble a sound . . . *"UGH!"*

Keep in mind since January 2000 to October 2019 the S&P is slightly up over 100 percent, but if carefully reviewed that equates to a whopping 5.6 percent yearly for all that risk, which most retirees can't handle. With two significant stock market drops in that period, it can really affect the portfolio returns. For young people who are working it may be okay, but for retirees who are taking out money to live on . . . that's a lot of antacid medication!

CHART J

So be careful with numbers that most advisors use—as you can see, they'll always cast them in the best light to make the sale. Telling prospective clients they lost 50 percent isn't very uplifting. Showing average returns of 73 percent per year gets their attention and their money.

Don't be afraid to challenge their numbers by asking for the compounded annual growth rate. They can't mask that figure.

MARKET VOLATILITY: THE FARMER'S PLOW

When using averages, it's easy to get lured into thinking you know where your stock's heading, especially over the long run. If a stock's earning an average of 10 percent per year, it makes people believe it'll just keep chugging along at a reasonably steady 10 percent rate. No stock does that. Viavi proved it many times over. Why are averages so difficult to rely on?

Investors buy and sell shares based on news, and because news arrives into the market randomly, stock price changes are random. Sometimes the news is positive, and sometimes negative. As investors react to the news, however, it creates small random shocks to stock prices, which is called volatility. There's a mathematical way to measure it, but that's not important. What's important is that you understand these small random fluctuations can greatly alter the price of a stock over time. As an analogy, if you toss a coin 10 times, you'll get a certain sequence of heads and tails. However, if you toss it another 10 times, you shouldn't be surprised that you'll get a different sequence. Even though it's the same coin with the same probabilities for heads or tails, the outcomes are very different. Those same random fluctuations apply to stock prices, and they are just one reason predictions can easily fail.

Millions of shares of stock may be traded each day from investors around the world. Some are buying; some are selling. Some orders are large while others are small. There's no way to tell when these trades will arrive at the exchange or the effect they'll have on the current stock price. Rarely, however, will any series of trades, even if small, have zero impact on the stock's price. Just watch any actively traded stock, and you'll see the price change a penny or two nearly every second.

Now think of each trade arriving at the exchange as a coin flip. If it lands heads, the trade pushes the stock price a tiny bit higher. If tails, it pushes it a touch lower. When the closing bell rings, these random fluctuations—the volatility—may force the stock price higher or lower based on nothing but chance, and that can lead stocks down different paths. In other words, if those identical fluctuations arrived at the exchange in a different order, you'd get a different closing price.

It goes against our intuition. You'd think that if a stock's price oscillates a little higher and a little lower, these effects would cancel out and there'd be no real effect on the price. But is this the case?

Unlike most scientific experiments, we can't run a test over and over of the same stock on the same day, so it's easy to overlook the effect that this randomness can have, especially over long periods of time. However, we can simulate a stock's random behavior.

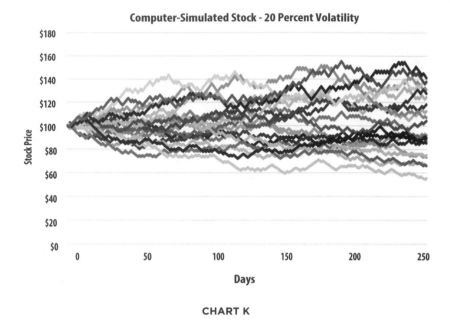

CHART K

Above is a chart showing a computer simulation of hundreds of hypothetical identical stocks starting at $100 and trading with 20 percent volatility for a full year, or about 250 trading days.

The above chart was essentially created by a computer flipping a coin. If it lands heads, the stock rises a tiny bit. If tails, it falls a tiny bit. Volatility is a mathematical calculation that shows how much "a little bit" really means. However, you could get a similar-looking chart by using a pencil and paper. Just flip a coin and make your $100 stock rise or fall one dollar depending on the outcome of the flip.

Just as coin tosses yield different results due to randomness, so will stock prices. Even though all stock prices started at $100 and traded for the same number of days at the same volatility, they end up at different prices after one year. And in some cases, it could be quite different. In one year, 20 percent volatility may make some of those stocks trade as low as $40 while pushing others as high as $160. That's a lot of possibilities for one year. You'd think identical stocks would land in the identical spot assuming all other conditions are the same. Randomness, or volatility, ensures they won't. Keep in mind—this wide range has nothing to do with news, earnings, interest rates, or anything else that could drive a stock's price higher or lower. Those are completely separate issues from volatility. We're simply looking at the effect that small, random jolts can have on a stock's price over time.

Interestingly, at the end of the year, if you tallied all the closing stock prices, you'd get a bell curve, just like the coin flips in the previous chapter. In other words, most of the stock prices will land near the center, but there will be occasions when they can drift far away. It's counterintuitive, but think about tossing coins. If you flip a coin 10 times, on average, you'll get five heads and five tails. If heads bump prices higher while tails push them lower, on average you'll get very little effect, and the stock's closing price at the end of the year will be close to where it started at the beginning of the year. In other words, stock prices are quotes and are most likely to land in the center, and that's exactly what the bell curve shows.

However, "most likely" doesn't mean all the time. If you flip a coin long enough, you'll see occasions where you get eight or more heads in a row. In those cases, the stock's price may get pushed much higher above the curve's center. Conversely, you'll get times when tails will dominate, and the stock's price gets pushed far below the center of the curve. It doesn't happen often, which is why those extreme stock prices don't fall below the center of the bell curve, but it does happen. When setting your financial plans, don't ever confuse "unlikely" with "impossible." In the above simulation, the chance of seeing our $100 stock above $120 or below $80 will happen about 34 percent of the time.

The longer the investment is held, the wider the variations become. Over a two-year period, that same $100 stock may fall to $15 or rise to $185 based on nothing but market volatility.

As an investor, however, you only see the year-end result of the stock you're holding, and it's easy to overlook an important point. The final stock price is the result of nearly an unlimited number of possible paths that could have occurred. Just because your stock may have earned 10 percent this year doesn't mean it's going to do the same thing next year even if market conditions and volatility were identical. It's an overlooked risk since we never see all the possible paths, but that doesn't mean the risk wasn't there. Remember, the most dangerous traps are those you can't see, and the concept of volatility is a big one. Using long-term averages is a special kind of trap because you can see real stock prices and calculate real averages. You can plug them into real financial models and get real answers. Few people realize the year-end closing price is one of the thousands of possibilities that could have occurred.

Even though you may be using long-term averages for your projections, don't be surprised if they don't come true. Sometimes they'll be better; sometimes they'll be worse. Rarely will they be on target. One thing is certain, half the time: your returns will fall below the average. You must allow for that in your long-term plan and know how to make the right adjustments when returns fall short. It's one more reason to have annual reviews to ensure your mice stay on the same page, or they may end up in the same trap.

WHY THREE BLIND MICE MISS BY MILES

Because of their widespread use, averages are convenient and addictive. The more they're used, the more they're accepted, and the more advisors rely on them for accuracy. Whenever you sit with an advisor, accountant, or attorney, there's no question they're going to use market averages for their calculations.

If you need $100,000 in 10 years to pay for your children's college and expect to earn 10 percent each year, you'll need to invest $488 per month. If you assume 8 percent, you'll need $547 per month, or about 12 percent more. Just because the calculations are easy doesn't mean they're correct. If the assumptions behind the numbers are wrong, so are the answers. Computer programmers call it GIGO[59]—garbage in, garbage out. As the previous section showed, stock prices can show extreme swings just because of volatility, or the small random daily shocks to stock prices. It's a big problem, and that's why it's impossible to predict where a stock's price will go.

In the stock simulation, we assumed a constant 20 percent volatility every day for 250 trading days. Steady volatility, however, will never happen. It was done to show how volatility by itself can impact a stock's price. However, that 20 percent figure will change, sometimes significantly, during the year, as new information reaches the market. It could be inflation warnings, trade wars, gas prices, terrorist attacks, commodity prices, even something President Trump tweeted and about a bazillion other things. Remember, investors react to news. Under normal conditions, some markets report good earnings that may push a stock up 2 percent. However, if it's a raging bull market, it may push it up 10 percent. Conversely, if there are inflation fears, the stock price may actually fall. Different economic conditions cause investors to react differently to similar news. All this random news changes volatility. Part of the year, we may have 20 percent volatility. In a short time, it could be 40 percent. Later, it could be 10 percent. In other words, volatility is volatile. In short, no rate of return, no matter how carefully calculated or conservatively estimated, is stable. To show how much it can change, there's an index called the Volatility Index, or VIX,[60] which calculates the volatility of the S&P 500 index.

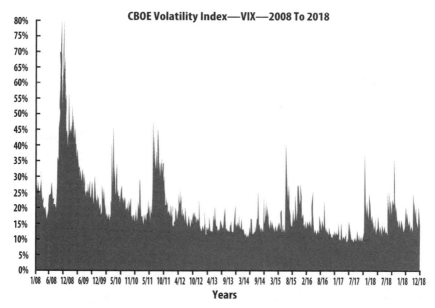

CHART L

For the 10-year period from 2008 to 2018, the VIX had a low of 9 percent and a high of 81 percent. The VIX always spikes during times of fear, which is why that high occurred during the Great Recession of 2008. If that looks high on the chart, during the Crash of 1987, the VIX doubled that level and skyrocketed to 160 percent. The chart clearly shows the S&P 500 typically chugs along at about 20 percent per year. That's the long-term historical average. However, like most other averages, there can be large deviations from that average, from 9 to 80 percent. Because volatility changes over time, it can cause any stock-return estimate to be off target. It will cause your three blind mice to miss by miles. Here's where the trap unfolds.

Depending on which years are considered, the S&P 500 has generated long-term returns in a range of somewhere between 7 to 10 percent per year. Out of convenience, advisors will pick a number in this range as the rate of return you can expect to earn year after year. To compensate for the possibly of falling short, they'll often pick a number toward the lower end of the range. An advisor may say, "The long-term return has been 10 percent, but let's be conservative and use 8 percent per year for our calculations."

The problem is that few advisors understand just how volatile that assumed return is. They think it means you're going to earn reasonably close to 8 percent every year. However, this figure is big and the volatility surrounding that number is about 20 percent, or two-and-a-half times as much. That may not mean much to investors, but to put it in perspective, it's about saying your child's height could fall somewhere between a gerbil and a giraffe. That much volatility creates a tremendous amount of possibilities for future stock prices, and because of that, using a single number as a long-term assumption isn't going to work.

When advisors use a single number, they're trying to project expected returns decades into the future with market rates that have a bipolar disorder. Imagine what happens when your three blind mice try to project your plans 10 years, 20 years, or more into the future. If you have $100,000 to invest today and want to know how much you can expect in 30 years, an advisor may whip out a financial calculator, punch in a few numbers, and confidently say, "Assuming 8 percent per year, you'll have just over one million dollars in 30 years. And because we're assuming 8 percent rather than 10 percent, you should be safe and easily on track for success."

Yeah, just like the mouse who built its nest in the wheat field.

If you invest in a $100 stock today with an expected 8 percent return, 20 percent volatility might make that return as low as *negative* 2 percent per year or as high as 14 percent. How much of a difference will that make?

If you invested $100,000 into this stock, you could end up with as little as $71,000 or as much as $5.2 million after 30 years.

Imagine thinking you're going to end up with one million dollars in 30 years but end up below $100,000. Keep in mind: this wide range has nothing to do with news, earnings, interest rates, or anything else that could drive a stock's price higher or lower. Those are completely separate issues from volatility. Instead, we're just considering the effect of the variations in the possible returns. I hope that got your attention. It's why financial planners need to focus on risk management and what to do if things go wrong. Murphy's Law says they probably will. It's not a problem if you plan for it and know how to build portfolios to hedge that risk. It's a problem when you're blindsided.

The biggest mistake many advisors make is to assume that the single return number selected is what you'll receive every year. Good financial advisors understand there'll be ranges of possibilities, so they must also plan for "what if."

A LOOK AT 100 YEARS OF RETURNS

The previous sections showed conceptually why volatility is such a problem for investors. But now let's look at actual market data to see just what 20 percent volatility can do to 10 percent returns. For the 20th century (1900 to 1999), the market has generated the following returns by decade.

Decade	Average Return Per Year
1900s	11.7%
1910s	5.58%
1920s	17.0%
1930s	5.19%
1940s	10.2%
1950s	21.1%
1960s	8.71%
1970s	7.53%
1980s	18.3%
1990s	19.1%
2000s	1.21%

TABLE C

The average return earned through this 100-year period is about 10 percent, but as shown previously, this average has an enormous amount of variation. During the decade of the 1900s, the market returned exactly 10 percent, but that was the only time it was even close to the 10 percent average for the entire century.

Long-term averages only produce accurate calculations if you invest over the entire period. For instance, a $1,000 investment in 1900 would have earned an average of 10 percent per year and be worth nearly $14 million in 2000. That's an accurate calculation since you're using the 10 percent average across the entire 100-year period.

However, even though 10 percent is the long-term average, you can't use it across any time period of your choosing and expect to get accurate results—remember GIGO. If you invest $10,000 at an average of 10 percent per year, you'd have $26,000 at the end of a decade. Well, if the long-term market average is 10 percent, will you end up with $26,000 at the end of every decade? Had you invested $10,000 in 1930, you'd have ended up with $9,400—a 64 percent shortfall. On the other hand, investing $10,000 during the 1990s earned 18.2 percent for a total of $53,000, and you more than doubled your $26,000 goal.

Even though the long-run 10 percent average was assumed for both decades, one left you well above your goal and the other left you severely below. Long-term averages are a dangerous tool to use across shorter time periods. Does that mean you should use shorter time frames to figure out the average?

That's worse.

Each decade comes with large variations, too, and the uncertainty is even greater for short-term planning. For example, the previous table showed, in the 2000s, the average return was 1 percent, but the following table shows the decade broken down by year. Once again, the story is the same: large variations from the average.

Year	Average Return Per Year (includes Dividends)
2000	-9.11%
2001	-11.98%
2002	-22.27%
2003	28.72%
2004	10.82%
2005	4.79%
2006	15.74%
2007	5.46%
2008	-37.22%
2009	27.11%

TABLE D

None of these are remotely close to the 1 percent return earned across the entire decade. If you were invested from 2000 to 2002, you lost 38 percent of your money. That's a big hit, especially if it was the year you expected to retire or send your children to college. From 2003 to 2006, you earned 73 percent—much better. But if you invested across the entire decade, you earned 1 percent per year, or about 10.5 percent on your money overall. Looking at the return across the entire decade paints a very different picture from what happened within that decade. If your plan was expecting 10 percent per year for 30 years, one-third of your time vanished. To add insult to injury, the paltry 1 percent wasn't enough to outpace inflation. Market returns are volatile, and they'll easily throw your targets off track. You can get long streaks of negative returns. You can also get long streaks of positive returns that leave them below your expectations. Trends up and down can last much longer than people expect.

DOES HISTORY REPEAT ITSELF?
—BABY BOOMERS BEWARE

Personally, I do believe history repeats itself, especially when it comes to the stock market. And yet the quote you will often hear from Mr. or Ms. Advisor is, "Over the long run, the stock market outperforms other asset classes." Say what? Now going on my 37th year in the profession, that record is still playing. Can someone please wake up and smell the coffee? Just try asking your advisor a very simple question. "How long is the long run?" I'm quite sure you'll hear a pin drop. At my workshops or during my radio shows, I often share the cycle of market history, which I'm still amazed hardly anyone is aware of. Let me see if I can explain. Let's start in the year 1899 and we will go to 2019. Is that long enough for you?

We all know there are good years and bad, as I went over in the previous chapters, but now let's add one more dimension. You're about to retire in just three short years, so you put 100 percent of your monies in the stock market. The stock market is on a tear and you don't want to miss out. You convince yourself, "Hey, why not? I'm about to retire so let's add more points on the scoreboard. I mean the retirement account. I deserve to retire in dignity, not disgrace, and it's only three more years—let's go for it." It's 1999 and you're excited. Heck, you may even mortgage your home, pull out cash, and double down. Sound familiar?

Let's take a look.

You see there are periods where the market made nothing—"bear market"—followed by a "bull market." As Wall Street says, the market slept like a bear (0 percent) and ran like a bull (12–15 percent).

Now let's review the S&P 500 for close to 100 years:

Bear Market 0%	Bull Market 12 to 15%
1899–1921 (22 yrs.)	1921–1929 (8 yrs.)
1929–1954 (25 yrs.)	1954–1966 (12 yrs.)
1966–1982 (16 yrs.)	1982–2000 (18 yrs.) 2nd Greatest
2000–2019?	Who Knows

TABLE E

As you compare the left side (bear market) and notice the good years wiped out the bad years but the right side (bull market) charged ahead despite a few down periods.

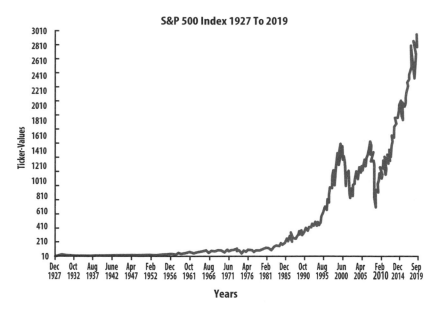

CHART M

By the way, had you retired in 2000 to 2019 and not taken any money out at all, your money grew approximately 76 percent (nice, right?), until you divide it by 19 years for 4 percent per year for all that risk.

So how long is long term? Well, history suggests a full bear-bull market cycle is over a 35-year period.

If you're in or near retirement, I suggest you heed Paul "Bear" Bryant's famous saying: "Offense sells tickets and defense wins championships."

As I stated before, money is emotional and that can affect your health and well-being. If you are still working now but lived through the correction in 2000 to 2003 or the crash and downturn of 2007–2009, it may be a dim memory, but if you were retired during these times, I bet you had serious concerns about how the correction would affect your retirement money. Imagine having $300,000 dwindle before your eyes to $180,000. That kind of shrinkage will take a toll on everyone's emotion and health. It may be time to play strong defense with your retirement.

Since I believe history repeats itself, there could be a third market correction around the corner that could be worse than the previous two. As Edmund Burke states, "Those who don't know history are destined to repeat it."

MUTUAL FUND MADNESS: THE TWR TRAP

Stock return averages are deceptively complex, but there's a related trap when investing in mutual funds. Most of the time, your three blind mice will use mutual funds, as there are a lot of benefits, especially with costs and diversification. As a benchmark, they'll look at the fund's 10-year returns and use that figure in your financial plans. For instance, one may say, "This fund's long-term average is 10 percent, so if you invest $500 every month, you can expect to have $102,000 in 10 years."

The math is correct if you want to base the answer on bad assumptions.

When mutual funds advertise a rate of return, it's called a *time-weighted return*, or TWR[61], also called a money-weighted return. The time-weighted return is a mathematical way of stripping out the effects of cash deposits or withdrawals. Without these adjustments, a fund's performance could look exceptionally good or bad just because of investors' money flowing in and out of the fund, and not because of the fund's performance.

It's easier to understand with an example. Let's say you bought $10,000 worth of Marvelous Mousetrap Fund on January 1, and it's worth $15,000 at year-end. It looks like a red-hot investment, as you made 50 percent on your money. But would you feel the same way if you discovered your advisor bought another $10,000 worth halfway through the year? Now it's ice cold. You've invested $20,000 total, but it's only worth $15,000, so you have a large overall loss. It was the additional money deposited that made the performance look so good—not the fund manager's skill. The same thing can happen with real mutual funds. If money pours into the fund, the asset value increases, and so does the fund's overall value.

On the other hand, what if you invested $10,000 at the beginning of the year, and the fund was worth $8,000 at the end of the year? It looks like a 20 percent loss. However, if your advisor sold $5,000 through the year, you have a net investment of $5,000 that's now worth $8,000, so it's a fabulous return. The point to see is that cash deposits and withdrawals can unfairly make investments look better or worse. As an investor, what you'd really like to know is whether the fund gained or lost the value of its holdings based on its abilities, not because of investors' deposits and withdrawals. That's what time-weighted returns show. If you see a fund that has an advertised return in its prospectus, say 10 percent per year over the past 10 years, that's a time-weighted return. It looks good. It sounds official. But despite the long-running track record, it's not the return you can expect on your money. I call it the TWR trap. The reason is that few long-term investors would have invested 100 percent of their money up front and held for the 10-year period. Why?

They don't have it.

It would be nice if advisors could figure out a single lump sum that clients need to invest today to reach future goals. Your children need $100,000 in 10 years for college? Sure, just write a check for $50,000 today and you're all set. It normally doesn't work that way. Instead, investors must put money away at periodic times, say every month or quarter. Over the years, prices fluctuate, so they end up buying some shares above the average price and some shares below the average price. That means some of their money will be making gains, while other dollars are taking losses. The overall return depends on the amount of money invested in the fund and the returns realized during those times. This is called *dollar-weighted returns*, or DWR[62]. Think of these as your personal returns—not those the fund reports.

To see why dollar-weighted returns can be so different from time-weighted, let's say the fund started the year at $50, rises to $65 mid-year, and then falls to $55 at year-end. If you invested $1,000 at the beginning of the year and held to the end, you earned 10 percent on your money, as you paid $50 and it's worth $55 after one year. However, let's say you were, instead, splitting up your investments over time, perhaps every six months. If you invested $500 at the beginning of the year and $500 six months later, you're in for an overall loss. Your first $500 earned 30 percent when the fund rose from $50 to $65 and is now worth $650. However, at that time, you invested another $500, so you have $1,150 in the fund. During the next six months, however, it dropped from $65 to $55, or over 15 percent. Because you have more money invested during this price decline, it carries more "weight" to your total performance. Overall, you've invested $1,000, but your position is now worth $973 at year-end. Without getting into the math, that's a 3.5 percent dollar-weighted loss even though the fund's time-weighted return shows it rose 10 percent through the year. To succeed with long-term financial planning, you must understand what the numbers mean, and financial math can play mind tricks even for those considered to be professionals like a nationally recognized investment club.

THE BEARDSTOWN LADIES WHO BEAT WALL STREET (ALMOST)

In 1983, a group of 16 older women formed an investment club in Beardstown, Illinois, which came to be known as the Beardstown Ladies[63]. They achieved national attention and authored a best-selling book, *The Beardstown Ladies' Common-Sense Investment Guide*, after posting 23.4 percent returns from inception through 1994, rivaling the returns of Warren Buffett. That's an impressive track record. With all the success and hype, four more books followed.

It was so eye-catching that it came under scrutiny when a personal finance counselor noticed their returns weren't audited and the club had no documentation to back up its claims. In defense, the club hired Price Waterhouse, which showed the returns were 9.1 percent during the twelve-year period—certainly not bad, but subpar when you compare it to the S&P 500, which returned 17.2 percent per year over the same time. By taking the club's advice, investors took additional risk and received half the returns. Why was there such a discrepancy between its 23.4 percent claim and the 9.1 percent actual result?

The returns included new investments made by its members.

That's right; the club didn't know the difference between time-weighted and dollar-weighted returns. Still, even if they had no financial experience at all, how could anyone not know that your bank balance will increase as you deposit more money? They just kept making deposits and chalking up the gains to stock-picking skills.

Here was a nationally recognized club whose financial acumen was apparently so strong it had an urban legend status. How could a small group of nonfinancial professionals consistently beat the market? Well, the answer was now embarrassingly apparent. Whether it was intentional, accidental, or just plain ignorance about finance, it missed the point. Millions of investors took the club's advice and ended up taking big losses or missed opportunities, and all because the members didn't back out the deposits from the calculations.

It led to a class-action lawsuit against the publisher, Hyperion.[64] (Nothing like a good ol' lawsuit to get your money back.) Were investors compensated for the complete lack of professionalism and egregious oversights? Well, sort of.

The publisher settled by offering anyone who bought the club's books to swap them for other Hyperion books. I'm not kidding. That was it. If anyone's long-term financial plans were completely derailed because of the bad advice, at least they had an extra book or two to read during retirement.

Unfortunately, most advisors are tricked into thinking the expected return is the easiest part of the business—just use the long-term average. A careless use of averages is probably the biggest problem. New clients have come to me because their financial plans have fallen behind. Their previous advisors told them they could expect to earn 8 percent, 10 percent, 15 percent, or whatever number they decided on. The problem isn't that their numbers were necessarily mathematically wrong. It depends on how many years of history you want to use to make your estimates. The problem is, they assume those numbers will be reasonably stable through time. Instead, they'll drastically fluctuate year after year. That changes the math, changes your plan, and changes your future.

If averages are making your head hurt, it means you understand the severity of it. Your headache can be cured with aspirin. But if just one of your three blind mice has a single whisker caught in a trap, by the time you find out, it may be too late. To have a successful financial plan, you must realize there are extraordinary fluctuations in long-term averages, but all too often, they're the single numbers used by advisors, accountants, and attorneys. When setting up your plan, it's not a safe assumption to use long-term averages of the distant past and project them into the future. Making financial plans based on a single long-term average is a mousetrap baited with a fresh piece of Swiss cheese. It's the ultimate temptation for a mouse. Imagine when there are three, and blind ones at that. Financial planning is about managing risk, so you must account for the possibility that those averages won't hold, and it's far more likely they won't, no matter how hard you try. "The best-laid plans of mice and men often go awry."[65]

MOUSETRAP #5:
THE BEST-LAID PLANS OF MICE AND MEN

After reading this chapter, it should be obvious that selecting a single rate of return as a long-term guide for your portfolio is a daunting task. However, it's this fact that leads to one of the biggest financial planning traps when you have multiple advisors. The single most important thing you can do when setting up your portfolio is to decide on the level of risk that allows you to accomplish your goals. That's defined by the rate of return you're seeking on your money. Set that rate too high, and you're taking too much risk to support the goal. You'll likely fail with disastrous consequences. Set it too low, and you'll definitely fail—it just won't be a disaster. Just like Goldilocks, you don't want risk being too hot or too cold; it must be just right. By setting the risk levels correctly on your required rate of return, you have the best chance of success.

Even if there's disagreement among advisors, and there probably will be, it's okay. What matters is that everybody comes up with an agreement on how the portfolios are to be managed. Think about professional football teams. Each has a head coach, offensive coordinator, defensive coordinator, and other members of the staff. Each coach has individual styles and philosophies on how those positions should be played. However, all must keep their strategies in line with that of the head coach. If the head coach says it's going to be a running game, then a running game it is. Each coach may disagree with that game plan, and that's okay. In fact, if each were the head coach of that team, different strategies may be carried out. However, there are a lot of ways to win a football game, and any single strategy isn't necessarily the only solution. What matters most is that everybody agrees with the plan and sticks with it. If each coach followed his own agenda, and kept it a secret from the others, the result would be chaos. Do the same for your financial plan. Pick a strategy but coordinate all efforts.

The problem occurs when you have multiple advisors. Each may have an agenda that doesn't correspond to your overall plan. For instance, one may have a desire to keep your assets safe and grow their assets under management, which yields a nice bonus at year-end. By keeping you in relatively safe assets, you won't lose money, but you'll miss your targets by a long shot. At the other extreme, another manager may set risk levels too high, as he may receive bonuses based on performance. Alternatively, he may want to win your business and encourage you to transfer other assets to his company, so he's going to do his best to impress you with his stock-picking skills. This almost always happens when a client takes some money to a new firm and says, "I have more, but just want to see what you can do with this money." That's an automatic signal to the advisor that the competition is on time to take on additional risk.

You must have a common goal for the team, and all advisors must agree on that goal. If not, it's like a football team with one player focused on setting a new NFL record, another player trying to impress the cameras and crowd, and another player trying to avoid injury since it's his last game before switching to a new team. Even though the crowd sees one team on the field and assumes everyone's playing to win, there are internal conflicts due to differing goals, and that will probably set them up for failure. Even though each player may have accomplished his individual goal, collectively they may lose the game. It's not a promising way to win a football game, and it's no way to set up your financial plan.

Of course, this is why you hired multiple advisors in the first place— let them handle the details. However, by working with three blind mice, it puts you right in the center of the team because you are, in effect, becoming an advisor. You must manage how they're managing your money. You've promoted yourself to head coach for a subject you know little about. You've got some mice running left, others running right, and some running on a hamster wheel.

MICE IN A MAZE: THE PROBLEMS BEGIN

When you hire multiple advisors, each will use different expected rates of return for a variety of reasons, but they won't necessarily be the rates that are best for you. Imagine sitting with your three blind mice. Mouse #1 thinks you'll earn 8 percent, Mouse #2 says 10 percent, and Mouse #3 believes 12 percent.

It might sound like a good plan, and actually lead some people to think they have a layer of diversification here. After all, some of your money is being invested at different rates of return. However, remember that the market doesn't care what anybody thinks, including mice. Just because your advisors think you'll earn a certain rate per year has absolutely no bearing on what you'll actually earn. That's up to the market. As shown in this chapter, those predicted rates are far more likely to be wrong than right. True, some may be better than expected, others may be worse, but it doesn't mean they must average out.

Trap #1: The first trap is set when one of your advisors falls short. Let's say the first advisor was expecting to earn 8 percent per year but only earns 4 percent per year after five years. Just as when a football team is behind, it must take a little more risk to catch up. And that's exactly what advisors will do. However, what if this advisor knew that your other two advisors were up 20 percent for the past five years and overall your portfolio is well ahead of schedule? There's no reason to play catch-up. But because this first advisor is blind to the other two, he exposes your money to additional unnecessary risk.

Trap #2: A second trap occurs when setting rates of return among three different advisors. For instance, let's say your investments with Mouse #1 rise 15 percent, Mouse #2 gains 25 percent, and Mouse #3 loses 10 percent. Overall, it sounds like a great year, and looks like you made an average of 40 percent. How much money did you make?

Your annual gain doesn't just depend on how much each advisor earns; it also depends on how much money each one manages. If Mouse #3 is your attorney managing a million-dollar trust, a 10 percent hit is a $100,000 loss. If the other two mice hold $100,000 each, you made $40,000 with them. Overall, you lost $60,000, or 5 percent for the year. This is quite a different outcome from the 40 percent average you thought you made. Here's a good example where diversification would have greatly helped. If the attorney lost 10 percent, it was an asset mix that went down when clearly others went up. After all, two of your other advisors made 15 percent and 25 percent returns. Had they been connected, all your money would have been distributed among these assets, and you'd have earned closer to 40 percent, depending on how the money was allocated. No matter what the gain turned out to be, it beats a 5 percent loss.

Trap #3: Because returns are so erratic and hard to predict, there's no doubt that multiple advisors will come up with different returns each year. In some years, the differences may be large. In others, they may be close. Even if they're close, it appears that the differences aren't a big deal. However, the small discrepancies compound over time and they can become big deals years later. In the chart below, the bold line shows the value of $100,000 over a 30-year period earning an expected 8 percent per year. The gray line shows what happens if you're wrong and earn only 6 percent per year. Notice how the difference between the two lines widens—that's the error in your estimates getting bigger and bigger over time.

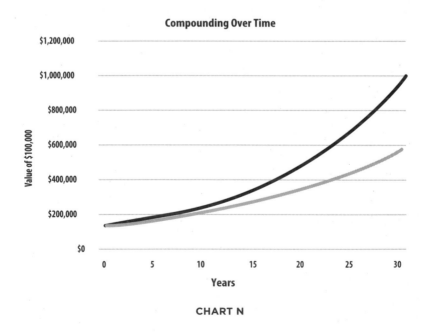

CHART N

After five years, the differences aren't too great. By earning 6 percent, you'd have about $134,000 rather than the $147,900 you expected by earning 8 percent. You're off by 9 percent. However, after 30 years, it becomes $574,000 versus $1,000,000. You're off by 43 percent. Imagine if the differences were off by 5 percent or 10 percent.

Trap #4: Advisors should focus on things that are known, how markets will respond under various conditions, and structure portfolios accordingly. The best approach to financial advising is risk management. The best advisors are those who understand how to manage the twists, turns, and volatility that the market throws at you.

However, as managers adjust portfolios to changing market conditions, they may sell some assets, buy others, and possibly even take short positions. The problem is that with more advisors, the chances for overlap greatly increase. Your financial advisor, for example, may buy a broad-based mutual fund while another may buy an inverse broad-based fund to hedge recent gains. Each manager may have good reasons for buying the two funds, but, unbeknownst to everyone including you, those funds are cancelling each other out. Your money's earning as much as if it were stuffed under your mattress.

A good financial planner risk manager knows how to compensate when plans fall below average and how to hedge those returns when they're above average. The hedges in the profitable years offset the losses in the losing years. The trick is about risk management, not predicting market returns.

MANAGING RISK, NOT UNCERTAINTY

In the financial markets, there's a difference between risk and uncertainty. Risk can be quantified and managed. It's imperfect knowledge, but at least we have an idea of the probabilities. Uncertainty, on the other hand, exists when the event is unknown, or the probabilities are unknown, such as the 9/11 terrorist attacks. Financial planning requires managers to manage the risks that are known.

Unfortunately, most advisors set up long-term financial plans by assuming a constant long-term rate of return. It's one of the riskiest variables in the financial markets, and yet it's the one that most advisors assume to be constant. Instead, you must accept the returns the market gives you. You can't predict the returns you're going to get, but you can play the cards you're dealt.

Good advisors will make tactical use of dollar-cost averaging, constant-dollar averaging, bond laddering, and time diversification to hedge the volatile nature of returns.

The highest standard in the financial industry and the legal system is a fiduciary duty, which means the advisor (the fiduciary) acts 100 percent of the time with your best interest of the principal (that's you) in mind. No decision should be based on commissions or the advisor's interests. The most important thing you can do is decide on your financial goals and share them with all advisors. The goals ultimately define the risks to be taken and the strategies to be used. But when you have independent advisors operating with separate goals, it creates hazards. When all use single rates of return for long-term planning, it sets wheels in motion that violate all the fundamental principles of risk management. While the best-laid plans often go awry, there's no reason to make planning more difficult by assuming a single rate of return over decades of investing.

> **PLANNING TIP:** Review and monitor you're spending habits with future prices in mind.

Luxury is anything that feels special. I mean, it can be a moment, it can be a walk on the beach, it could be a kiss from your child, or it could be a beautiful picture frame or special fragrance. I think luxury doesn't necessarily have to mean expensive.

CHAPTER 6

TRAP #6

Hidden Costs Can Rob You Blind: The Biggest Traps Are Those You Can't See

"Just remember, if you give a hundred and ten per cent, I get twenty per cent of that."

Remember when your mom or dad said, "Turn out the lights when you leave the room," or "Close the door; we're not heating the world," or, the most famous: "Money doesn't grow on trees"? I also use the same line on my children. Heck, I'll never forget the night I came home from work and my 18-year-old daughter, Meredith, greeted me at the door like a puppy wagging its tail excited to tell me about her day. She was so thrilled to tell me all about her job she was about to accept in New York City. Like a cheerleader cheering for his team, I was ecstatic for her as she kept repeating, "$720 dollar a week, Dad, $720 dollars." I think she had it spent already. All she could taste, feel, and see was the $720 a week. She hit the lottery in her young mind. Then the bombshell came when she asked, "What do you think?" I froze as so many thoughts darted through my head. I surely didn't want to throw cold water on her fire. Then it came to me—"the teacher will appear when the student is ready." So in my ninja stealth manner, we sat together as I asked many questions so she could give me her insight. I asked her to add up the cost of gas and tolls (MPG and inflation), wear and tear on the car, and time in the car she could be doing something else (time value of money); it was a three-hour round trip assuming no traffic, and let's not forget taxes that would be deducted. Yuck. As she ran the numbers, the excitement seemed to dwindle out rapidly. I remained silent, which was a miracle for me. Then, as if a light bulb went on, she turned to me, smiled, and said, "Dad, I'm worth way more than $9.73 per hour." This small, teachable moment will surely last a lifetime as her critical thinking awoke and she realized her value and how to weigh things.

It's not how much you make; it's how much you keep of it that counts. It's a powerful Wall Street saying reminding individual investors that costs matter. After all, it doesn't matter if you earn $100 or if you earn $120 and pay a $20 fee. Money saved is money earned, and there's no sense in making your financial plans more difficult by paying high fees, especially when they're not necessary. There are other choices. However, it's easier said than done. Many fees are hidden, and if you're not aware of them, you can step into traps that can quickly erode your long-term financial plans.

To make things more difficult, some of these hidden money-eaters are not true costs, but instead, misinterpretations behind the math of investing. As you read through this chapter, you'll uncover traps you never knew about and some you've probably already stepped into. To succeed with retirement planning, you must understand the hidden costs that can rob you blind.

UNMASKING THE HIDDEN FEES

Mutual funds are often marketed as having no fees or commissions, which makes it sound like 100 percent of your money is working for you. Rather than buying shares of stock, many fee-based advisors will suggest buying their "house" mutual funds for no commissions. What could be better than an investment with no commissions? A lot.

All mutual funds, whether load, no-load, or even ETFs, have fees associated with running them. These are called the Annual Operating Expense (AOE), or sometimes the Annual Operating Expense Ratio (AOER). The AOE includes management fees,[66] administrative fees, and another called 12b-1 fees. Management fees are used to pay the managers and others who run the fund, and typically range between fractions of 1 percent to several percentage points. Think of these as an advisory fee you're paying for the manager's expertise. Administrative fees are used for expenses like office rentals or for administrative staff that cannot be covered by management fees. The 12b-1 fee must be authorized by the SEC under Rule 12b-1 to charge such fees, but these are used to cover expenses for advertising, mailing prospectuses, and other administrative procedures. The 12b-1 fee is usually regulated to 1 percent per year.

Don't expect fee-based advisors to point these fees out, however. Instead, the SEC only requires that they hand you the prospectus, which is a lengthy legal document that, like your economics chapter on inflation, is another literary sleeping pill, although this one's double strength. Sleeping sickness aside, in the eyes of the law, you've been warned. But, depending on the fees, your investment may be doomed.

To understand how expenses impact your investment, let's look at a simple example using a 2 percent AOE. Recall from Chapter 1 that most mutual funds report a single closing value each day, which is called the net asset value, or NAV. It's simply the fund's value after subtracting its expenses from its assets. Let's say the fund's NAV is $50 today. The next day it rises, and the fund calculates its NAV at $51. However, the fund isn't going to report a $51 value. Instead, it deducts its expenses first, which we're assuming are 2 percent of the one-dollar gain, or two cents. Rather than seeing a NAV of $51, it'll get reduced to $50.98. The implicit fee simply takes from investors by reducing the value of the gains. Because investors don't write a check to pay these fees, they're easy to miss, but they're every bit as real.

What happens if the fund's value falls?

It shouldn't come as a surprise that the fund always charges a fee. Let's say, instead, the NAV fell one dollar from $50 to $49. Before reporting this $49 NAV, however, the fund will deduct its two cents and report it as $48.98. The fee reduces the fund's value whether it rises or falls. This fee is deducted from the fund's assets each year. Two percent certainly doesn't sound like much, and that's exactly what the fund wants you to think.

Yes, 2 percent appears insignificant when compared to the 15 percent or 20 percent normally left at restaurants, or to the $5 or $10 tip you may give to the bellhop for bringing your luggage to your hotel room. The difference is that you're not doing it *every single day* on very large investment values. By charging 2 percent each day, these small costs compound, or magnify, over time. This is where hidden costs begin to get scary.

WHAT A DIFFERENCE
1 PERCENT MAKES

If a fund charges 2 percent, it deducts $20 per $1,000 invested. If you have $100,000 invested, you're being docked $2,000 every single year. However, as your account value grows, the fees grow, too. They compound over time. For example, if you invest $100 per month and earn an average of 8 percent per year, you'd have $17,410 after 10 years if your fund charges 1 percent. But with 2 percent fees, your balance falls to $16,470.

The extra 1 percent steals 5 percent of your earnings.

After 15 years, however, the extra 1 percent will take 8 percent. After 40 years, it embezzles 24 percent of your entire balance. If you amass one million dollars after 40 years, the fund would eat up $240,000 in fees. The chart below shows how the losses increase over time.

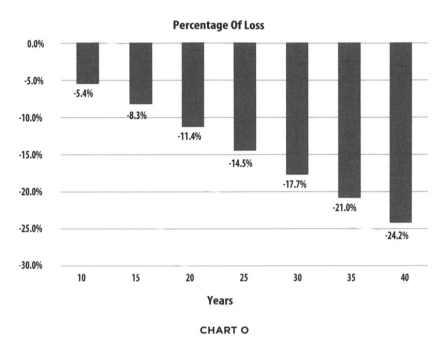

CHART O

The additional 1 percent takes away roughly an extra 3 percent every five years. Each additional 1 percent charged by the fund leaves you with a lot less money. In fairness to the funds, these fees normally don't stay fixed over time. When a fund is brand new, it has a fixed amount of expenses that must be spread over a smaller investment base. That means the AOE will likely be much higher. However, after the fund draws new investors, those same expenses are being spread out across a larger asset base, so the AOE should theoretically decrease over time. However, that's not always the case. Sometimes, funds that are doing well will increase their fees just because investors are willing to pay them. Depending on the type of mutual fund, you'll see different fees charged. The average is around 1.5 percent, but it's not uncommon to see 2.5 percent, and many hedge funds charge as much as 20 percent. Be sure you fully understand the operating expenses your funds are charging. Most brokers have an incentive to hide them.

THE COST-EFFICIENCY OF SPY

Now that you understand the benefits of diversification from Chapter 4, it's even more eye opening when you consider the benefits of investing in an S&P 500 mutual fund, or an ETF, such as SPY. Because the SPY is passively managed, there's no expertise necessary to manage the fund. There's no fund manager making decisions of what to buy and sell. Instead, the fund is automatically rebalanced to mirror the percentages of all stocks in the S&P 500. Because it's passively managed, the expense ratios are super small. For instance, the SPY's expense ratio is just 0.09 percent. To put it in perspective, a 2 percent fund is charging 22 times as much. Let's compare two different investors. One deposits $100 per month into a fund charging 2 percent expenses. The other does the same thing but charges just 0.09 percent expenses into the SPY. Both earn 8 percent per year. How will they fare over time?

The following chart shows the SPY investor in bold and the 2 percent fund in gray. After 26 years, the SPY investor in black earns $342,378 while the other earns $174,902—almost exactly half. Take your choice. It's either money in your pocket, or out.

Because an S&P 500 fund is the same no matter who controls it, you'd think the fees would be identical. However, a real financial industry puzzler is that many S&P 500 funds charge vastly different fees. For instance, the Schwab[67] S&P 500 Index Fund (SWPPX) charges 0.09 percent, State Street Global Advisor[68] S&P 500 Index Fund (SVSPX) charges 0.16 percent, and USAA[69] S&P 500 Index Fund (USSPX) charges 0.25 percent. You'd think that competition would force the fund managers to charge the same prices to be more competitive but the markets show otherwise. The only explanation is that investors don't know about these fees, or

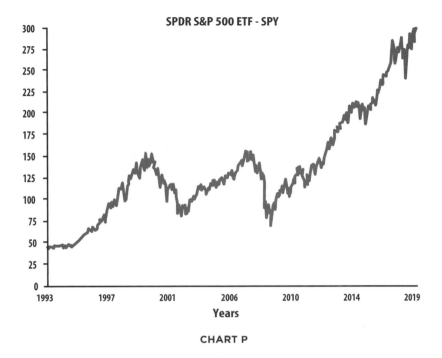

CHART P

they don't know what a difference they make. Operating expenses add up quickly. As Benjamin Franklin said, "Beware of little expenses. A small leak will sink a great ship." These expenses, however, may be the least of your fears, as we're just beginning to uncover the hidden costs.

TURNING OVER MORE ROCKS

If these AOE fees weren't bad enough, many brokers charge commissions to buy their funds. Once again, it may not seem like much to pay a $5 or $10 fee, but if you look at that as a percentage, it can be quite large. If you put $1,000 into a fund but pay a $5 commission, it's another 0.5 percent fee, and it's charged every time you add money to that fund. In addition, you may get smacked with other fees such as a custodial fee, which is usually charged quarterly or annually just to "hold" your account. Brokers justify them as a way to cover expenses of mailing account statements, providing phone support, and other services. Some may also charge "inactivity" fees, which means you'll be charged another fee if you're not doing enough trading in your account. Hidden mutual fund fees, combined with these other costs, are key reasons why most investors miss their long-term targets. You must account for them in your planning.

However, you can't just count the costs you can see. Traps are set for those who don't understand that opportunity costs are just as real. An opportunity cost is any cost that is due to missing an opportunity rather than having to pay a fee. When it comes to mutual funds, there are four additional costs—cash, trading fees, slippage, and taxes that are almost always overlooked, and they can also be among the biggest.

IDLE CASH HAS A COST

Most actively managed mutual funds never keep 100 percent of the cash invested. Instead, they keep cash available for redemptions (when investors sell shares), and they'll keep it available should some good market-buying opportunities arise. However, by keeping investors' money in cash, there's an implicit cost because it's money that's not being invested. Imagine if you gave $100,000 to your advisor and the markets returned 10 percent for the year. However, you get your statement and find your money's been sitting in cash and earned virtually nothing. You'd certainly feel like there was a $10,000 "loss" or "cost" with his decision. Most passively managed funds, like the S&P 500 index funds, keep very little in cash. Instead it's all invested to mirror the index. However, most actively managed funds keep quite a bit of cash on hand, and the cost of the idle cash can run as high as 1 percent per year.

MUTUAL FUNDS PAY COMMISSIONS, TOO

Trading fees are another overlooked category. Actively managed funds constantly buy and sell shares in an attempt to beat the market. They see Apple Computer has risen while Amazon.com has fallen, so they sell

Apple and buy Amazon. Then, after it's risen significantly, they sell. But now it's approaching earnings, so they sell. After the earnings are released, they buy. They're constantly chasing stocks, and each time they trade, they pay commissions. Naturally, their fees aren't as large as the ones paid by retail investors. However, the size of the transactions can be monstrous. Many of these funds will place orders for 10 million shares at a time. So even though the fee percentage may be small, the total dollars they spend add up—and they're charged to the fund.

There's a related phenomenon called *window dressing*, where actively traded funds will buy the hottest stocks of that quarter or at year-end, so that they appear in their quarterly reports. It makes for a much more alluring presentation when investors see, for example, that the FANG stocks (Facebook, Amazon, Netflix, and Google)[70] were the stellar performers of the year and they all just happened to be chosen by the fund manager, too—what a genius. Little do they know that these stocks were just purchased while the report was going to print. Actively managed funds do a lot of buying and selling many times back and forth in the same stocks, and there are costs.

Finally, as mentioned in Chapter 1, funds may engage in "style drift,"[71] where the manager is allowed to drift, sometimes substantially, from the fund's stated objectives. Just because a fund may have returned 10 percent per year over a significant time doesn't mean the fund manager will stay on that course. You have no control over the decision, but you do have money riding on this.

THE COST OF THE BID-ASK SPREAD

For every asset traded on an exchange, such as stocks, bonds, options, and others, there's a bid to buy and an offer (or asking price) to sell. The bid is the highest price at which someone will buy right now, while the offer is the lowest price at which another will sell. The difference between the two is called the bid-ask spread. For instance, let's say a stock is bidding $30 and offered at $30.20. This means you can currently buy it for $30.20 (since another investor is willing to sell at that price) and you can sell it for $30 (since another investor is willing to buy at that price). Notice, however, that if you were to buy it for $30.20 and immediately sell it for $30, you'd lose 20 cents, or about 0.7 percent. As with the mutual fund expense ratios, it doesn't appear to be a big cost. However, when mutual funds are buying and selling hundreds of millions of dollars' worth of stock multiple times through the year, the costs become very real. That rapid turnover can easily add another 1 percent to trading costs during the year.

PRICES ARE SLIPPERY

Slippage, or market impact costs, is another hidden cost of funds. If a fund manager places a large order to buy or sell, it often causes the bid to fall or the offer price to rise. Using our previous example with an offer price of $30.20, it doesn't mean that you can buy all the shares you want at that price. Instead, the market is a live, continuous auction, and there are only a limited number of shares available at that price. For example, perhaps that's another trader's order to sell 500 shares at $30.20. In market terms, the "size" of the market is only 500 shares at that price. Once those shares are purchased, unless new sellers enter the market, the offer price will be raised to reveal the next lowest seller, maybe $30.30. If a fund manager places an order to buy 20,000 shares, he'll get *some* filled at the current $30.20 price, but others may get reported back at $30.30, while others may be even higher at $30.40. Once the entire order is filled, the market may settle down back at the $30.20 level. These price discrepancies are due to slippage. Because the manager was filled with some prices higher than the current market price, his average cost is also above the market, and that means he needs the stock's price to rise somewhat just to break even. The price slippage has the same effect as paying a commission. It's another cost that must be overcome before profits show.

Slippage doesn't end with the purchase. When the manager decides to sell the shares, he'll incur the same effects just in the opposite direction. Let's say the stock price has risen and is bidding $40. However, if he places a large order to sell, he'll get some shares filled at the current $40 price, but may get others filled lower at $39.90, perhaps others filled at $39.80, and still others at $39.70. Although he intended to buy at $30 and sell at $40—a 33 percent gain—slippage reduced that profit. He may have purchased at an average price of $30.20 and sold at an average price of $39.70, a 31.5 percent gain. In other words, he's unable to lock in his expected gain because prices "slip" when he's executing large trades. That's a cost. The fund manager doesn't write a check nor do the clients, so it's an implicit cost due to the market's inability to absorb that many shares at once. However, they'll affect your bottom line just the same.

UNCLE SAM AFFECTS YOUR PLAN

Taxes are another overlooked cost of funds, and in many cases, far bigger than expense ratios. As an investor, the only returns that matter are after-tax returns since those are the only ones you get to keep. An investment earning one million dollars isn't worth much if there's a 99.9 percent tax associated with it. Because passively managed funds have very little turnover in the stocks they own, their after-tax returns are relatively high. For example, for the 10-year period ending in 2017, SPY averaged a 9.63 percent return but 8.92 percent after taxes, for a 92 percent tax-efficiency rating (8.92/9.63 equals 92). In other words, the fund keeps about 92 percent of all money earned. On the other hand, actively managed funds often have tax-efficiency ratings of 85 percent or less. That's because a lot of their returns are given up in the form of short-term capital taxes, wash-sale violations, and other unfavorable tax consequences.

VOLATILITY:
MARKET WHIPSAWING CARRIES A PRICE

Stocks are up. Stocks are down. Bulls are in. Now they're out. Anyone who's invested for any length of time knows the stock market is a constant struggle between the bulls and bears. A stock may rise 10 percent by the end of the year, but it also has a lot of ups and downs along that path. Those ups and downs are a mathematical concept called *volatility*.

Volatility is another type of cost at work stealing your money and it's camouflaged. These costs, however, aren't like mutual fund expenses or commissions. Instead, they're mathematical effects, but they'll chew through your profits just as quickly.

Without getting into the details, don't think of volatility as prices rising, falling, or even going sideways. Instead, volatility is a measure of how far a stock's price drifts from its average. For example, if a stock trades for $100 today and the same price at the end of the month, it has a 0 percent return. However, if it traded with a low of $90 and a high of $110, it had some pretty good variation in prices and volatility during the month. If it traded in a wider range, say between $80 and $120, it had even more volatility even though the 0 percent return was the same. A stock's return has nothing to do with its volatility. A stock price starting and ending at $100 in one year can exhibit tremendous volatility while a stock rising from $100 to $200 during that same time may have low volatility. Volatility, again, is the idea of stock prices moving back and forth along a longer-term path, or what most investors call whipsawing. The technicalities of volatility aren't important. What's important is that the back and forth stock price motions impose another hidden cost—and it can be a big one.

For example, let's say a stock rises 10 percent one year and then falls 10 percent the next. Most investors think they're back to even, but the math shows something quite different—you've actually lost 1 percent. A $100 investment would rise to $110 after the first year, but losing 10 percent the next makes it worth $99. The reason is simple. You added 10 percent to $100 during the first year but subtracted 10 percent from a bigger number in the second year. The result is an overall loss. That's bad enough, but the problem compounds. A gain of 20 percent followed by a loss of 20 percent doesn't mean you're down twice as much. Instead, you're down 4 percent, or four times as much.

Losses also compound over time. Let's go back to our mutual fund with a NAV of $50 and say you invested $10,000. But now let's say it rises 2 percent to $51 the next day, then falls 2 percent the day after that, and it repeats this every day for a full year. It sounds like you'd be back to even, but you'd see your investment is valued at only $9,512, a 5 percent loss. The point to understand is that volatility reduces your returns. It acts just like a commission every day. The more the market whipsaws, the more the value of your account shrinks. Volatility is yet another reason why diversification is so important. With a well-diversified portfolio, you'll certainly see some investments rise while others fall. However, you're far more likely to get a consistent overall increase in your portfolio rather than a lot of whipsawing, which can easily happen when holding only a few stocks.

Volatility, like inflation, is a thief in the night. If you don't understand that the day-to-day price changes will slowly erode your returns, you're setting yourself up to miss your long-term targets. Not accounting for volatility is costly.

MOUSETRAP #6: HIDDEN COSTS CAN ROB YOU BLIND

Hidden costs are one of biggest reasons investors struggle to reach their financial goals. It's up to the financial advisor to account for these when setting up the financial plan. However, it's easy to overlook these fees and their impacts on long-term plans. The list of hidden fees is long, and the effects are far reaching. Here's a few common ways that investors are hurt by working with three blind mice.

First, financial advisors are notorious for using simple averages to devise plans. If a client needs to earn 8 percent per year to accomplish his future goals, it's easy to believe a fund that's returned an average of 10 percent per year will do the trick. But now you should understand the trap. That average is a time-weighted average and not at all representative of what the client will receive over time. Market volatility will reduce returns even further. The more volatility, the more money it eats away. And if those funds have high fees, then a good portion of your returns get eaten away over time. And, it gets worse.

An accountant may audit your financial plan and verify the fund's returns are on track to meet future financial plans or even far ahead of schedule. What if the accountant doesn't know additional money has been added to your account? And you didn't know to inform him? Can attorneys miss the hidden fees?

Attorneys may know the law, they may even know the judge, but they don't necessarily know the math of investing. Your attorney may approve of a mutual fund for your conservative trust fund[72] but not understand what a difference 0.09 percent and 0.25 percent can make over time. What if there's a broad-based fund that has a better track record, but also carries a front load with a five-year contingent-deferred sales charge? How do you make comparisons now? The questions aren't easy, but the right answers are critical for your success.

Hidden costs are another key reason you need a liaison to connect your three blind mice. It only makes sense to have one person who understands the financial calculations and how they'll impact your decisions, but who also oversees the actions of others that affect your future plans. The financial industry, however, doesn't require it. Your attorney and accountant won't volunteer it. And that means you need to understand it.

CHAPTER 7

TRAP #7

The Madness Of Mice Versus Markets: Trying To Profit From Stock Market Patterns

"We have three confirmations, the crystal ball,
the magic 8-ball and the coin flip, all say to buy."

CartoonStock.com

People love patterns. The need for recognizing patterns is an ancient instinct, wrapped in our DNA, designed for survival. Our cave-dwelling ancestors quickly learned whether that rustling in the bushes was a saber-toothed tiger about to attack, or a rabbit passing through that would make a great snack. It was the difference between eating or being eaten. Today, patterns are used for different reasons, and profits is right up at the top of the list. We may not have the fear of being attacked by a tiger or a T-Rex, but a quarterback would certainly like to know if he's about to be blindsided by a 300-pound linebacker. Sporting events are entire industries built on patterns. What will most players do most of the time? Teams pay big bucks for answers.

Canadian broadcaster Peter Gzowski[73] said, "The best of the best athletes in all sports understand the game so well, and in such detail, that they can instantly recognize and capitalize upon emerging patterns of play."

With today's technology, it's easier than ever to detect patterns, and if profits can be found, you can be sure they're being tracked. Tech giants like Google and Facebook record your every move, every search, every purchase, to figure out your buying habits. Is it worth the effort?

In April 2018, Facebook reported record earnings of nearly $12 billion just for the quarter. That was up 49 percent from a year ago, and mobile advertising has accounted for 90 percent of the company's earnings since 2012 when it entered that market. Consumer buying patterns are very big business.

If there's money to be made, you'll find people looking for patterns. It's hard to believe, but there are even consulting companies hired to assist attorneys with jury selection pools. Jo-Ellan Dimitrius[74] was hired by the O.J. Simpson defense team to design jury questionnaires to identify people who would be most likely to render a not-guilty verdict. Crazy, right? Well, it's nothing new. She did the same thing for the Rodney King trial, the McMartin preschool trial, and the Night Stalker trial. For defense attorneys, they're seemingly impossible cases to win, when defendants have been convicted in the court of public opinion. Gaining a small edge to win an against-all-odds case can potentially mean tens of millions of dollars over their careers. Paying a consultant to identify patterns, no matter how small, amounts to peanuts.

Pick any industry, and you'll see that people look for patterns to gain an edge. If patterns are rewarding for other industries, they should pay off many times over where money is the game, where the best of the best can instantly recognize and capitalize upon emerging patterns of play in the stock market. It sounds like another great idea for making money. Why get rich slowly when you can take financial shortcuts through profitable patterns?

It's a hard thought to dismiss and an easy trap to fall for.

That's right. Searching for stock market patterns isn't going to be worth your time. If anything, it'll lead to false confidence and even bigger future losses. The problem is that many financial advisors use market timing as part of their practice, as it's an easy way to command higher fees. What will you get in return? A portfolio that underperforms in the market. It's a big trap if you're working with one of these advisors, but if you're working with three blind mice, it creates a financial disaster.

LOOKING FOR FOOTPRINTS

If everyone else makes money by studying patterns, it shouldn't come as a surprise that entire businesses have been created to study every conceivable stock market pattern to uncover potential profit-making gems. For example, do stock prices usually rise after announcing a stock split? If an analyst issues a buy recommendation on a stock, will you make money by purchasing shares? If a stock's price has been rising, how long does it usually take before it reverses? Do prices perform better on Monday than Friday? What about April versus October? Every conceivable question you can think of and then some has been studied. The reason is simple. If you could find recurring patterns where stock prices rise or fall after certain events occurred, you could turn Wall Street into an ATM machine. Buy the shares at the right moment and rake in the profits. It beats working for a living.

The answers to these questions don't have to be glaringly obvious either, as it wouldn't take much of an edge to make patterns worthwhile. If you were certain that stocks reacted a certain way 55 percent of the time, it's all you'd need to know to make an insane fortune. You don't need to be right all the time; you just need to be right most of the time. Las Vegas makes a killing by creating small favorable edges, sometimes less than 1 percent on its games, which means many of the games lose nearly half the time. Small edges, however, add up over time. If you've ever visited any of the casino hotels, you'd see they're living large on small advantages. It seems that small advantages can be found by looking at patterns. It's obvious you can wait for good news, buy the shares, and profit as the price rises from the good news.

It's obvious, and wrong.

For nonfinancial professionals, it's hard to understand why, but if you've ever been stuck in five o'clock traffic, the rationale is the same and equally frustrating.

STUCK IN RUSH-HOUR TRAFFIC

Dale, my best friend, and his fiancée came up from Jacksonville, Florida, for a visit. My wife and daughter came along as well, and we went to the Big Apple for a tour of the 9/11 Memorial and Museum (you really must visit). Then we went for dinner and a Broadway show. It was 4 p.m. bumper-to-bumper traffic, with all the trimmings of blowing horns and people shouting. He looked over at the speedometer and GPS and said, "Damn, I've never seen a trip of 3.1 miles that would take 45 minutes." Jokingly, I told him to get out and find me a good parking spot.

Why couldn't we get there any faster during rush hour? Surely we could have just moved into a quicker lane, right? Well, partly true. The problem is that you're not the only one stuck in traffic. Everyone's stuck and everyone's trying to accomplish the same goal—all are searching for faster lanes. Are there blocked lanes? Accidents? Maybe slow-moving semi-trucks? What's the radio traffic report saying? Every kind of information they can find to get home quicker is being used. The problem is that when everyone tries to get home faster, they all end up going slower.

If you spot a faster lane, you may decide to switch. However, in doing so, you've added one more car to the lane, so it slows down a bit. Conversely, the lane you left speeds up a little for the opposite reason. If all drivers actively search for faster lanes, the faster lanes slow down, and slower lanes speed up. The process continues quickly until all lanes end up going the same speed. In other words, you're stuck in traffic. If it's any consolation, at least you have a better understanding of how financial markets work.

TRAPPED IN TRADING TRAFFIC

Getting stuck in traffic is exactly what happens when news reaches the stock market. Rather than occurring during rush hour, it happens every second of the day. All investors have a big incentive, not to get home quickly, but to find profits quickly. Investors aren't searching for faster lanes and roadblocks; instead, they're on the lookout for any news or information that means a stock's price may be heading higher. Upon hearing that news, investors rush to buy the stock, just as drivers react quickly if they see a small lane opening during rush hour. If you hesitate, you'll miss it. The second the news hits, the stock exchanges get flooded with buy orders, and the price rises in response. The score is measured in dollars, so nobody's going to intentionally make a bad investment.

For example, let's say news hits the market that suggests a $100 stock will be worth $120 in one year. The stock will trade very close to $120 today, discounted slightly for the *Cost of Carry*,[75] on that money. If the stock rises to $105 instantly, that's like the lane slowing down. However, it's still worthwhile to switch, so more investors pile in, and the stock rises to $110; it's getting less attractive, but still worth buying. The process continues until it's trading close to $120. When the current stock price reflects all available information, its price stabilizes. You're stuck in trading traffic. Remember from Chapter 2 that price equalizes risk. So yes, when news hits the market, it spells profits. It's like drivers spotting a faster lane—everyone quickly buys the stock.

Now, you may be thinking there's still hope. What if you were among the first people to hear the news and you could buy the shares for $100, or $105, or $110, as it was climbing? Wouldn't you make big money? Yes, you would, but you'd also be dreaming.

In a digital world where profits are the prize, you can't imagine how quickly investors respond. For instance, on Friday, March 10, 2017, Mobileye[76] (MBLY) closed at $47.27. After the closing bell, Intel (INTC) announced it was buying the company, in cash, for $63.54 per share on August 8. That could be easy money, right? You didn't even have to be fast, as you had the next four months to think about it. However, on Monday morning, the *first trade* on the opening bell was $61.50 and hovered around that price all the way through the acquisition date five months later as shown in the chart below.

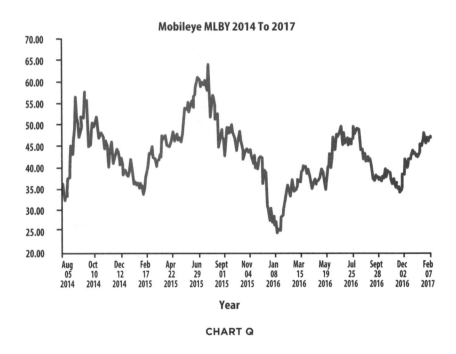

Mobileye MLBY 2014 To 2017

CHART Q

Notice the sharp price zigs and zags prior to March 2017, but the price jumps vertically on the announcement and flat-lines from there. It may appear there was still a little bit of free money since you could pay $61.50 and sell for $63.54 in August, but the stock traded at the slight discount to account for the lost interest while waiting for the money, and there were also two dividends to be collected. It all balances out. The point to understand is that all that information got immediately filtered into the stock price on the very first trade on the following business day. Was it because investors got to think about it during the weekend? Not at all. Had the announcement been made during market hours on Friday, the stock's price would have traded at $61.50 in less than one second. News travels fast.

HOW FAST IS FAST?

It's hard to believe information can travel that quickly. But remember, this is the business of money operating with 21st-century technology. This isn't Wall Street in the 1800s when news traveled by smoke signals and people traveled on horseback to get to their brokers. The only thing investors must do is press the "buy" button, and anyone can do it, even from their phones. It's not just a game of information—it's a game of speed. Knowing the information is one thing, but reacting to it is where the money's made, and that's an entirely different story altogether. How fast is fast?

It's difficult to describe, as speeds are measured in units of time that don't mean much to most people: milliseconds and microseconds or thousands and millionths of seconds. To understand how fast the game is played, large brokerage firms purchase space at the exchanges to engage in high-frequency trading (HFT) where computers can trade a mind-boggling 10,000 times per second. At those speeds, a longer connection cable makes an ever-so-slightly noticeable difference in processing speed, so companies pay big money to get as close to the exchanges as they can. Author Michael Lewis[77] described in his bestselling book *Flash Boys* how a company called Spread Networks[78] paid $300 million to lay cable in as straight a line as possible between Chicago and New York. And for what reason? It shaved three milliseconds (3/1,000 of one second) of trading time between the two exchanges. The human eye blinks at about 300 milliseconds, or 100 times slower. Each time you blink, a super computer can trade one million shares of stock based on information arriving into the market. Milliseconds of time mean millions of dollars.

The instant news is announced, computers, not people, are waiting with digital fingers on the "buy" buttons. And people think they can take the time to get online, log on to their broker's website, enter their user names and passwords, uncheck a bunch of annoying pop-up ads, type up the order, and place a trade based on news they heard 10 minutes ago? They're showing up to an Indy 500 race on a mule cart—with square wheels. News travels unimaginably fast, and because everyone is trying to profit from the same information, all known information is priced into the current stock price instantly.

The idea that the current market price of any asset, stock, bond, mutual fund, or any other entity reflects all known information and is therefore considered fair by all investors is called the *efficient market theory* [79] or EMT. By "efficient," it just means that all market information is reflected into the current price. Therefore, if you hear on CNBC that Goldman Sachs[80] just issued a buy recommendation on Facebook, it doesn't pay to rush out and buy the shares expecting to ride the wave of free profits as the news makes its way through the world. Even if you're lucky enough to be staring at your computer the instant the news drops, a computerized trading desk in Manhattan picked it up 30 seconds ago. That's long enough to trade 300,000 shares ahead of you, and it was just one of thousands of computers doing the same thing. The second you hear the news, the perceived value has already been priced into the shares. That's fast.

Interestingly, even if you buy shares on the news, it doesn't mean you can't make money. Instead, it means any profits you make are due to future news and not the news you heard. Without knowing it, you paid for those profits. The stock market works in strange ways, and that makes it an easy trap for do-it-yourself investors.

Fun fact: Do you know how Wall Street got its name? During the 17th century, Dutch settlers living on Manhattan Island were terrified England was planning an attack, so they built a wooden wall (known as "de Waal Straat") for protection. Its association with the financial industry didn't occur until over 100 years later, when the New York Stock Exchange rented a room on Wall Street (Initials: SMM).

NOBODY CARES WHAT YOU THINK

The market doesn't care what you think. To predict the market, you must correctly guess what everyone else thinks. The only reason a stock price rises is because everybody else thought it would rise, not because you thought it would. If you trust your money to one person's opinion, you're setting yourself up for failure.

The market knows far more information than any single person.

How many times have you seen where "good earnings" are reported, but the stock price plummets? Or maybe the CEO steps down, but it causes the stock's price to rise? It's not enough for you or your advisor to do in-depth research on the company's future sales or earnings. The market is forward looking, so today's information is old news. If a company releases "good earnings" but also announces negative news for the next quarter, the stock price will fall in anticipation. Yet, many novice investors scratch their heads in disbelief and can't understand why the stock price fell when the earnings were great. To predict the market, it's not enough to predict the prices. It's not what you think that matters. You must predict what everybody else thinks, and that should give you a better idea as to why it's so difficult to predict prices.

STOCK PRICES ARE LARGELY RANDOM

Because information arrives in the market randomly, nobody sees it coming and stock price changes are essentially random. Trying to predict whether a stock's price will rise or fall at any moment amounts to trying to predict whether a coin will land heads or tails. It's hard to believe, but look at these one-year charts for four different stocks.

What patterns do you see? Are there areas where the stock price clearly rallied, or dropped? Can you see times where the price reached a top or bottom and then quickly reversed as if investors realized it was too cheap or expensive? Lots of patterns are visible, and it's easy to make up corresponding stories to fit the pictures. For example, when the stock's price

A Computer Simulation

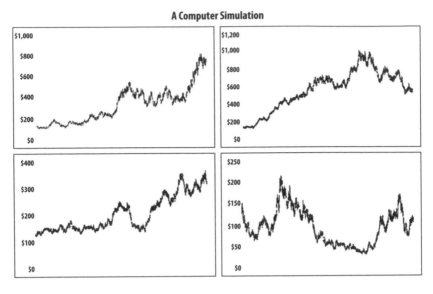

CHART R

falls near a particular low point, investors must believe it's a bargain price because it tends to rally. Next time it reaches that price, we should buy. Or when it's trading higher in another particular price range, it tends to fall, so investors clearly believe the price is too high. Next time it reaches this high, we should sell. Do you also see sideways patterns where the stock consolidates after making large moves up or down? Those must be investors in a holding pattern, perhaps waiting for the next earnings report. It's easy to believe these explanations because the pictures are so convincing. Your eyes can't possibly be deceiving you. The patterns are clearly there and there's an unsettling surprise.

These aren't stock price charts at all. All four charts were created on a computer by flipping coins to determine whether the imaginary stock price would move up or down and rolling a pair of dice to generate the difference. They're nothing but meaningless random patterns and computerized cloud formations. Flip them long enough and you'll see some crazy-looking patterns just as you will with stock charts. Most people would think you'd get a lot of sideways, choppy motions with coin flips and dice, but you get beautiful and impressive patterns from randomness.

However, that doesn't mean that these patterns necessarily tell a story. It doesn't mean you can therefore follow the news and predict how any stock's price will react. Even though these look like real stock charts, if you tried to predict future prices based on what happened in the past, you'd fail miserably. If you can't distinguish computerized stock price charts from real price charts, you must question whether the information contained in a real stock chart will yield any meaningful profits. It's no different than looking at the sequences of heads and tails over the past 100 flips and trying to use that information to predict the next flip.

But people love patterns, and it's so easy to think it can be done. If financial markets weren't price efficient, anyone could buy shares upon hearing the news and earn easy money. The entire world could be employed by opening a brokerage account and listening for news.

A TALE OF TWO JUICY SCANDALS

The year 2012 was not kind to Best Buy.[81] With its stock down 80 percent under CEO Brian Dunn's leadership, including closure of dozens of stores, the electronic retail company's stock continued to plummet when Dunn was discovered having an inappropriate relationship with an employee at the company.

Do you think you can trust Facebook? Think again. In March of 2018, data firm Cambridge Analytica[82] revealed the social media company had collected information on users' friend networks and "likes" in order to map out their interests, using that information to target people with relevant ads. Shares plunged nearly 20 percent in the aftermath. That's a $119 billion loss, causing founder Mark Zuckerberg to lose his standing as the third richest person in the world. (He's now ranked a measly sixth.)

So if you think a company you invested in will continue on a high-earnings path, remember, someone in that company might be taking active steps to ensure its doom.

THE CHARTS (DON'T) TELL ALL

There are people in the financial markets called technicians, or chartists, who "read charts" and try to predict where stock prices will go based on price patterns. They'll talk about support and resistance, consolidations, flags, pennants, head and shoulders, and many other patterns. I've shown charts like these to market technicians, and many exclaimed, "Wow, which stock is this? It's forming a textbook-perfect head-and-shoulders pattern and you should buy shares today." They're not so happy when I tell them they're cloud formations. If random patterns can fool people who are self-proclaimed experts at reading charts, they'll certainly fool the average investor. However, each failed prediction makes your long-term investment plan more difficult. Remember, a stock that falls 50 percent must rise 100 percent just to break even. Losses have dramatic impacts on your financial plans, and trying to predict random patterns is no way to finance your future.

Everyone is looking for small advantages, and that means everyone is paying close attention to potential patterns. If a pattern leads investors to free money, don't think you'll be the only one using it.

To revisit a prior question: Can some people make money because they're the first to hear big news? Sure, they're the big brokerage firms that have news teams parked in every corner of the world, own supercomputers on the exchanges, have teams of MBAs, CPAs, and all other kinds of professional alphabet-soup designations just waiting for news to analyze. Or they're Martha Stewart. The game is fast and only the strong survive. For every buyer there must be a seller, and for every winner, there must be a loser. People who aren't good at deciphering information get washed out of the market quickly. The people who survive are really, really good at figuring out just how much information is worth. Some people will make money by quickly reacting to news. It won't be you. Stock price changes are random, and you can't predict coin flips and dice rolls to make consistent money.

PRICES AREN'T PERFECT
(BUT THEY'RE CLOSE)

Not to be deterred, there are people in the financial markets who bash EMH,[83] the Efficient-Market Hypothesis that is based on some of the wild price rides we've seen. They say if all information was priced into securities, we shouldn't see such large price swings. That misses the point. The theory doesn't say prices are perfect. Instead, it says that, on average, they shouldn't be consistently high or low any more than a point spread in a football game should consistently favor the home or away team. If prices weren't correct, on average, we'd be right back into a market where people could make free money acting on the news. In other words, if prices were always too low following the news, it would still pay to buy. If they were always too high, it would pay to sell. Prices aren't perfectly efficient, just as all lanes in rush-hour traffic aren't moving at identical speeds. Instead, prices must be out of line just enough to make it worth someone's while to act on the news and switch lanes if perceived prices are too high or low. Prices aren't perfect, but they're pretty good guesses, on average. The only way you'll beat the market by listening for news is if you know something the entire market has missed.

THE VALUE OF INFORMATION

As long as there are financial markets, you'll find people who want to sell their stock market prediction services. As long as there are people who want to get rich quick, there'll be people willing to sell the dream. It's an easy market to enter. Just get on TV, YouTube, or create a web page and make a convincing presentation that you're the world's best stock predictor. How can they prove you wrong? It requires no experience, no degrees, no certifications, and no morals. Use phrases like "proprietary trading algorithms," or "back-tested trading strategies with 84.6 percent accuracy," or "high-profit trades with little risk." People will believe you.

There's an entire industry willing to sell expensive online trading systems as much as $100,000 for their secret sauce.

Why would anyone claiming to have a goose that lays golden eggs be willing to take a relatively small flat fee to invite competition? Businesses normally pay hundreds of millions of dollars to keep competition out. These people, however, are willing to sell you their infinitely valuable information for next to nothing. It makes no sense, until you realize the information they're selling is virtually worthless. They're guessing at coin flips. The only value comes from selling it.

Information only has value if it will alter a decision.

Knowing that the home team lost its starting quarterback for the next football game doesn't give you an edge at placing a bet in Vegas. Everyone knows, and it's built into the point spread. If someone's selling information based on past prices, news, technical formations, or any other public reason, it's already known to everyone else, too. It doesn't give you an edge, so the information is worthless. Be careful what you pay for.

TATTERED TEA LEAVES AND CRACKED CRYSTAL BALLS

Turn on CNBC, and you'll see many guru guests talking about why the market's going to go up and an equal number saying why it must go down. The thing that's always fascinated me is that these guests give just one or two reasons to justify their predictions. The Fed's going to lower rates, or the U.S. dollar's value will rise, or the Cyclically Adjusted P/E Ratio is getting too high. To new investors, it sounds brilliant. To good financial advisors, it's senseless.

The world has nearly eight billion people generating $78 trillion worth of goods and services covering 195 countries, 180 currencies, more than 20 stock exchanges, and all controlled by 10 powerful central banks. And yet, each of these is connected by invisible gears. When one turns, they all turn. No matter where news may break out in any corner of the world, it starts a chain reaction that can send shock waves through the financial markets.

Think about Nick Leeson,[84] the lone rogue trader who bankrupted Barings Bank, and nearly caused a U.S. financial meltdown. He was hired as a super-whiz advisor to trade derivatives in Singapore because of his ability to read markets. The Kobe earthquake, something nobody saw coming, sent the Asian markets tumbling along with the company's money. The only thing Barings got was a note saying "I'm sorry" before he fled to Germany leaving the company with a $1.4 billion loss. It's not like the bank was a newcomer to financial risk either. Founded in 1762, it financed the Louisiana Purchase and the Napoleonic Wars. It knew about risk. And yet, one trader sunk the entire operation. If there are any problems with your multiple advisors, you'll miss them, too. If a single trader can't predict the markets, perhaps a small group of really smart people can, right?

Long-Term Capital Management (LTCM) was a hedge fund founded by John W. Meriwether,[85] former vice-chairman and head of bond trading at Salomon Brothers. He added Myron S. Scholes and Robert C. Merton, who shared the 1997 Nobel Prize in Economic Sciences,[86] as advisors for a sophisticated trading strategy. Certainly, they must have known what they were doing and likely were worth the 25 percent advisory fee plus 2 percent of assets. But then the Russian government defaulted on its bonds—something nobody anticipated—and caused LTCM to need a $3.6 billion bailout from over 15 banks including the Federal Reserve. News travels randomly. Nobody sees it coming. And that's why people can't predict the markets.

The September 11 terrorist attacks caused the Dow to fall 684 points, or 7 percent, which at the time was the largest one-day point loss in exchange history. By the end of the week, the index dropped 1,370 points, or 14 percent. It had nothing to do with interest rates, inflation, earnings, or other economic issues that experts talk about. Yet it had one of the biggest impacts on the financial markets in modern-day history. Nobody saw it coming.

All these events created some of the biggest, most overwhelming crashes in stock market history for one simple reason. Nobody predicted them. News arrives randomly in the markets. Sometimes it's good, sometimes it's bad, but we never know when or to what degree. If there are unknown events that can dramatically move markets, there's no way anyone can make consistent predictions.

THE INDISPUTABLE MATH OF MARKET TIMING

Market timing doesn't pay off in the long run, and simple math shows it won't work. The market is made up of active and passive investors. Active investors are those who attempt to time the market while passive investors buy and hold a broad-based index, such as the S&P 500. It doesn't matter which numbers we use, but let's say 75 percent of advisors are active while 25 percent are passive.

If the overall market earns 15 percent, as measured by the S&P 500, passive investors must also earn 15 percent since they buy and hold the entire market. Active investors, however, will buy and sell according to what they think will happen. On average, active investors must also earn 15 percent since that's what the overall market returned. However, some investors will beat the overall market, but to do so, another active investor must have lost. The trouble is that active investors spend far more in commissions and missed opportunities to get the same returns, on average, as passive investors. As a result, active traders, on average, underperform passive traders.

To make the point, Dalbar,[87] a financial market research firm, looked over the past 20 years and found actively managed equity funds lagged behind the S&P 500 by an average of 4.6 percent per year, partly due to poor market timing.

SELLING STOCK-PICKING SERVICES

No matter what the research or math may say, competition is tough, especially in the financial planning business. Many have found it's more lucrative to sell stock-picking services, market timing software, or proprietary trading algorithms rather than creating solid, long-term plans for clients. If they can convince clients about their stock-picking skills and how they'll make a fortune by only buying the best stocks and dodging the risky ones, the price of their services goes up dramatically. It's an easy sale. Who wants to take 20 years to build wealth consistently and slowly, when someone claims to be able to get you there in a fraction of the time?

If you think about it, it's just a bad arrangement. Whether they're right or wrong, they get paid their fees, but you're taking all the risk. If they happen to pick some good stocks, though, they'll tout it loud and clear on their website to the rest of the world and entice more investors into their services. If wrong, they simply won't mention it. No matter how many examples are given that successful stock picking is an impossible thing to do consistently, there will always be people who are talked into paying for stock-picking advice. It's an expensive trap since you'll pay a fortune for the advice but most likely underperform the overall markets. You're better off finding a financial planner who can allow you to safely reach your goals rather than spending tons of money on people who proclaim to have some sort of cosmic connection with the market.

THE MARKET-TIMING QUEEN

While working as an analyst for Shearson Lehman, Elaine Garzarelli[88] made an eerily psychic prediction. On October 12, 1987, she appeared on CNN television where she predicted an imminent market collapse. One week later, on October 19, Black Monday, the Dow fell nearly 23 percent to post the largest percentage drop in stock market history. No other crash has come close. Her prediction was so accurate, not only with the timing but the magnitude, how could it not be skill?

She was crowned and glorified by the media as the stock market prediction queen. Shearson quickly promoted her to Chief Quantitative Strategist, and, as a bonus, she was given her own mutual fund to manage: the Smith-Barney/Shearson Sector Analysis Fund. Financial shows praised her. Magazines honored her.

Unfortunately, investors followed her.

By mid-1994, the fund was up 38 percent during her five-year reign. It sounds impressive, until you consider that it underperformed the Dow by nearly 50 percent. By closing your eyes and investing in an index fund, you'd have done a lot better. After Garzarelli made a series of awful predictions, Shearson fired her in 1994. Not wanting to be dethroned, she started her own financial prediction newsletter in 1996. How did it perform?

By May, the market was in a definite bullish trend, and the Dow eclipsed the 5,700 level for the first time. Everyone could see the pattern forming, so she told her subscribers to buy. The market quickly fell over 400 points.

She then flipped directions to follow the herd on the bear-market bandwagon. The pattern was clear that the market was falling, so how could she go wrong? She was, and a bull market began, and by 1997, the Dow approached 7,000. If the pattern hadn't been clear previously, it was now—the bulls were back. So, she flopped back and recommended buying again. Within four months, the market dropped below 6,400, or about 8 percent. Her newsletter recommendations were a constant flipping, flopping, and floundering with few predictions ever working in her favor, as if the market conspired against her. The cosmic connection was broken. The publisher finally folded the newsletter that same year after losing 30,000 subscribers due to her bad market-timing predictions. It was hardly a fairy-tale ending for the market-timing queen. How could someone who made the world's best market-timing call in history turn out to be so wrong?

For the past 100 years, there have always been lots of people predicting the markets would crash. Turn on CNBC, and you'll hear dozens of people each week saying the markets are about to crash. You don't hear about them. You just hear about the one who got it right. It's like doing a rain dance for days on end until it finally rains and then claiming it was the dance that caused it. Very rarely do any of the gloom-and-doom predictions come true. But if hundreds of people keep making predictions long enough, just like a rain dance, eventually someone will get it right and you can be sure that person will capitalize on that "prediction" to the fullest.

State lotteries work the same way. Most of the time, someone correctly picks six numbers to win the lottery each week. That doesn't mean you should buy his best-selling book *Make a Living Predicting Ping-Pong Balls*. In fact, it's not uncommon to see multiple people win. Are they all psychic?

It may seem that way, but with about 23 million combinations, if tens of millions of tickets are sold, you'll get multiple winners. Mathematically, it's more surprising when nobody wins. Don't ever be impressed by any form of "prediction" where the number of people guessing vastly outweighs the number of possibilities. If you flip a coin 10 times, it would be highly unusual to get all heads. However, if you have 1,024 people in a room flipping 10 coins each, you'd expect one person to flip 10 heads in a row. If you increase the number of people in the room to 2,000, there's an 85 percent chance that someone will do it. With 3,000 people, the chance increases to 95 percent. The probability for success doesn't rely on skill. It only depends on the number of people trying. When you have thousands of guests on CNBC each year, somebody will guess it correctly.

Mathematician Ronald Graham[89] said, "Math is sometimes called the science of patterns." Whenever we see stock market patterns, it's easy to think they must be predictable. Randomness, however, is also a mathematical concept, and it also produces incredible patterns, none of which can be predicted. If you put your trust or your money into advisors who try to predict markets, you'll find the patterns don't give you any added information. They only help you to see what you want to see.

Don't think it can't happen to you. The entire nation was fooled for over a decade by Elaine Garzarelli. If your long-term plan spans 30 years, one-third was wasted by trying to take a shortcut with mice who try to master the markets.

MOUSETRAP #7:
THE MADNESS OF MICE VERSUS MARKETS

The best reason for hiring an advisor is to keep your long-term goals on target, make you understand the potential risks, provide a voice of reason when markets kick up a dust storm, and clearly convey the difference between probable and possible.

For any financial goal, the trick is to balance risk and reward. Unfortunately, many advisors think the trick is to avoid risk, and that's why they turn to reading charts and listening to financial gurus on television, all to avoid falling prices. If avoiding risk is your top priority, then make it easy on yourself—keep your money in bank CDs. If you don't trust banks, bury your money in a coffee can. If you want diversification, bury one can in the front yard and another in the back. You should also see that's no way to accomplish financial goals, unless it's to have your money wilt away from inflation. On the other hand, if you take too much risk, you may earn far more than you dreamed of or you may also lose it all. Those are extreme outcomes, which is what you're trying to avoid through risk management. Find the right level of risk, and you'll most likely accomplish your goals. Goal setting is critical, as it defines the risks you should be taking. Selecting the wrong level of risk is the biggest risk of all.

Interestingly, good financial advisors don't worry about risk. I know it sounds odd, but the reason is that market prices can't be predicted. Risk is part of the process. It's what creates the potential rewards you're seeking. Instead, good financial advisors manage potential risks and the ranges of possible outcomes. They don't guess as to what rate of return you're going to earn each year for the next 30 years or which risks will be present.

Despite this commonsense view, the financial markets are a perfect breeding ground for advisors trying to capitalize on patterns. What better way to avoid risk than to buy when the market's at the bottom and sell when it's near the top? It's easy for an advisor to tell clients he has a proprietary algorithm for timing the markets. It's also an easy way to charge higher fees. The only thing it provides is false confidence to unsuspecting clients.

Many advisors use some type of market timing, and it's a problem by itself. However, it creates a deadly problem when working with multiple advisors who don't communicate with each other—your three blind mice.

IT'S HARDER THAN YOU THINK

The biggest problem with market timing is that an advisor must be correct, not once, but twice, before the strategy pays off. He must be right about when to sell, and he must be right about when to get back in. Even though timing the markets amounts to guessing coin flips, let's be overly generous and assume an advisor has a 70 percent chance of calling a market top and a 70 percent chance of calling the bottom. By simple rules of math, he has a 49 percent chance of being correct on both—not even as good as a coin flip. You can either pay for advice or do better by flipping coins for free.

However, what happens if three or more of your advisors are trying to time markets? To earn profits, all must be correct at the same time, and the odds are virtually zero that it's going to happen.

CONTRARIAN VERSUS MOMENTUM INVESTING

Many types of market-timing investment strategies exist, but most fall into two camps: contrarian investing and momentum investing. Contrarian investing[90] goes against the market. Investors sell as prices rise and buy as prices fall. Sometimes you'll hear this called "fading" the market. On the other hand, momentum investing,[91] also called swing trading, moves with the market. Investors buy shares after good news is announced, hoping to ride the momentum as buyers jump in. But once prices begin to fall, they sell.

It sounds simple enough, but there's an interesting dynamic that develops with your portfolio depending on which style you're using.

For example, if your advisor uses a contrarian style, your portfolio is getting longer (more market exposure) as prices are falling, and it's getting shorter (less market exposure) as prices are rising. Sometimes you'll hear this called "fading" the market.

On the other hand, if your advisor follows a momentum strategy, your portfolio is getting longer (more market exposure) as prices rise, and shorter (less market exposure) as prices fall. The two strategies work against each other.

For long-term success, you ultimately must be long on shares (own them) when prices are rising. However, if it's difficult enough for one advisor to be correct twice, imagine if all three advisors must be correct and long at the same time.

DISCONNECTED ADVISORS
MEANS UNKNOWN RISKS

If you have different advisors engaged in any type of market timing, they're not all buying and selling at identical times. If the timing is different, the risks are different. When advisors engage in market timing of any kind, the first trap is that your money is being managed under unknown levels of risk.

If you had one advisor, or multiple advisors who communicated, different risk levels are part of good diversification. However, when advisors are using different strategies, nobody knows what levels of risk you're holding. The risks—the very things your advisors are trying to manage—are unknown. Even though your meetings with each advisor may have given you the impression that your money was being well managed, it was actually being led straight into a trap.

It's not because your advisors didn't know what they were doing; it's because none of them knew what the others were doing.

CHAPTER 8

TRAP #8

Retirement Planning Without Plans: Failing To Plan Is Planning To Fail

WHY WE ALWAYS FAIL

CartoonStock.com

Former professional golfer Doug Sanders[92] offered great, workable advice for retirement planning: "I'm working as hard as I can to get my life and my cash to run out at the same time. If I can just die after lunch Tuesday, everything will be perfect."

Successful retirement doesn't depend on hope. You don't need to hope for unrealistic returns, the best market predictions, or for guessing six numbers correctly on a state lottery. It certainly doesn't depend on hoping you run out of time.

It depends on planning.

Most Americans, however, don't plan, partly because they expect Social Security to take care of their needs. In fact, the Social Security Administration said that one-third of retirees receive nearly all their income from its payments. Considering the maximum payment anyone can receive who retires in 2018 is $2,788, it's not much.

In my Social Security workshops and in meeting with potential clients, I want people to know how to really maximize all their benefits from the 567 different options available to them. With all the new changes and options, it's not as simple as it once was. Over the years, I've found the #1 choice compared to the #2 could mean an extra $100,000 to $200,0000 or more over one's lifetime with no do-overs. This precious benefit is being rushed into rather than taking the necessary time and coordinating with spouse's benefits, pension option, investments, and savings in light of taxes. If one does not seek the right advice, it could be disastrous in the long run, and the number one fear is outliving one's money when there is so much life left to live.

A 2016 Willis Tower Watson[93] survey showed that 23 percent of Americans don't expect to retire at age 65. Relying on Social Security isn't a good plan either. On the administration's website, it says, "Your estimated benefits are based on current law. The law governing benefit amounts may change because, by 2034, the payroll taxes collected will be enough to pay only about 77 cents for each dollar of scheduled benefits." In other words, the boat is sinking.

Receiving just 77 percent of your expected benefits is a nice way of saying you're losing 23 percent. Social Security was never intended to be a sole source of income. Instead, it was designed to be a supplement, but with a 23 percent expected reduction—at least so far—it's hardly going to count. Instead, you must plan for a retirement without the traps. And I don't mean by lunch next Tuesday.

PLAN #1:
GET OUT FROM THE MOUNTAIN OF DEBT

Planning for retirement isn't just about setting aside money for the future; it's also about getting rid of debt. Money saved is money earned. You shouldn't be working hard at building a nest egg so you can pay off a mountain of debt. But many people are. At the end of 2018, the Federal Reserve[94] released its latest numbers on household debt. The results are frightening. The average American carries nearly $17,000 in credit card debt, $30,000 for auto loans, and $50,000 for student loans. That's nearly $100,000, and that doesn't factor in mortgages.

If you ever find someone in financial trouble, it's likely due to one of two reasons. I won't mention any names, but they rhyme with MasterCard and Visa. Credit cards are not necessarily dangerous because of high balances, but because of high interest rates. The compounding force creates a trap few people can escape from.

To put things in perspective, let's run some numbers. Each bank uses different criteria, but assuming you must pay a minimum of 2 percent of your balance each month, subject to a $10 minimum, a $5,000 balance at 18 percent takes (ready for this?) 46 years to pay off. And when you finally do pay it off, you'll have paid $14,000 in interest alone. For the average American with $17,000 in credit card debt, it'll take 66 years to pay off. An 18-year-old who racks up that much debt will be 84 years old once they pay off the card under those terms. They're serious traps.

Credit cards are so difficult to pay off because of compound interest. In other words, when you make a monthly payment, most of that money goes toward interest, so the net payment paying down the principal is relatively small. Even though you may be sending relatively large payments each month, you're only scraping a few dollars off the top of the mountain of debt. It's distressing, but there's a financial planning trick you can do to pay down the debt quickly. The sooner you pay it off, the sooner that money goes to your financial plan and not the banks.

Fun fact: Think you have enough credit cards?[95] As of 2013, over 1.6 billion credit cards were in use. If laid side by side, that spans over 86,000 miles, enough to circle the world 3.5 times.

A LITTLE EXTRA GOES A LONG WAY

With a $5,000 balance and 2 percent minimum, your first payment would be $100. How long do you suppose it would take to pay off if, instead, you paid an additional $100 per month? Most people think it would cut the time in half to 23 years. Instead, it will take a little over three-and-a-half years with only $1,600 interest. By paying a little extra each month, you're applying that money directly to the principal balance, and the mountain of debt isn't so big. But the bigger benefit is the principal reduction not only avoids the interest for next month but for every month until it's paid off. It's reverse compounding in your favor. What if you have multiple cards with balances? Fortunately, there's an invaluable trick for that, too.

DEBT SNOWBALLING

If you have multiple credit cards with balances, try a simple trick called snowballing for quick debt reductions. Line up all your credit card debts according to dollar balances—smallest to largest. Send additional money for the first card, but pay a nominal amount above the minimum for the remaining two. Once the first card is paid off, roll that payment over to the second card in addition to the payment you've been making. In other words, you've been making that payment before, so there's no reason you can't continue. Instead, you're just applying it all to the second card. When that debt is eliminated, add that payment to the payment you've been making on the third card. Like a snowball rolling down the hill, the payments gradually get bigger for each card, and the bigger they get, the faster the debt melts away.

For instance, let's say you have balances of $2,000, $4,000, and $6,000 across three cards. With the same terms above, it'll take 60 years and $35,000 in interest to pay them off, but watch what happens with snowballing.

Let's say you'll send an extra $150 per month for the first card, but $25 additional per month for each of the remaining two. The first card will take 13 months to pay off with $206 in interest.

Now that it's eliminated, continue what you were doing and pay $25 extra on the remaining two cards. However, roll the $150 additional payment you were previously making on the first card and apply it to the second card, for a total of $175 additional each month. That'll take 21 months to pay off with $1,200 worth of interest.

Finally, continue sending the extra $25 per month on the third card, but now also roll over the $175 extra to it for a total of $200 extra. That'll take another 29 months with $4,700 in interest. In total, you'll take five years and $6,100 in interest. It's a lot, but it beats taking 60 years and $35,000 worth of interest. By paying a little extra each month, the time is reduced by 91 percent and the interest by 82 percent.

In this example, you committed an extra $200 every month until all cards were paid off. Compounding is a very powerful force. What do you suppose would happen if, instead, you committed $300 each month? In other words, you'd spend an additional $250 per month on the first card and continue making the additional payments of $25 on the remaining two.

That mountain will now crumble in three-and-a-half years with just $4,400 worth of interest. Committing an additional $100 per month reduces the time and interest by another 30 percent.

TAP INTO SAVINGS IF NECESSARY

I purchased my first car in 1980 at age 21. A 1977 VW Diesel Rabbit 50mpg—efficient, and a powerful car—at only 12.75 percent. I was thrilled. I did it—my first loan. I was driving 211.6 miles every weekend from Nyack College to work in Toms River, New Jersey, on the weekends. I have to say, the excitement wore off after the fifth payment and I wanted to work harder and get out of debt. Lesson learned? I hated debt, as it made me a slave to 1st National Bank of Toms River.

Perhaps all people hate paying credit card bills and car loans, and understandably so. It's really painful to see that money flying from your account each month but getting nothing in return. It's also why many people pay the minimum amounts. Unfortunately, some advisors make things worse by getting clients on a financial plan where they're making monthly contributions to brokerage accounts, IRAs, or 401(k)s without attacking the credit card[96] debt first. When paying off 18 percent debt or far more, it's mathematically the same thing as finding an investment paying 18 percent.

It sounds strange to say that paying off credit cards is the same thing as an investment, but given the fact that you have credit card debt, it's part of your financial plan, whether you want it to be or not. You must put dollars away where they serve you best. What if the tables were turned and you could lend the credit card company money at 18 percent? Would you do it? If you said no, you don't need a financial planner, you need a psychiatrist.

If you loaned $12,000 at 18 percent, the monthly interest you'd receive from this wonderful investment would exactly equal the amounts you're paying each month on the above three credit cards—you're effectively debt free. Being freed from a debt is the same thing as earning that money. However, if you took your $12,000 and stuck it in a savings account paying 1 percent per year, but continued to pay 18 percent on the cards, you're losing 17 percent per year. That's planning without a plan.

To get ahead, you must get rid of the tremendous drag created by high-interest-rate debt. It's so devastating that it can even be beneficial to withdraw money from other sources, including a 401(k) plan. You can usually borrow from your 401(k) at a relatively low interest rate. However, it gets even better, as many companies allow you to pay the interest back to yourself. In other words, you may owe 5 percent on the money, but it all goes back to your account, including the interest. By borrowing the money, the biggest cost is that you may miss out on any potential market gains, but again, how often does the market return 18 percent per year? The best financial plans find the optimal steps to take to put you in the best future position. Rarely does a better financial opportunity come along than paying off credit card debt. It may be painful, but it's deadly to hang onto it. Just ask your psychiatrist.

Fun fact: Before the Equal Credit Opportunity Act of 1974,[97] single women could not own credit cards and married women were unable to get cards to establish separate credit from their husbands.

DON'T STOP AT CREDIT CARDS

Once credit cards are paid off, you can use the snowballing technique to tackle other debts, too. Just continue rolling those extra payments you were making on the credit cards and put them toward your cars, home, student loans, or other debt.

For example, you can shave nearly nine years and $92,000 worth of interest off of a 30-year, $300,000 mortgage at 5 percent by adding an additional $300 per month. The chart below shows how much quicker you'll pay off your home. The dark area of the chart shows how your home will be paid off by paying the monthly $1,610 mortgage. If you pay an additional $300 each month, your schedule shifts from the dark area to the lightly shaded area.

Mortgage Amount

Years

CHART S

SMALL DEPOSITS MAKE BIG DIFFERENCES

It's not uncommon for advisors to be met with resistance when clients are shown the difference an extra hundred dollars every month can make toward a car payment, credit card payment, or even a mortgage. In their view, it's not going to make a difference toward their retirement, but it is money they could be using today. Why make things tougher today if those dollars aren't going to help much in the future? It's a wrong view, and exactly why so many investors fail with retirement planning. There's no doubt that an extra hundred dollars here or there isn't going to make a monumental difference in the total, but it will make a big difference incrementally. The faster you pay off high-interest-rate debt, the sooner you *don't* have to be making those monthly payments. It's money in your pocket, and that's as good as money earned.

You must think incrementally. If an extra hundred dollars per month can knock three years off a six-year car payment, you'll have three years of saving $500 per month. If an extra $300 per month can strip nine years off a 30-year mortgage, it's now nine extra years you can be saving the monthly mortgage. A similar trap happens when investors start an IRA late in life. By maximizing annual deposits, it may only be expected to grow to a value of $50,000 at retirement. That's not going to fund your retirement, although it could end up paying off your home at that time. To succeed with financial investing, think incrementally. Any time any-one can show you a way to pay off debt sooner, build equity faster, or just start putting a few extra dollars away each month, it all counts. Money saved is money earned if you think incrementally.

PLAN #2:
BUILD AN EMERGENCY FUND

Most financial advisors recommend at least six months' worth[98] of living expenses parked in liquid cash, which means it could be converted into cash within a day without penalties or facing adverse price fluctuations.

By this definition, it normally limits you to a savings account or money market account. Don't put emergency cash in the stock market, even if the investment is labeled as conservative. Prices can change drastically in a single day, and there's nothing you can do should you need the money on that date. It's also best to avoid bank CDs and IRAs as sources of emergency cash, as they usually charge a 10 percent penalty for early withdrawal.

Like all financial plans, there's a balancing point. You can have too little, or you can have too much. If you're emergency fund has too little, there's a good chance you may deplete it and end up relying on credit cards. On the other hand, you don't want to sock too much money away, as there's an opportunity cost. It won't be earning much interest, if any at all. Your emergency fund should cover necessary expenses such as mortgage, car loans, student loans, and other obligations that must be met. Don't put money away for frivolous expenses, as the money is expensive to hold. By building a sizable emergency fund, you're in a better position to stay with a steady financial plan. Planning for an emergency is much easier than scrambling for funds if an emergency arises. There's another advantage to having a properly sized emergency fund. Should you lose your job, you won't be forced to take the one that comes along just because you need the money quickly. That almost always leads to a lower-paying job, and that cuts into your time of finding a better one. A good emergency fund counts for far more than people realize.

PLAN #3:
SELL YOUR HOME AND DOWNSIZE

If you're behind in retirement plans, there are steps you can take today to put them on the fast track. A big option is to downsize by selling your home. However, people overlook this because they just compare the differences in the monthly mortgages, and if you're just looking at those numbers, it'll probably never seem advantageous to downsize. Like most financial decisions, however, there are many overlooked connections. For instance, mortgage expenses usually account for 30 percent or more of a family's income. By selling your home, you may be able to fully pay for a smaller home and pocket the difference. The balance can be used to pay off credit cards, create or add to retirement accounts, and build emergency funds. The connections go far beyond that. A smaller home will drastically cut monthly expenses, including lawn maintenance, electricity, and utility bills. Smaller homes may also not require housekeepers, landscapers, pool maintenance, and other workers to help with daily upkeep. They're cheaper to furnish, carpet, paint, tile, and re-roof. They're cheaper to insure and are charged fewer taxes. The savings go far beyond reducing the monthly mortgage payment.

Another choice is to consider renting, especially if you think moving may be a possibility once you retire. Rentals may be cheaper, which allows you to build your retirement accounts faster or pay off credit cards sooner. Many rental communities cater to the 55-plus crowd and offer amenities such as swimming pools, gyms, walking trails, and social activities as part of the rent, and those benefits may also reduce monthly expenses. Millennials who find it difficult to buy a home are also always looking for places to rent. Proper downsizing requires good planning. Too many times, newly retired couples will downsize to save $1,000 per month in mortgage payments and then pay $1,200 per month in homeowners' association (HOA) dues and other fees. Be sure you're accounting for all costs, including taxes. You don't want to go through the bother of moving, expensive in itself, only to find that your monthly expenses are higher. Plan carefully.

PLAN #4:
GUARANTEED CASH FOR LIFE

After downsizing, you may end up with a sizable amount of cash. Another alternative to consider for retirement planning is to buy either an *immediate annuity* or a *deferred annuity*[99]. Annuities are insurance products where you receive a continued stream of income, usually a fixed amount, over a given time. While many types of annuities exist, two of the more common are *immediate annuities* and *deferred annuities*.

IMMEDIATE ANNUITIES

A popular annuity among retirees is the immediate annuity. The idea is simple—you pay a fixed amount today and the insurance company begins paying you a steady stream of monthly income, usually beginning within the next 13 months. The size of the payments depends on age, gender, interest rates, the amount you paid, and various other factors. To give you a basic idea, a 65-year-old man investing $100,000 would probably receive $580 per month for life. Women generally receive a touch less—say $540, because they have longer life expectancies.

If the insurance company pays as long as you live, it's called a life annuity, but you can also get them for a fixed amount of time, perhaps 10 or 20 years.

You can also buy a joint and survivor annuity, which will cover your lifetime plus another's, which is usually your spouse. Because the chance for both to die is less than for either one individually, the monthly payments will drop a bit—say maybe $450 per month. Immediate annuities are a great solution for people to turn a large amount of money into an immediate stream of income. For soon-to-be retirees who sold their homes, businesses, received inheritances, or cashed in on a 401(k) plan, immediate annuities can offer a great solution. One of the drawbacks with immediate annuities is that there's a big penalty, generally 10 percent or more, if you need to access the cash for an emergency. Always be sure you're using cash you can live without.

People are often wary of immediate annuities because they feel it's a big risk if they die sooner than expected. It seems like you got shortchanged on the deal. However, insurance is designed to hedge risks. It's not designed to necessarily make you money, but to ensure you don't encounter a cash-flow shortage during retirement. Just as with car insurance, you don't buy it hoping that you get into a wreck to make the most of your contract.

Fear of not getting your money's worth is not good financial planning. The reason for the annuity is to guarantee you'll always have a fixed amount of money coming in each month. It may be a risk to you to die early, but it's also a risk to the insurance company if you live much longer than expected. Just as diversification sharply reduces the negative outcomes, the insurance companies gain this same quality by pooling the risks among large groups of people. Don't consider annuities a risk. Consider them a benefit.

DELAYING BENEFITS WITH DEFERRED ANNUITIES

Deferred annuities account for about 80 percent of all annuities, and they're the insurance industry's answer to a savings account. The idea behind a deferred annuity[100] is the same as an immediate annuity, but the big difference is that you significantly delay the time, say 10 or 20 years, before you begin receiving your monthly payments.

During this time, you'll make payments to the insurance company, which is called the accumulation phase. Most people make monthly payments, but you can elect to do a single lump sum, or a combination of the two. By combining the two methods, your account values grow much faster and larger. Other companies offer flexible premiums where you can choose to make premiums whenever you'd like and in any amount you choose. It's not a bad idea if you have a long time until retirement, as it offers a way out without voiding the contract should an emergency arise. It's a nice benefit; however, the drawback is that it's easy to skip payments if you're not required to make them.

No matter which choice you make, you keep making the monthly payments until the contract matures, at which time you enter the payout phase, which is when the deferred annuity is converted to a regular annuity. If using a deferred annuity, during the accumulation phase, you're effectively funding your retirement by paying into a savings account. Because of this, you're allowed to make limited annual withdrawals, generally within the first several years.

It's possible to back out of the contract entirely should you unexpectedly need to access the cash, but it's not without cost. Charges can range from 7 to 20 percent, but generally fall one percentage point for each year until there are no more fees. However, the IRS may impose a 10 percent penalty if you withdraw the money before age 59 1/2. Annuities can be invaluable planning tools, but that's assuming you plan for them properly. Be sure you have all other expenses well covered first.

Interestingly, the Employee Retirement Income Security Act (ERISA) of 1974[101] made it possible for annuities to be purchased in IRAs or Keogh accounts[102]. Just because you're allowed to, however, doesn't mean it's a good idea. These are tax-deferred accounts, as are annuities, so it's not a benefit to wrap them inside another tax-advantaged account. The only exception may be if you're sitting on a large amount of cash and about to retire, and you may decide to use some of your money to buy an immediate annuity to provide income for life.

THE BIGGEST DEFERRED ANNUITY BENEFITS ARE:

- **No Annual Contribution Limits:** Unlike IRAs or other tax-deferred accounts, you can save as much as you wish. That allows you to put away more money for retirement, especially with those who may have cash to invest and need to catch up.
- **No Required Distributions:** For traditional IRAs, you must begin withdrawing money at age 70 1/2, but annuities aren't subject to this rule.
- **Guaranteed Principal:** You're guaranteed to receive your principal (the amount invested).
- **Higher Interest Rates:** Investors can get higher yields. Because of the deferral, insurance companies can invest in longer-term bonds, and since insurance companies have larger pools of money, they can get better bond yields than individual investors.
- **Tax-Deferred Savings:** When you buy an annuity, you're not taxed on the money until it's withdrawn. This allows

you to grow your money tax-deferred and accumulate savings quicker.

THE BIGGEST DEFERRED ANNUITY DISADVANTAGES ARE:

- **Reinvestment Risk:** Immediate and deferred annuities pay a fixed payment each month, based on interest rates at the time you enter the contract. If interest rates rise, you'll miss out on the opportunity to earn higher interest rates since you're locked into a fixed rate.
- **Commissions:** Annuities are a lucrative business for brokers and you'll pay relatively steep commissions, up to 10 percent or more. However, you can combat these fees by using direct-sold annuities since there is no insurance agent involved. Consider firms like Fidelity, Vanguard, and T. Rowe Price to reduce the cost of annuities.

VARIABLE ANNUITIES: BUYER BEWARE

"Bad news—that's just for the lawn."

CartoonStock.com

Whether you choose an immediate or deferred annuity, you're guaranteed to receive a fixed monthly income. The big difference between the two is whether you begin receiving that money now or in the future. However, there's another popular annuity called a variable annuity[103]. It's similar to the deferred annuity in the sense that you're making monthly payments that accumulate over time. With a variable annuity, however, you're investing those funds into the stock market through a selection of stock or bond funds, much like the choices you'll get if you have a 401(k).

By investing your monthly payments, you have the chance to increase your future payouts and you could also reduce them, too. With a deferred annuity, the insurance company takes the risk by investing the funds. With the variable version, you're taking the risk, although the insurance company does guarantee a small minimum, say 3 percent per year. How much will you receive each month when it's time to collect? That depends on how your investments performed. Variable annuities act like a mutual fund tied to an insurance policy. Like most insurance contracts, you can get insurance on top of insurance. You can purchase a death benefit rider, which guarantees a minimum amount to your heirs. If you invest $100,000 and the market value is less when you die, your heirs still collect the $100,000. You can also get step-up benefits where the insurance company guarantees certain increases in that payout each year.

You can purchase another beneficial rider that will lock in your annuity's highest value each year on the contract's anniversary. If your $100,000 grows to $120,000 at any point during the year, the company "locks in" that value on the anniversary date. It's the high-water mark, which means your value can never fall below it, but it may rise above depending on market conditions. All these benefits sound great on paper, but most financial advisors suggest investors steer clear of variable annuities.

First, they're expensive. You'll pay a large sales commission, usually 7 percent or more. I call this annuity "broker friendly." You fill in the blanks why. There's also a surrender fee if you cancel the contract within a certain time, say six to eight years. A hidden fee is the "mortality and expense" charge, which averages about 1.25 percent per year. It compensates the insurance company for mortality risks and other risks associated with the contract. Finally, you'll get hit with administrative fees, which can run 3 percent per year. While each fee may appear small, collectively they can double the cost for you to construct a similar market portfolio through your financial advisor. However, there's one final fee, and it's a big one—taxes.

All annuities—not just variables—are taxed as short-term capital gains regardless of how long you've held them. Most investments receive favorable long-term capital gains treatment if held for more than one year, which means most investors would be taxed between 0 to 15 percent. Only the highest bracket would be 20 percent. Annuities, however, tax everyone as ordinary income, which could be as high as 37 percent. However, even this tax treatment isn't as straightforward as it sounds.

There are exclusion ratios, so not all annuity income is taxed as ordinary income. If you invested $100,000 into an annuity that pays $500 per month for life starting at age 62, the IRS' expectancy tables say you can expect to receive that for 23.5 years, or 282 months. Your annuity's value is therefore $500 * 282, or $141,000. Your exclusion ratio is the $100,000 invested divided by $141,100, or 70.9 percent. From the $6,000 you'll receive from the annuity each year, you can exclude 70.9 percent, or $4,254, as income. That's because it was essentially just a return or principal, but everything over that amount is taxed as ordinary income rates.

Variable annuities are not necessarily all bad, and there are limited times they make financial sense. One of the more unknown uses is for asset protection. About 75 percent of the U.S. states protect variable annuities from creditors. Other forms of retirement savings, including IRA accounts, are easier for creditors to access through the courts. For those in high income brackets or those vulnerable to lawsuits, you may want to remember variable annuities to guard against creditors. Unless asset protection is part of your retirement plan, variable annuities should probably be forgotten.

UNCLE SAM WANTS HIS CUT

Most assets get a "step-up" basis upon your death. That means your heirs' cost basis is marked at the current market value, not the price you paid. For example, if you bought shares of stock for $10 per share but sold it for $100 per share, you'd own capital gains on the $90 difference. However, if your heirs received those shares valued at $100 on the date of your death, their cost basis is $100. They could sell the shares and owe no taxes. If they sold the shares for $110, they'd just owe taxes on the $10 capital gain.

However, no annuity—fixed or variable—receives a step-up basis upon death. If your heirs receive one million dollars from an annuity, they owe taxes on it. I've seen cases where heirs are in a relatively low 15 to 25 percent tax bracket but get launched into the highest bracket when they receive the annuity. A good financial advisor can show you better ways to leave money to heirs excluding your Uncle Sam, of course.

PLAN #5:
PURCHASE A MEDICARE SUPPLEMENT

The United States spends more on health care than any other country in the world. It was reported in 2018 that more than $1 out of every $3 of health-care spending may be ascribed to Medicare and Medicaid. Health-care costs are spiraling out of control, increasing far greater than the rate of inflation of even most home prices. It's no cause for concern for soon-to-be retirees, but one of the best defenses you can do is to file for Medicare upon turning age 65.

To be eligible, you must be a U.S. citizen, legal resident, and lived in the U.S. for at least five years. You must have also worked at least 10 years in a Medicare-covered employment and earned the required credits for working and paying into the Medicare system. However, provisions are available for those under 65 who have certain disabilities and illnesses, such as kidney failure that requires dialysis, a kidney transplant, or Lou Gehrig's disease[104]. If you currently get Social Security checks, you'll automatically be enrolled. You'll receive your Medicare card three months before your 65th birthday and the benefits begin immediately on the first day of the month of your 65th birthday. To understand the benefits of Medicare supplements, you must first understand the basics of Medicare Parts A, B, C, and D.

MEDICARE'S ALPHABET SOUP

Medicare Part A is hospital insurance. It helps to cover expenses for inpatient hospital care, nursing facilities, home health care, and hospice, excluding the services of physicians and surgeons. Any U.S. citizen or legal resident, provided they've been in the U.S. at least five years, who is fully insured under Social Security, receives Medicare Part A without a monthly premium. Unqualified individuals must pay a premium for Part A.

Part B is medical insurance, which is partly funded by the Social Security payroll tax. Once you enroll in Part A, you're automatically enrolled in Part B unless you opt out. However, it's not advisable unless you or your spouse receive insurance from an employer. If you opt out, you may face a stiff penalty for signing up later. Medicare Part B[105] monthly premiums are automatically deducted from your Social Security check. The standard premium for 2019 is $135.50 per month.

Medicare Part B assists with payments not covered by Part A, which include medically necessary services or supplies to diagnose or treat your medical condition, including fees to physicians and surgeons. It also covers preventive services such as flu shots or screenings.

Part B also covers other medical services such as inpatient and outpatient services, X-rays, clinical research, ambulance services, durable medical equipment, mental health, partial hospitalization, second opinions before surgery, and outpatient prescription drugs. Medicare coverage is good, but it doesn't cover everything. Some things not covered are long-term care, routine dental or eye care, hearing aids, acupuncture, routine foot care, dentures, and cosmetic surgery. Medicare also limits the services covered and the amount it will pay if your doctor doesn't accept Medicare's approved payment in full. If that happens, you're responsible for the difference. If you need services not covered, you must pay for them yourself, and that's a big risk that must be accounted for in your financial plan.

SUPPLEMENTAL COVERAGE: MEDICARE PART C AND PART D

To reduce health-care payment risks, the Balanced Budget Act of 1997[106] created the Medicare Choice program, which allows people to supplement their Medicare coverage by using independent insurance companies that have contracts with the government and approved by Medicare. That's where Medicare Part C and Part D come in.

Medicare Part C, also called Medicare Advantage, is like an HMO or PPO.[107] You must have Part A and Part B to enroll in Part C. If you enroll in Part C, you'll get the benefits of Parts A and B. However, Part C allows you to receive all your health-care services through a provider organization rather than through the list allowed under Parts A and B. While there is a monthly fee, these plans may offer significant benefits that'll lower costs. It's possible to even get Part D benefits as well.

Part D[108] is also voluntary and is essentially an insurance policy for prescription drugs, so it is also called the Medicare Prescription Drug Plan. You must opt in by filling out a form in an approved plan, but you must have Medicare Parts A and B first. You'll pay an additional monthly fee for Part D, but depending on income and other factors, financial aid may be available through Medicare's "Extra Help," which covers 85 to 100 percent of the fees.

Once you have Part D, you'll pay a small supplemental fee for any prescription drugs or supplies, which are covered by monthly premiums of Medicare enrollees.

It seems you'd be well covered with Parts A through D, but there's a big risk for upcoming retirees. Like most government programs, Medicare is on the brink of collapse. As health-care costs spiral out of control, prices are going up and Medicare's solvency is going down. In 2017, Medicare Trustees projected that the trust fund financing Medicare's hospital coverage will be depleted in 2029.[109] Medicare may not have much time to make changes, but you do.

MEDIGAP POLICIES

If you elect to have Medicare Part A and Part B, all medical costs won't be covered. Many things like prescription drugs, copayments, vision or dental care, hearing aids, eyeglasses, and private-duty nursing are considered part of your out-of-pocket expenses. However, you can buy extra coverage to cover these costs, which is often called Medigap,[110] or Med-Sup policies.

Just as Medicare Parts C and D are issued by private insurance companies, retirees can purchase a separate Medigap policy, which covers the payment differences not covered by Medicare Part A or Part B.

If you choose to buy a Medigap policy, you should do it within the six months of turning 65. During this time, insurers can't refuse a policy—even if you have a preexisting condition. After this time, there are no guarantees you'll be able to get coverage. Medigap insurance is different from Parts C and D, as they provide Medicare benefits, but a Medigap policy supplements Parts A and B. These policies may also cover copayments, coinsurance, and deductibles. More importantly, many offer coverage outside the U.S.

If you have a Medigap policy, Medicare pays its share of the Medicare-approved amount but the Medigap policy picks up the balance. That leaves you with known medical expenses, more money in your pocket, and no monthly worries.

PLAN #6:
BUILD A BULLETPROOF PORTFOLIO

Once you're basics for finances and insurance plans are sorted out, you can then move on to a portfolio that'll provide a lifetime of income and even weather the market corrections. For example, you can create a mixed portfolio—say 60 percent in stocks and 40 percent in bonds. The stock portion should be well diversified, such as an S&P 500 mutual fund.[111] You can certainly supplement this with a few favorite stocks, but you should not build your entire portfolio on what you think will happen.

The general rule is to withdraw 4 percent of your portfolio value, adjusted annually for inflation. For example, if you have one million dollars in assets, the first year you could withdraw $40,000, and if inflation is 3 percent, you could draw $41,200 the next year, and so on. Using this as a guide, a portfolio like this will generally last about 30 years. When markets are doing well, you'll sell shares of stock to provide income. However, when times are bad, you'll use your bonds cash so you won't be forced to sell your shares at rock-bottom prices. How do you know your bonds won't be trading below face value? That's where a bond ladder comes in.

Start by selecting the longest maturity you wish to hold—for example, a 10-year bond. The bonds are held mostly for market downturns, so you want to be sure you have enough cash for several years if you should need it. It's usually recommended to use somewhere between five- and ten-year bonds. Whatever maturity you choose, it represents the highest rung on the ladder.

Next, invest equal dollar amounts in successive bond maturities beginning with one-year bonds all the way up to your maximum maturity. For example, if a 10-year bond is your longest maturity, put 10 percent of your money in a one-year bond, 10 percent in a two-year bond, and so on all the way up to the 10-year bond. Each maturity is a different rung on the ladder.

By building your ladder this way, you'll always have a bond maturing each year at full face value. Recall from Chapter 3 that if you must sell a bond prior to maturity, you may end up getting far less than the face value if interest rates have risen significantly. The bond ladder prevents that from happening. Each year, you'll have a bond maturing at full face value.

If you don't need to tap into your bond proceeds for that year, when the one-year bond matures, take the proceeds and roll it into a new 10-year bond and your 10-year ladder is reestablished.

Regardless of the bonds you use, one common theme is you must use investment-grade bonds but also diversify among Treasury notes, corporate bonds, municipal bonds, or others. Even though these all may be investment grade, you don't want bonds to end up in default such as what happened in late 2013 with the city of Detroit's unsecured general obligation (GO) bonds. Investors were left holding the $600 million loss. The city has decades to recover; investors don't.

For those with smaller portfolios, you can use bank CDs (Certificates of Deposit) rather than bonds to create bond ladders. Investors often make the mistake, though, of using CDs issued by the same bank, which may not always offer the most competitive rates. Instead, shop around. When one CD matures, you can take the cash to another bank offering higher yields. As long as the banks are FDIC insured, your investments are guaranteed. Also, be sure you understand the bank's policies for early withdrawal; most have heavy penalties of 10 percent or more so be sure it's money you can part with.

Once the portfolio is established, here's the basic idea—when stocks are doing well, you'll sell shares to get your cash. Doing so, you're selling at relatively high prices. On the other hand, if we fall into a bear market, or, worse yet, a prolonged recession, leave your shares of stock alone. Again, there's no benefit in selling your shares at the bottom. Instead, take cash from the bonds. Each year, you'll have a bond maturing to full face value, so there's no risk of having to sell your bonds far below face value to access the cash. The average recession lasts about two years, so by having a 10-year bond portfolio, you'll have more than enough safe money to get you through. When the economy picks back up, you can sell shares of stock to replace the bonds you sold.

This is designed to just give you a basic idea of what a well-constructed portfolio can do for you in retirement. There are new issues for today's investors. For instance, with the nearly nonexistent interest rates, withdrawing 4 percent per year may be a little aggressive. These are all things your advisor can talk over with you, but at least you have the idea of what you are trying to accomplish by establishing a retirement portfolio.

MOUSETRAP #8:
RETIREMENT PLANNING WITHOUT PLANS

One of the biggest risks for retirees is to start with a relatively large portfolio and just use it to live from. Money goes a lot faster than most people realize. In 2009, *Sports Illustrated* estimated that 78 percent of NFL players are bankrupt within two years of retiring,[112] and 60 percent of NBA players are flat broke within five years of retiring. Scottie Pippen, who played for three different teams during his career, lost $120 million in career earnings in 2010. That's what happens when your retirement plans don't include a plan.

Part of the reason this happens is that, during working years, people are busy through the week and just have the weekends to go out to dinner or enjoy a good movie. During retirement, though, every day is a weekend. There is more time for golf, tennis, visiting grandchildren, and, of course, dinners and movies. You may even want to take up a new hobby such as painting or sailing. People often fail to account for this when they're setting up their plans.

This chapter should give you an idea of the complexities that go into setting up a thin financial plan. But can you imagine what happens if you have multiple advisors all attached to your plan? One may be trying to sell you on investments while another may suggest buying a variable annuity. They're all trying to get your cash into investments that also benefit them. But how many told you to pay down the credit cards first? Very few will. Again, they want that cash to go into products where they earn commissions.

On the other hand, accountants are extremely conservative. There's nothing necessarily wrong with that, unless they are controlling a large part of your money and not communicating that with everybody else. Accountants have an insatiable need to make sure that debits equal credits, but sometimes they're not going to add up when you're dealing with risk. It's impossible to put risk in terms where it can be measured as debits and credits. Still, accountants want to see these balances, so they often create values that are meaningless to risk managers, but at least make the spreadsheets balance. It may be what they need to do to follow their professional standards, but it's not necessarily what you need to do to follow your plan.

Attorneys can fall into a similar trap. They're not financial professionals seeking a strategic allocation of funds to help you reach retirement goals. Instead, their profession isn't worried about the risk you're incurring, but who's to blame if something does go wrong. Read any legal disclaimer, and you'll see it's filled with who's to blame and who pays if things go wrong. And because they're holding your money and don't want to be blamed, they are generally overly conservative with your money. Remember, that doesn't come without cost. You're always faced with inflation costs, and if your attorney is holding bonds for you, you're definitely facing interest rate risk. Good financial advisors can always tell your bond's *duration*, which is, loosely speaking, a mathematical measure showing the percentage of change in your bond's price if interest rates change by one percentage point. For example, if interest rates rise 1 percent and your bond falls 5 percent, that bond's duration is five years. What's your cost? You'll never know because your three blind mice haven't spoken to each other. If your retirement is being laid out with unknown costs, unknown risks, and unknown destinations, you're faced with the biggest risk in all financial planning.

You're planning without a plan.

CHAPTER 9

TRAP #9

Tres Ratones Ciegos (Three Blind Mice): Financial Planning Is Dangerous, If You Don't Speak The Language

It's often said that language is the source of misunderstandings. Use the wrong word, misinterpret another word, or let body language speak for you, and messages get mixed. How about tweeting or texting? Two people can read the same message; one is thrilled while the other reads the same message as an insult. Finance is a language, too, and unless you understand the terms, concepts, theories, and math, information gets lost and so does money.

Most investors have no idea about the language of finance. It's not their fault, and to their credit, that's why they're using a financial advisor. Unfortunately, many advisors don't understand the language either. Just because you may be doing business with a well-known firm doesn't mean the advisor is a financial expert. It's easier to get hired as a financial sales agent if you previously sold Xerox copiers than if you earned a PhD in finance. In fact, having a strong knowledge of finance may actually hurt applicants, as they're more likely to question management's actions if they don't correspond to sound financial principles. Financial firms want to hire aggressive salespeople, not potential whistle-blowers.[113]

But traps can easily be set and masked in the language of finance. To succeed with your goals, you must have a plan, but more importantly, you must understand what your plan says. In this chapter, I'll walk you through many of the terms you're likely to hear or that'll be dodged that can set traps you'll never see coming.

THE FIDUCIARY STANDARD

If you're seeking professional investment advice, it's reasonable to assume that the person you're dealing with must put your interests first. You expect it from doctors, lawyers, accountants, and any other professional position, so when it comes to managing the bulk of your wealth, you'd certainly think it applies there, too.

It's reasonable, and wrong.

It all depends on the type of standard your financial advisor must abide by. In the industry, there are two key standards: a fiduciary standard and a suitability standard. Quite simply, a fiduciary standard means the advisor must put the client's interest first. No product, no advice, and no actions can benefit the advisor over the client. Generally speaking, fiduciaries can't accept commissions, kickbacks, referral fees, payment for order flow, or any other compensation for their advice. The advice must be what's best for the client. It's the highest standard in the industry, and the fiduciary is derived from the Latin *fidere*, to trust.[114]

However, there are other types of advisors, such as brokers, insurance agents, sales representatives, and even some financial advisors who fall under the umbrella of a suitability standard. These advisors simply need to give advice that is suitable based on your account profile. If two mutual funds are suitable but one doesn't charge a fee while another charges a fee, it's acceptable for them to suggest the commission-based product. It's not okay for a fiduciary. The word "suitable" doesn't translate to "your best interests." If that connection is broken, so is the trust.

However, the standards are even more complicated, as there are four main types of advisors and fiduciaries and each operates under different standards.

The first type of advisor operates as a fiduciary under the SEC (Securities and Exchange Commission)[115] or as a state-registered investment advisor (RIA). For an RIA, the fiduciary duty is bound by Section 206 of the Investment Advisor's Act of 1940.[116] This section simply says that advisors must be transparent with clients about their advice, fees, and disclose any potential conflicts of interest. As part of the process, advisors must list on Form ADV all affiliations with related people or outside entities, outside employment, and potential conflicts that could arise while acting as an advisor, provided they're not deceptive, fraudulent, or manipulative. For instance, if the advisor has affiliations with broker-dealers or outside money managers, receives commissions, or gets paid a fee for referring clients, it must be stated.

These advisors may work for firms that own related insurance or real estate businesses that do pay commissions provided they're disclosed. If this is starting to sound confusing, imagine how clear it will be in the contract you're required to sign.

Second, there is a Department of Labor (DOL)[117] fiduciary. These advisors are held to a fiduciary standard but only for retirement advice. If they give advice on 401(k) plans and IRAs, they act as a fiduciary. However, if that same advisor gives advice in a taxable account, the fiduciary relationship doesn't hold. Advice that may be allowed by the SEC provided it's disclosed may not be allowed under the DOL standards.

A third type of planner is the CFP (Certified Financial Planner),[118] which requires advisors to pass rigorous exams and pledge to abide by the board's standards. However, even this standard is limited, as the advisor must be offering "material elements of financial plans" to be held to the CFP fiduciary standard. It's therefore possible to hold a CFP designation, but act in a non-fiduciary capacity.

On the plus side, the CFP standard is the broadest in scope, as it applies to all types of financial planning, not just retirement planning as with the DOL standard. The weakness is that it's the least enforceable, as the CFP board isn't a regulatory body. As a client, you cannot sue for breach of CFP contract like fiduciary breaches under DOL and SEC.

The CFP board holds some power and may investigate client complaints, but clients can't get compensated for bad advice. The reason is that a CFP advisor doesn't sign a fiduciary contract. The worst the board can do is strip away the advisor's CFP designation, but it has no legal significance if you've suffered damages. You can't file a court claim stating the advisor had his CFP designation stripped as proof of wrongdoing. In fact, the advisor may continue to work for the firm but just wouldn't be able to list the CFP designation.

Finally, there is a voluntary pledge that advisors may take under many self-regulating agencies such as the National Association of Personal Financial Planners (NAPFA),[119] XY Planning Network (XYPN), and the Center for Fiduciary Excellence (CEFEX),[120] which is one of the strictest standards and requires an annual audit of its advisors. Regardless of the organization, they're all voluntary, and advisors simply agree to abide by the fiduciary standard. However, each of these organizations carries its own definitions of appropriate fiduciary behavior. Advisors who take the pledge cannot accept any commissions at all, while DOL, SEC, and CFP will allow fees. But like the CFP, a voluntary pledge isn't enforceable. However, some organizations require advisors to sign a fiduciary contract with each client and that does make it enforceable.

Just because an advisor says he's a fiduciary doesn't mean there'll be no conflicts of interest. To successfully navigate through the Valley of the Shadow of Death,[121] you must understand the differences between advisors and fiduciaries and the different types of fiduciaries.

When you have three blind mice managing separate portfolios, acting on their own beliefs, and operating on different fiduciary standards or none at all, each is changing their small piece of your total portfolio. Each person may be acting in good faith, but their actions may have unintended consequences. They don't know, but the bigger trap is that you'll never know until it's too late. Good financial planning doesn't just depend on risk. It doesn't depend on negative correlation. It depends on trust.

FEE-ONLY VERSUS FEE-BASED

It's not hard to see that there's a lot of room for confusion among clients as to what they're getting from an advisor, but there are other terms that muddy up the waters even more. Because fiduciaries can't accept commissions (the exception is the DOL standard for non-retirement accounts), most will charge a flat fee for their advice, which is called a *fee-only* structure. They're not getting paid for selling products. Most charge a small percentage of assets under management (AUM).[122]

However, because of the recent push by the industry to move toward fiduciary standards, companies that follow a suitability standard have found a way to mask the language. They advertise themselves as *fee-based,* which is designed to make it sound like the same structure as fee-only. It's not. With a fee-based advisor, you're working with someone who gets paid for selling certain products, and that's most likely to be a conflict of interest. You must ask yourself, out of all the thousands of potential financial products out there, how likely is it that the exact one you need just happens to be the one your advisor is trying to sell? If you're working with a fee-only advisor, chances are it's a good choice. With a fee-based advisor, it's nearly guaranteed there are better choices and for less money. Remember the difference between fee-only and fee-based. One word makes a difference.

ADVISORS, AGENTS, AND BROKERS

Or, What my broker has made me.

When shopping for a financial planner, you'll run across some who call themselves agents, some who call themselves brokers, and still others who refer to themselves as advisors. In general, advisors are those who have financial planning skills, understand markets and finance, and can construct a portfolio to help you reach financial goals. Most of the time, advisors are fiduciaries, but as described previously, that's not always easy to tell. An advisor may qualify as a fiduciary, but only if acting in a certain capacity. On the other hand, brokers and agents are salespeople who are paid commissions to sell you products. The term "broker" or "representative" is usually used for stockbrokers who are employed by a brokerage firm, while "agent" is usually a self-employed person acting on behalf of another company. To make things even more difficult, many brokerage firms have now begun to label their brokers as advisors.

Advisors and fiduciaries operate on a transparency standard. Their goal is for the client to understand everything from how your money is being managed to the fees being charged. They're also required to send clients a copy of Form ADV, which shows how the firm is structured, so there are no hidden relationships. Brokers and non-fiduciaries operate on a disclosure standard. As long as it's disclosed, no matter how muddy the language, the client's been informed. It's the caveat emptor[123]—buyer beware—standard of the industry. No matter what you call them, you can be sure these people act on a suitability standard, not a fiduciary standard.

The problem with a suitability standard is that it will apply in any situation depending on how you want to define it. For example, stockbrokers and brokerage firms are governed by the Financial Industry Regulatory Authority (FINRA),[124] which is a self-regulatory agency (SRO)—the industry's watchdog. By creating this SRO,[125] the industry keeps the SEC off its back. However, it's the fox guarding the hen house. FINRA is funded primarily by annual dues from member firms, including assessments based on gross income, a fee for each broker, and a separate charge for each branch office. And with $845 million in revenues for 2016, if you file a complaint against a broker from a large firm, you can be sure you'll have virtually no chance of winning the dispute. Further, depending on the number of arbiters, a FINRA hearing can top $3,000 per day, which is usually split between the parties. Even if you decide to arbitrate without legal counsel, you'll likely lose and still pay $10,000 or more. It's one more deterrent to protect the industry.

Another reason it's difficult to win a FINRA case is the way they've defined suitability. FINRA Rule 2111[126] says it "requires a firm or asso-

ciated person to have a reasonable basis to believe a recommended transaction or investment strategy involving a security or securities is suitable
for the customer." It's all based on the information obtained through
reasonable diligence of the firm or the associated person to ascertain the
customer's investment profile. The investment profile is based on FIN-
RA's Know Your Customer rule, which requires firms to take relevant
information on the customer's financial objectives, risk tolerances, and
more. However, most firms won't accept an account unless clients check
the box that says speculation is part of their plan. They'll tell you it's there
so that they are not limited in their selections, but they're really trying
to cover themselves in the event of a complaint. If you say speculation is
part of your plan, you can probably forget about complaints being a part
of it, too.

So how do you define what is "reasonable" and "suitable"? FINRA
gives no way to define or measure it. There's no checklist of things that
must be done or avoided. It only requires the broker to have a reasonable belief it was suitable. In 2010, FINRA adopted a new suitability
rule to include suitability for investment strategies, including the recommendation to hold securities. The rule, however, says the suitability
standard depends on whether the recommendation was suitable when it
was made. FINRA states that any strategy recommendation, including
holding, doesn't create an ongoing duty to monitor and make subsequent
recommendations.

If you lose 30 percent of your portfolio because an advisor recommended bitcoin,[127] how will you ever convince an arbitration panel that
the investment wasn't suitable at the time the recommendation was made?
If the client's suitability form includes "speculation," bitcoin may top the
list. Sure, after the fact, it's easy to say it didn't work, but the suitability
rule says it only needed to be suitable at the time the recommendation
was made, without any ongoing duty to monitor it. If the client earned a
million dollars from that same investment, no complaint would be filed.
It's only because things went wrong. How would you prove the broker
didn't have a reasonable basis for making the recommendation? A reasonable person would assume that the argument all comes down to risk.

How much risk did the broker expose you to with this by recommending the securities? It turns out, that's even a thornier problem.

Fun fact: In 2013, after shutting down online drug marketplace "Silk Road"[128] and seizing the bitcoins, the FBI became the second largest bitcoin holder[129] in the world (after founder Satoshi Nakamoto).[130]

RISK:
IT'S ALL RELATIVE

Many suitability standards talk about risk and how an additional asset will alter the client's overall portfolio to losses. Even risk, however, has a language all its own. Is the client trying to reduce the portfolio's volatility? Or the maximum loss? Or the chance for any loss? Or is the goal to reduce inflation risk, default risk, interest-rate risk, reinvestment-rate risk, call risk, liquidity risk, systematic risk, business risk, political risk, or exchange-rate risk? I could go on, but you get the idea. If your goal is to reduce portfolio volatility, a large bond purchase may do the trick. However, if it's a 30-year, zero-coupon bond, it may have ensured you'll miss your goals, subjected you to unacceptable inflation, interest-rate risk, and reinvestment risk. Was it suitable? It depends on how you define risk. Unfortunately, suitability standards don't dig that deep. Instead, they just say if the investment is "suitable," then it's acceptable.

No matter which risk is identified, its suitability also depends on whether the advisor is defining risk in *relative* or *absolute* terms. An absolute risk measures the size of the entire risk while a relative risk just measures the percentage change in risk. As a simple example, if you buy a lottery ticket, the absolute risk is large, as you're nearly guaranteed to lose. However, if you buy a second ticket, you've doubled your chances to win, so in relative terms, you've increased your probability of winning by 100 percent. How should you look at the purchase of the second ticket? Did it increase your chances for success and therefore reduce your risk? Or did it double the amount of money you're nearly certain to lose?

The same thing can happen when building a portfolio. Here's a simple example. Let's say your office has a football pool. I know this wouldn't be much of a pool, but to keep the math easy, let's assume it's just you and one coworker in the office. Each week, the pool circulates the office, and players wager whatever amount of money they wish. Their winnings correspond to the percentage of dollars contributed. Let's also assume that each team has a 50 percent chance of winning each week. The sheet makes its way to your desk, and you see your coworker bet $10 on Team A. With only two people in the pool, it appears the only choice you have is to bet on Team B. If you put $10 on Team B, you're either going to double your money or lose it all. As I've mentioned previously, financial risk managers avoid extreme outcomes, and making it all or losing it all is as extreme as it gets. Most people would see this as a risky bet, and if you put your money on a single team, they're correct. If you continued to play the football pool each week, you and your coworker could expect to break even in the long run. But is there something else you can do? This is where finance gets very interesting.

You could hedge by betting $10 on Team A and $10 on Team B. You're now guaranteed to win part of the $30 in the pot. And yes, part of your money is guaranteed to lose. The idea of a hedge, however, is to give up some of the upside in exchange for not losing it all. It's a form of diversification. What happens in the long run?

Half the time, you'd lose $5, and half the time you'd win $10. For example, if Team A wins, you'll collect half the pot, or $15. Because you paid $20 total, you lost $5. If Team B wins, you'll keep all $30, and because you paid $20, you made $10. In the long run, you'll earn $2.50 per bet. To see why, on average, you'll win once out of every two weeks. If you lose $5 the first week and win $10 the next week, you're up $5 over the course of two weeks, or $2.50 per week. A single bet in the football pool is risky—you can win it all or lose it all. Now here comes the all-important question. By taking two risky bets, did you increase your risk?

The answer is no, because you can expect to earn nothing under the first strategy of betting $10 on a single team, but will earn $2.50 per week by hedging. The same idea, on a more complicated level, can be done in a portfolio. By combining risky assets in ways that offset each other, you can reduce the portfolio's risk. The key here is another complicated financial term called *negative correlation*,[131] which simply means when one investment is up, another is down. In the case of the football pool, your bets are always perfectly offset, as each week you'll have a winning and losing ticket. That's what created the puzzling long-term positive gain. A key financial concept says that investors are only rewarded for risks that can't be diversified away. It's one more reason why investors are better off with a well-diversified basket of stocks rather than having a single person pick a handful of potential winners. Negative correlation is the reason.

A fiduciary advisor can help you construct negatively correlated assets in your portfolio. However, this powerful concept also creates a shield to hide behind. A sales representative in close contention for winning the trip to Tahiti may put you in a risky position, but claim it was a benefit to you in context of the overall portfolio. Don't think these firms haven't figured that out. They're the same firms that created the term *fee-based* to throw investors off guard. It's easy for them to claim it was suitable under the circumstances at the time. Unless you're willing to file a claim and hire an attorney and financial professionals to argue otherwise, it's a financial trap from which you may not escape.

However, think about what happens when you have multiple advisors and you're blind to whether they're even fiduciaries or not. One may, in good faith, close out one position that appears risky. However, they don't know it was placed intentionally as part of a hedge. By selling the position, they've actually increased your risk. The irony is that you don't know it, and they don't know it. However, if you had an advisor who could synchronize all your advisors, it would be clear whether it should be closed or not and you'd know why. The biggest lesson to learn about risk is that a good portfolio is delicately balanced. Blindly change the number of shares, ticker symbols, industries, or sectors, and you'll change the risk-reward balance—maybe for the worse.

SHORT-TERM OR LONG-TERM RISK?

Risk is difficult to assess, as it depends on assumptions. For instance, let's say you're given the opportunity to flip a coin and will earn 25 percent on your money if it lands heads, or you'll lose 22 percent if it lands tails. Should you take it?

The calculation many advisors use is to look at the average, or the expected value. If there's a positive expected value, it's an acceptable risk to take. In other words, if you win 25 percent half the time and lose 22 percent half the time, you'll earn 2.5 percent, on average. There's an edge working in your favor, just like a casino, so there's no reason not to accept the deal. However, anything can happen with just one flip of the coin. Because there's a positive bias, does it make sense to repeat this gamble many times? It seems like it would be an even better deal. After all, casinos make their money by offering games that have a house edge. In the long run, the casino must win. It seems like an advisor may turn down a single bet but would be stupid to turn down repeated attempts.

However, if your advisor takes the long-term view, you'll lose money. That's because multiplying your money by 25 percent and then subtracting

22 percent leaves you with a loss of 2.5 percent. Even though there's a positive edge in your favor for a single play, it leads to financial death for a long-run bet. If your financial advisor says he has an investment portfolio that has a built-in positive edge, you'd be thrilled and sign the contract immediately. What you'll find, however, is that your account balance will slowly dwindle away despite having a favorable edge. It seems like a paradox, since the casino always wins in the long run. The difference here is that you're compounding these rates of returns on one single portfolio, and that changes the math. It's an interesting financial fact that when returns are volatile, your cumulative growth rate will fall below the expected value over the long run.

The point to understand is that there can be a very big difference between short-run risk and long-run risk, depending on how the problem is worded. If you don't know the language, you won't know the difference.

And how would this ever be proven in arbitration? In this example, it's easy to show there is a definite positive edge, so any losses can be attributed to a string of bad luck, but that doesn't mean it wasn't suitable at the time the recommendation was made.

FUND INCUBATION: PERFORMANCE MADE EASY

Traps are easily set in the financial industry because investors don't speak the language. Whether they're intentional or not doesn't matter. What matters is that they're easy to step into, and you may not have any means for backing your way out. One of the more common traps happens within the mutual fund industry with a practice called *fund incubation*. Fund families are always looking for hot new products to sell. Whether it's one that specializes in artificial intelligence, fintech,[132] or battery-operated cars, the funds take a risk by launching a new product and having it flop. To avoid this, fund families are legally allowed to start many smaller funds with limited amounts of money. They're not open to the public and aren't advertised. Generally, they'll operate these funds for two or three years, and then check the performances. If the performances are good, they're brought to market. If not, they're simply forgotten. The process creates an unfair bias for those funds. To the investor, it looks like these fund managers are good stock pickers, market timers, or just amazing at managing risk. The trouble is that anyone could come up with a handful of remarkable performing mutual funds if given the chance to try hundreds of times. It's just like the coin-flip example we saw in Chapter 4, where if enough people are flipping, someone is bound to get 10 heads in a row. It doesn't mean you should be willing to pay them a lot of money to do a repeat performance. Yet, that's exactly what happens in the mutual fund industry. They take lots of chances until they find a fund that shows a remarkable performance, even though it may be purely by chance. Investors, however, unaware that this even goes on, look at the track records in the prospectuses and are misled into believing those numbers are repeatable. Maybe they are, maybe they're not, but the problem lies in that you're making a decision with biased information.

BACK-TESTING: DIGGING FOR GOLD

Another bias that results in the stock market is called *back-testing*. With today's technology and lightning-fast computer speeds, it's possible for companies to test how various strategies would have performed by creating simulations over the past 50 or 100 years. For example, how would your portfolio have performed had you only bought stocks in January with P/E ratios[133] below 15 when they were at their 52-week lows and sold in May? What if you only bought stocks that paid dividends greater than 2 percent whose prices were above their 50-day moving average? Some of this back-testing software has thousands of criteria to choose from. A lot of times brokers and advisors make use of these "proprietary strategies" to convince you they have a superior proven method for beating the market. It's just another bias that's creating the illusion.

If you throw enough questions into the computer, eventually you'll find a sequence that beats the market, and it gives the impression it's a good strategy and that you've hit gold. But it's simply the number of attempts that's allowing you to find such apparent gems. You could do a similar thing by flipping a coin[134] 10,000 times and go digging to the data and find some bizarre sequence that had a statistical significance. For example, every time three heads appeared in a row, followed by two tails, it was more likely for heads to appear on the next toss.

Coincidences work the same way. Perhaps you meet someone for a first date and find you have the same initials, were born in the same state, and have the same birthday. People get chills when they encounter situations like this, as there are too many coincidences for it not to be a mysterious force at work. Sorry to cut the cosmic connection cord, but it's easily explained.

If you knew you had three things in common when you first sat down, you would have predicted a long chat because of your common history. There were thousands of things that could have matched. Maybe you have sisters by the same name, fathers who work in the same profession, own the same type of dog, hate science fiction, and the list could go on for miles. Something was bound to match. People, however, don't see it that way. They just realize that three things on the million-mile list matched, so it must be a meaningful coincidence. That's exactly what happens with back-testing. Throw every possible combination of connections that could possibly exist into the computer, let it chug along for days and weeks, and eventually it'll spit out a list of things, a few strategies that would have beaten the market. But just as you didn't predict beforehand the things that would match with your dinner date, investors back then didn't pick the right combinations that would have beaten the market. Now, however, that they've reversed the process and are actively looking at every combination of possible strategies, it appears to be a winning strategy going forward. If you invest on that information, you'll find it's nothing but fool's gold.

If investors get behind, advisors often turn to higher-risk opportunities in an attempt to catch up. In doing so, many are misled into brand-new funds with stellar track records but are completely unaware it's a biased sample.

The problem that most investors don't realize is that every time you take a small hit to your portfolio, it forces you to need larger returns to reach your goals. For example, if your advisor plans to earn 10 percent per year on a $100,000 portfolio, you'll end up with nearly $673,000 in 20 years. But if your portfolio has fallen to $95,000 after 2 years, you need 11.5 percent per year over the next 18 years to reach that same goal. If it increases to $130,000 4 years later, you'll need to earn 12.5 percent per year for the remaining 14 years to reach the same goal. Because you're likely to miss it, your advisor may start increasing the risk in an attempt to make up the losses. By increasing the risk, you now have the chance of even bigger losses. For those who don't understand finance, it's hard to believe that accepting a bet with a favorable edge can lead to financial ruin because of compounding. Financial decisions must always be based on the full picture, the full portfolio, and all advisors acting in concert. If you allow one advisor to make an independent decision, it may be a good decision in isolation, but a terrible one for you, the investor. And always remember, three blind mice never pay the price. It's why you must keep them connected, even if you think they're acting as fiduciaries.

Finance is a different language, and like any foreign language, it's not easy to speak. If you're not a financial professional, you won't be able to keep your three blind mice connected. You won't know the right questions to ask, and you won't know how to interpret the answers they're providing. It reminds me of a joke about two translators talking on the deck of a cruise ship.

"Can you swim?" asks one.

"No," says the other, "but I can shout for help in nine languages."

All kidding aside, there are parallels with financial planning. If you don't know how to put together a long-term financial plan, you're left with the alternative of shouting for help. The difference here is that the answers will come back in different languages. Is it the language of an advisor—or a fiduciary? Is it the language of the SEC, DOL, or FINRA? Are they quoting rates of returns based on actual results or back-tested data? Or incubator[135] funds? These terms are just scratching the surface, but this chapter is designed to show that there are a lot of meaningful terms that'll have no meaning to you. And yet, you're supposed to make sense of them all and relate them back to your three blind mice. It's one thing to keep them blind, but it's an entirely different thing to try to speak to them in different languages.

MOUSETRAP #9:
FINANCIAL PLANNING IS DANGEROUS
IF YOU DON'T SPEAK THE LANGUAGE

Financial planning is difficult enough without having to complicate it with its own language. Because of the threat of lawsuits and a recent industry push for fiduciary relationships, stricter rules will have unintended consequences. Brokers will have the incentive to charge high fees for putting clients into ultra-safe investments, which only ensures they won't reach their goals.

However, there will always be firms that want to charge fees for selling products. It's a billion-dollar business, so there's no reason to expect they'll go away. The trick becomes in how you mask the disclosures. It becomes a game of words, not financial planning. If you ask your advisor if he's a fiduciary, he may say, "Absolutely, I'm registered with the Department of Labor." It sounds official, and you'd have no reason to question it. However, because you don't understand the language, you didn't understand that his advice only applies to retirement accounts.

This doesn't mean the financial industry is bad or that it's riddled with fraud. To the contrary, most advisors will have your best interests at heart. Instead, just understand, as with any industry, there will always be people who try to take advantage of others by hiding the truth behind words. The real problem for investors begins when you have multiple advisors. The more advisors, the better the chances you're going to end up with some that operate on a non-fiduciary standard. If one chooses to put you into a mutual fund with high fees, you may have been able to use that money in a different fund and meet your goals easier. However, you'll have no way to know because those choices are being masked in the language of finance.

I'm not saying it's necessarily bad to have multiple advisors. In many cases, it's a good idea, as you'll have people with specialized skills. The problem begins when all your advisors are pulling in separate directions, possibly not even acting in your best interests, and nobody knows because they're disconnected. A change to your portfolio by one advisor can have negative repercussions on a portfolio held by another. As a simple example, if you own an S&P 500 index fund under one advisor but another advisor who engages in market timing buys an S&P 500 inverse[136] fund, the two funds cancel each other out as if that money is parked in cash. However, neither advisor may agree that you should have that much money sitting in cash, yet that's what you're doing. For financial planning, consistency is a virtue, but that's provided you're hitting your target.

CHAPTER 10

TRAP #10
Planning To Retire, Without Planning To Change

After 40 years of hard work, a man retired with $5,000,000.00, which he had gained through courage, diligence, initiative, skill, and devotion to duty, thrift, efficiency, shrewd investment, and the death of an uncle who left him $4,999,999.50.

All good planning requires change. Conditions always change, and your plan must adapt. For instance, a football team may plan a passing game, but if it ends up 20 points ahead after the third quarter, coaches may switch to a running game. Prior to the start, nobody knew the outcome. Now the score is known, and because the probability of winning is so high, it only makes sense to reduce the risk of interceptions. The goal has changed from winning to "not losing." Financial planning works the same way and for the same reasons.

Twenty years prior to retirement, you didn't know what your portfolio would be worth. Now you do. Further, if you continue taking the same risks and there's a market correction, there's no time to make up for the shortfalls. Your income stops but your expenses keep going. You need to begin withdrawing money just at the time you should be buying. As you approach retirement, your plans must change. This is why financial experts separate the fields of money management from retirement planning. They're different stages with different risks. They need different plans. There are many people who continue using the same pre-retirement plans, and it's perhaps the biggest of all financial planning traps. Just because you've reached retirement doesn't mean your plans are over. They've just changed.

During working years, you're investing money, and all of that money is growing from capital appreciation. You're making use of the compounding effect—money making money. Of course, there'll be the times when we get the occasional bear markets, and possibly even severe corrections. However, none of that really matters because you're still in building mode. During these times, stock prices are low, and your monthly contributions will buy more shares, and that may actually accelerate your future gains. It can be a benefit, but only because you have time for stock prices to recover. In the early years, it's all about building, and time is your friend. As you approach retirement, however, those dynamics must change. You can't afford an interception with a minute left in the game.

For instance, let's say you were set to retire with a million-dollar portfolio just before the tech bubble[137] burst in 2000. The S&P 500 index's highest closing price was 1,527.46 on March 24, or roughly 1,530. The market dropped 49 percent, and never regained that level until seven years later, on May 30, 2007, just in time for the 2007–2008 financial crisis. The market then lost 55 percent, and you never saw your million-dollar mark again until February 19, 2012, when it first closed above 1,530.

From 2000 to 2012, your money went nowhere. That doesn't mean you could just sit and wait for prices to recover, because you began withdrawing money, and that created even more damage. You were withdrawing money from a shrinking portfolio, and you never received the benefit of buying shares at lower prices. It's another financial double-whammy and all because plans didn't change. But it gets even worse.

Most investors, as they watched their portfolio values disintegrate, sold near the lows. Remember how the math works. A 50 percent drop means you need a 100 percent increase just to get back even. However,

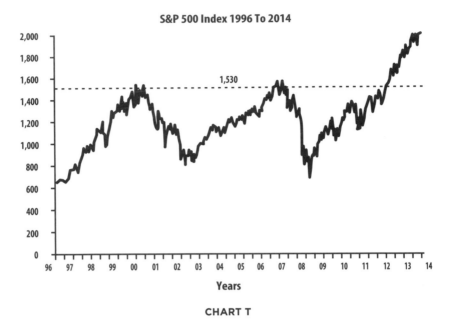

S&P 500 Index 1996 To 2014

1,530

Years

CHART T

it's also a 50 percent hit on a million-dollar portfolio. That's $500,000 that could end up disappearing. Even if you sold all your assets and went 100 percent into cash, you still had to withdraw money. That means when the markets recovered in 2003, you had fewer shares. Now it takes far more than a 100 percent increase to get you back to where you were. It doesn't take much to dig a hole, but it takes a whole lot of effort to climb your way out. If you were set to retire in 2000, that twelve-year period was pure devastation. But now let's look at another scenario.

Any 20-year-olds investing in 401(k) plans had their portfolios decline, too, but they were buying shares, not selling shares and withdrawing money. Further, they may have only had $10,000 invested, so a 50 percent drop wasn't difficult to recover. But from 2000 to 2009, they were buying, and their portfolios have skyrocketed in value because they loaded up on cheap shares that got catapulted to all-time highs in 2018. It's the same chart, same percentages, and same investments, but the outcomes are dramatically different depending on whether someone needed to withdraw money in 2000 or someone was continuing to buy. As you get near retirement, risks change, and that means your plans must change.

THE DISPOSITION EFFECT:
THE VALUE OF GAINS AND LOSSES

It probably goes without saying, but investors despise losses far more than the satisfaction they get from earning profits. In other words, if you have a $100,000 portfolio, a $10,000 loss has a far more powerful emotional effect than a $10,000 gain, which financial experts call the *disposition effect*,[138] or, more simply, loss aversion. Okay, it's not hard to believe, so why is it so important?

During retirement, you're not making deposits, so the current dollars have more value, and that accelerates the fear. You're more likely to sell shares when prices are falling, which is the worst thing that can happen, as you've now eliminated any chance for that money to generate future capital gains. In the previous S&P 500 chart, if you did nothing with your portfolio, it took 12 years to recover. However, if you sold at any time during those downturns, especially near the bottoms, you could easily end up more than doubling the recovery time. Maintaining the balance between necessary monthly income and desired capital appreciation is the real challenge of retirement planning. Once retired, you won't have the same ability to earn income as you did during your working years, so you're not able to withstand the same declines in portfolio values. Financial professionals call this the *risk capacity*,[139] and it declines, or at least should, as you approach retirement. Most people don't make these adjustments, and it's usually because of the various arrangements with financial advisors.

I've found that people fall into one of three categories, and no matter which you choose, you're likely to fall into traps. First you have the do-it-yourselfers. Second, you'll have those who use a one-stop financial advisor, where all financial decisions and investments are made by one person. Third, you'll have people who use multiple advisors. Regardless of the arrangement, financial traps can be set.

DIY:
SAVING ON FEES

Do-it-yourself investors often choose to tackle investing on their own to save on fees. It may be low on fees, but it's high on traps. First, they don't realize there's a tremendous amount of knowledge and experience that goes into making financial decisions, and they often end up making the wrong choices. For instance, during retirement, you're selling assets to generate income, and most do-it-yourselfers will sell the poor-performing assets and hang onto the ones that are red hot. Doing so, however, means they're making the portfolio more aggressive. Advisors not only look at the buying and selling decisions, but also how that will rebalance the account.

Second, few will refer back to the plan to see if they're on track, and for those who do, they often lack the financial or mathematical skills to align their portfolios with future goals. If you had a 20-year plan at 10 percent per year, but the market returned 8 percent during the first five years, what return do you now need to reach your goal? It's tough enough, but to answer it accurately and efficiently, you must include taxes, expected Social Security payments, inflation, and investment compounding just to name a few.

Third, they don't update their plans as markets or lifestyles change. A new job, the birth of a child, or changes to the tax laws can significantly affect your future plans if not accounted for.

Fourth, and probably the biggest risk, is failing to remain objective. In the legal business, there's a saying that an attorney who represents himself has a fool for a client. The reason is simple. It's hard to be objective when you're in the defendant's seat. Good attorneys don't represent themselves, doctors don't operate on family members, but for some reason, people feel they can remain objective when handling their own finances. The research says differently.

In a 2015 Natixis Global Asset Management[140] survey, 65 percent of investors said they struggle to avoid making emotional decisions during bear markets. But they also fail to remain objective during bull markets.

In 2014, the S&P 500 rose 13.7 percent, thus marking the third consecutive year of double-digit returns. The survey reported that 81 percent of investors expected double-digit returns going forward. Markets, however, gravitate toward a long-term average of about 7 percent depending on the time frame measured. That means you should expect markets to fall after experiencing above-average returns, and to rise after experiencing below-market returns. Investors, however, don't think that way. When times are good, they expect that things are only going to get better. Investors should have been adjusting for lower returns, but they did the opposite. That's a dangerous trap, but the reason they step into it is simple.

It's hard to remain objective when you're sitting in the defendant's chair. When people begin losing money, their first reaction is to sell. The better action is to get more aggressive when prices are down. It's so hard to do, but a good financial advisor can keep you from having a fool for a client.

To make things worse, do-it-yourself investing has become increasingly easy. There's no shortage of websites, YouTube videos, and robo-investment programs to help people handle their own finances. Today, nearly every bank and financial website offers robo-investing, where computer algorithms make decisions for you, and your investment purchases are conveniently debited from your account. You can even download phone apps to change withdrawal dates, the amount invested, or even the assumptions you gave the computer. However, these space-age planners are far more designed to sell products rather than create sound, comprehensive financial plans. Sure, they'll ask a few basic questions that make you feel like you're in control of your financial future. What's the expected rate of inflation you wish to use? What's your expected return?

If you don't know the answers, the computers will make suggestions based on long-term averages. These questions, however, aren't asked to make your plans more secure. They're designed to put the risk back on the investor. If goals are missed, the financial institution can say you entered the wrong data, and the more information it asks for, the less responsible the computer becomes. These computer programs simply perform calculations based on the numbers that you feed them. They're not designed to think. They're not designed to be customized to your needs. They're designed to sell. They may even tell you they're commission free, but as covered in Chapter 6, the hidden fees are probably well above industry average. Even the SEC has words of advice for investors. "While automated investment tools may offer clear benefits including low cost, ease of use and broad access, it is important to understand their risks and limitations before using them. Investors should be wary of tools that promise better portfolio performance."

Above all, you must use age-appropriate investments and continue to use realistic market data. Do-it-yourselfers may think they're saving money, but it's only because they never see the money they missed.

ONE-STOP-SHOP ADVISORS

While many people prefer to do their own financial planning, there are those who realize they need financial help, but they end up selecting a one-stop-shop advisor. Many great financial planners can be found, and most will put your best interests first. The problem is that you won't know it until it's too late. The first problem arises because there are no qualifications to be a financial planner. People who are totally unqualified can call themselves a financial planner, and many people do. Many even have criminal backgrounds. Advisors are required to disclose any regulatory, disciplinary, or criminal actions as part of the application process. For instance, applicants must disclose any client complaints involving $15,000 or more, being fired for investment-related reasons, and, of course, criminal convictions. Just because it's disclosed, however, doesn't mean they won't get hired. A 2015 CNBC survey[141] found over 20 percent of representatives filed some type of disclosure. A detailed look at 4,000 of those criminal disclosures revealed about half were for felonies. Over 25 percent involved shoplifting or theft. About 7 percent were charged with assault and 8 percent with fraud. Seven people were charged with kidnapping, and nine charged with rape. Surprising? At least two were charged with murder or intent to murder. To anyone in the industry, it's not all that surprising. Each year, outlandish stories appear that show just how far people will go to pull off a financial con. We've all heard the Bernie Madoff[142] story and other highly publicized cases, but few people realize just how rampant financial frauds really are or how far people will go.

In 1996, Sam Israel swindled $300 million from his Bayou Hedge Fund Group,[143] and later created fake accounting firms to send fake statements to investors to try to avoid getting caught. Once caught, he tried to fake his own death, but was later recaptured after being featured on *America's Most Wanted*.[144]

Stephen Trantel[145] was a successful oil commodities futures trader on the New York Mercantile exchange[146] but lost his job in 2001 after the market downturn that followed the September 11 attacks. He needed money to support his home, so decided to rob banks for a living. He robbed 10 banks before getting caught.

In 2009, Marcus Schrenker[147] tried to escape financial crimes that he ran through his investment firm, Icon Group. He also tried to fake his own death but chose a more extreme method by jumping from a $2 million private plane. His plan was to defraud an insurance company, the very industry where he was licensed. He pleaded guilty to securities fraud, sentenced to 10 years in prison, and required to pay over $630,000 in restitution.

If you've followed the financial markets as long as I have, you realize that these stories are nothing new. Every year, we hear of another big financial con, fraud, deception, or Ponzi[148] scheme. Stories like these show what some people will do for money and how far they'll go to keep it.

Honest investors, however, assume their advisor has the financial skills and criminal-free background that one would reasonably expect. Unfortunately, the financial markets are riddled with fraud, and you must be careful where you place your trust and money. As mentioned in the previous chapter, even acting as a "fiduciary" doesn't necessarily mean what you think it should mean. It has different definitions, and depending on the relationship, a fiduciary isn't always required to act in your best interest.

Investing under one roof has its benefits. You can see all of your investments in one place. You can see the entire financial plan. But when it comes to your advisor, you can't see the motives.

THE MULTIPLE-ADVISOR TRAP: THREE BLIND MICE

The third scenario, and probably most common, is when investors use multiple advisors. At a basic level, they may use one for financial advice, an accountant for taxes, and an attorney for trusts and wills. The trap here is the main point I've made throughout the book. Multiple advisors, three blind mice, and they don't communicate with each other. In fact, they have the incentive not to communicate, as it opens up their knowledge, strategies, and clients to others. Working with three blind mice is always a dangerous trap, but the trap has a stronger spring near retirement.

As you get closer to retirement, the rules change. You don't have time to make up for bad investments, bad markets, or bad timing. Once you actually retire, it changes again. It's now time to begin withdrawing money, and you must make sure the withdrawals balance with the rate of expected growth. In other words, if money's flowing out faster than account values are rising, you will run out. However, it's difficult to balance these cash flows when using multiple advisors for several reasons.

First, you're likely to double-up on investments. When the FAANG stocks[149]—Facebook, Amazon, Apple, Netflix, and Google—were hot, it was hard for advisors not to buy. How good would it look when the *Wall Street Journal* reports that these were some of the best performing stocks the market has seen in decades, but your advisors didn't buy a single share. Advisors realize this, and don't want to be the one to tell you they passed up the opportunity. As a result, all advisors buy and you end up being over-weighted in risky stocks. But you'll never know because they don't communicate with each other. Nobody knows what percent of your overall portfolio is being held in these stocks. While each advisor may be acting in your best interest, collectively they're not. You end up paying fees to be left in the dark but bearing all the risk.

Tax efficiency is another area to consider. Your IRA and 401(k) accounts grow tax deferred. If you're in the early stages of retirement planning, you should hold Real Estate Investment Trusts (REITS), bonds, and any actively traded portfolios in tax-deferred accounts.

Taxes also play an important role during retirement. When you're no longer earning money, strategies should focus on saving money, and taxes are one area where investors can capitalize. For example, let's say you have $20,000 in taxable gains for a year with one advisor and $20,000 worth of losses with another. If the two communicated with each other, you could end up with a lower tax bill. You must also consider how withdrawals will affect your marginal tax rates. Should you withdraw money from your traditional IRA, Roth IRA, or 401(k)? Or a little from each? If you don't know the answers, or if your advisors aren't communicating, you'll overpay taxes, underfund your investments, and pay fees to receive sub-optimal results.

For example, during a bear market, you should be selling bonds and buying stocks, but if left up to individual advisors, they'll do the opposite. Bond advisors want to see their assets under management increase in value, so they'll want to hold not sell. Stock advisors, on the other hand, don't want to report declining values, so they'll advise to sell. Both advisors believe they're acting in your best interest because they don't see your entire portfolio. If they saw your bond prices rising but stock prices falling, it would become evident that they should sell bonds and buy stocks. Because each only sees a portion of the overall portfolio, the decisions end up being different. From your perspective, it's better to sell bonds and buy stocks, but no individual advisor wants to be the one holding the portfolio that's declining or selling the one that's rising. The traps, however, don't end there.

Advisors are, rightfully so, fearful of losing money for retirees. As a result, they go low risk, but that ends up increasing the chances that your portfolio's growth won't keep up with the rate of withdrawals, especially after accounting for inflation. It's becoming an increasing problem as the marvels of modern medicine are allowing people to live longer. In a recent book by London Business School's Lynda Gratton, *The 100 Year Life,*[150] the number of people living to 100 years or more is becoming more common, especially in Japan, which has the largest proportion of centenarians in the world. When the country began keeping statistics in 1965, the number was just 153, but in 2017, it was nearly 68,000. As the demographics[151] change, so will policies on Social Security, which will likely continue to increase the full retirement age. Beginning in 2017, full retirement age is now 67 for anyone born in 1960 or later. Investors must be prepared to fund the majority of their retirements.

The key to surviving retirement isn't to take no risk. Instead, it is to take managed risks across the entire portfolio. To do that, however, your advisor needs to see all assets under management.

SURVIVING RETIREMENT TRAPS

I can remember so vividly that between the years 1995 and 2000, and then again from 2004 to 2007, the stock market was sizzling. Investors didn't want to miss out. Real estate values and the stock market were booming at an unprecedented rate, and most of us had not seen that in a long time. At the same time, interest rates were falling. What a perfect scenario to pull equity out of the house and invest it in the stock market. Heck, you could get a nice write-off and make millions. I can't imagine how many DVDs, seminars, and books were sold to capture the American dream—financial independence. What marketing hype. Perhaps you were one of them. So many investors around the U.S. wanted in, as they were listening to the drummers beat and observing the stock market continuing to grow like weeds in the garden. So many financial sales representatives, planners, investment guys and gals worked with the mortgage brokers as they got clients to cash out and invest.

While that carnival was going on and interest rates were dropping, real estate tycoons instantly arose. Perhaps you remember your friends buying homes and renting them out for little or no money down, many completely leveraged to the gills. Not knowing much about the real estate industry, realtors were in their heyday. Bidding wars on properties emerged and debt escalated. The real estate boom was on. Whether you knew what you were doing or not, the hype caught so many people. The American dream turned into the American nightmare in 2008, as real estate plummeted and stocks dropped almost 60 percent. Beware, temptation and greed is here to stay. Way to go, Adam and Eve.

Preparing for retirement is one thing. Surviving it is another. Bear markets will always happen, and you must make your money last. By using multiple advisors, however, the lack of communication means you're nearly guaranteed not to have a properly balanced portfolio during the times when it's most important. So what's the best way to ensure you don't outlive your portfolio?

Many strategies exist, and each should be customized to the needs and risk tolerances of the client. Just to give you some ideas of what a financial planner can do for you, let's say you have a million-dollar portfolio at retirement. The first step is to figure out how much you'd like to withdraw each year, adjusted for inflation. If you wish to withdraw $50,000 in the first year and inflation is expected to be 3 percent, you'd need $51,500 the following, and so on. Next, we'll keep about two years' worth of your annual needs in cash, so for this example, we'd park $100,000 in cash. Next, we take the remaining $900,000 balance and buy a combination of stocks and bonds. We'll want to diversify for both categories, and, in reality, we'd probably place the bulk in the S&P 500 index, which would also include smaller percentages from 5 to 15 percent in international funds, emerging markets, and real estate. To keep the example simple, let's say the stock portion is invested in the S&P 500 index.

Diversification is important regardless of the asset class. Bonds, even though guaranteed, are no exception. The reason is the price risk that can occur if you need to sell prior to maturity, which was covered in Chapter 3.

The best way to reduce price risk is to create a bond ladder, which means we'll buy bonds with varying maturities, say from 1 to 10 years. It's called a ladder because each bond maturity represents rungs of a ladder, and the height of the ladder represents the differences in maturities. What's the advantage?

Without a ladder, you're at risk if you need to sell bonds prior to maturity. For instance, if you put all your money into 10-year bonds but we enter a bear market shortly after, those bond prices may be well below the price you paid just at the time you need to sell them. Instead, by having a variety of maturities, the one-year bonds will have matured to their face value. If that money isn't needed, you simply buy new 10-year bonds. By always keeping a bond ladder, you'll always have some maturing soon, so there's no risk of having to sell below face value.

Of course, as prices change, the proportions will change, too. To keep the portfolio in its 60/40 balance, we'll "rebalance" each year. It's important to do each year, regardless of market conditions. This is one of the key areas where an advisor can keep you focused on goals. When markets are red hot, as they have been lately, investors never want to rebalance because they must sell shares of stock. As a result, the percentage held in stocks continues to increase. When the bear market strikes, these investors have the bulk of their assets in stocks and can take devastating losses. Instead, each year, if stocks are up, we'll sell enough to bring the percentage back down to 60 percent, and we'll take the sales proceeds and buy enough bonds to bring their percentage back to 40 percent. Notice the benefit of rebalancing. It ensures you'll buy low, sell high, and never allow your percentages to get too far out of alignment. Now that we have investments diversified between stocks and bonds, how does it help you?

Well, let's look at some statistics. Since 1930, most bear markets have lasted about 18 months, while the average bull market lasts five times longer, about 97 months, or just over 8 years.

When markets are rising, you'll sell shares of stock to generate the required income. Further, in a well-diversified portfolio, you'll also receive dividends, which can be coordinated so that you'll receive cash each month or quarter. In this example, you have $540,000 invested in stocks. If it returns 10 percent, you've got more than the required $50,000. That extra cash will go to buy more bonds at depressed prices. As long as market prices rise, continue selling shares and buying bonds. But stock prices don't rise forever. What do you do then?

When a bear market hits, there's no sense in selling shares of stock at depressed prices. Instead, you'll use your cash. Because most bear markets last less than two years, you should have plenty of cash to get you through. As the short-term bonds mature, you'll use those proceeds to buy shares of stock at the lower prices. However, if a bear market happens to last longer, you'll always have some bonds maturing that can generate additional income. Rather than rolling the maturing bonds to new 10-year maturities, you'll simply withdraw the cash from the maturing bonds. When markets recover, stock prices rise, and bond prices normally fall, and you'll go back to selling shares in the rising markets and replace the bonds and cash.

The key idea behind strategic retirement portfolios like this is to keep you from allowing the percentage of your portfolio from getting too heavily weighted in shares of stock, only to watch them get crushed in a short-term bear market. Most investors will sell out of panic, and it's the surest way to run out of cash.

Naturally, there are many variations of this basic strategy. Rather than using the S&P 500 for stock investments, you could put some cash into dividend-paying stocks that are selected based on their yields and payment dates. Most companies pay quarterly dividends, but you can choose stocks whose dividends are paid more frequently, almost monthly. There's a big selection of stocks to choose from that have high-dividend yields, some surprisingly high.

However, like all investment decisions, there are risks and trade-offs to consider. Most high-yield stocks don't have the potential for capital appreciation like their non-dividend-paying counterparts. Second, some companies have a long track record of paying high-yield dividends and doing so comes at their own peril. Many times, companies are fearful of cutting dividends because it sends a signal to investors that the company

Company	Ticker	Dividend Yield (August 2018)
Hi-Crush Partners	HCLP	24.7%
Sandridge Permian Trust	PER	18.5%
Mobile Telesystems	MBT	14.2%
Pacific Coast Oil Trust	ROYT	13%
Norbord, Inc.	OSB	11%
BP Prudhoe Bay Royalty Trust	BPT	7.3%
AT&T	T	6%

TABLE F

can't maintain the dividend. In other words, it's running out of money. While that may not necessarily be true, investors usually sell shares on the news of any dividend cuts. Rather than cutting dividends, companies may end up selling assets to maintain the high yield, but that also reduces its ability to generate future profits. The result can be a vicious cycle where the company ends up running itself into the ground. Remember, as we talked about in Chapter 1, the dividend yield only applies if you can sell the shares for the price you paid. For instance, if a $25 stock pays a one-dollar dividend (25 cents each quarter), the yield is 1/25, or 4 percent. If you buy 100 shares, you'll spend $2,500 and receive $100 in dividends, which means you earned 4 percent on your money. However, if the shares are trading for $19, you'll only receive $1,900 if you sell, for a total of $2,000 when you count the dividends. The result is that you spend $2,500 but end up with $2,000, which is a 20 percent loss. Before you go searching the Internet to buy the highest dividend-yielding stocks, you need to dig through the company financials to determine how that company is making those payments. Is it from volatile commodity prices? Or is it from a long history of great earnings? In other words, the size of the dividend isn't as important as the quality. This is another area where a knowledgeable financial advisor can help you select a good portfolio of dividend-paying stocks. Even then, you should only allocate a relatively small portion to these stocks.

PICKING YOUR PORTFOLIO

A third variation of the retirement portfolio is to allow for some active investing. With this strategy, your stock portfolio still includes the S&P 500, but you also get to select a handful of stocks you think will outperform the overall market. Even though the odds are against it, some people enjoy the thrill of the hunt, looking for the next big winner. That's okay, as long as it's not the majority of your investing philosophy. In exchange, you may outperform the index, but you may also underperform it. Still, for some clients who like to dabble in stocks, we can set up portfolios that allocate a small percentage to individual stock picks.

As with all financial plans, there are hundreds of variations, but the idea is to show what a well-balanced and strategically planned portfolio can do for you. The worst thing to do is put 100 percent into stocks and hope the market continues higher, and yet, that's what most do-it-yourselfers end up doing. The goal of a retirement portfolio shouldn't be focused on growth. It's about income. Yes, it's nice to have some growth to counteract inflation and provide for higher annual withdrawals each year, but the goal is never to aim for the highest returns.

THE BENEFITS OF RETIREMENT PLANNING

Financial planning has been studied in intricate detail for decades. The Society for Financial Counseling Ethics[152] was established in 1969, and we've witnessed many bull and bear markets during that time. Financial planners know what works and what doesn't. Yet, there are still people who believe financial planning is nothing more than a disciplined approach to setting aside money for the future. If markets continued to rise every year, maybe that's all you'd need to do. But the real trick isn't about how or where to invest. It's about understanding the history, the math, and the portfolio constructions that allow you to meet your goals. If you contribute too much each month, you'll pay with bigger sacrifices today. If you invest too little, you'll pay dearly for it tomorrow. Retirement planning is the science of finding the balance that's just right.

MOUSETRAP #10:
PLANNING TO RETIRE
WITHOUT PLANNING TO CHANGE

If that doesn't work, let's look at other retirement options.

Planning for retirement[153] is one part of financial planning. However, the risks are often overlooked because the dynamics change so sharply. You're no longer earning money, but need to withdraw it. You've also accumulated a large nest egg, which means it has further to fall should you get caught in a market correction. Trusting the retirement planning process to another is an important decision, and you must be sure the advisor acts as a fiduciary and puts your best interests first. Acting as your own planner may seem like it's the best decision. After all, nobody will look after your best interests better than you, right? It seems to make sense, but it sets a lot of traps.

First, people incorrectly judge how much control they have. When markets are rising, it seems like your portfolio balances are climbing because of your financial skills. Who needs a financial planner? Markets, however, don't always rise, and one of the biggest benefits of a financial planner is to help keep emotions in check.

Second, people take more risks when things appear safer. When market prices are rising, it seems there's no risk. Consequently, investors take more risk. It's the problem of unintended consequences economists have studied for a long time. For instance, as cars became safer with mandatory seat belts and airbags, people began to drive faster, closer, and take more risks. As a result, we've seen the net number of traffic deaths increase. Individual investors fall into the same trap when markets are rising. Not only do they not rebalance portfolios, but they do the opposite and invest more heavily in stocks.

Third, people get comfortable with familiarity and follow the Yogi Berra rule: "If it ain't broke, don't fix it." They believe the financial plan they've always used quite successfully must also work as they approach retirement or during retirement. However, as conditions change, risks change, and therefore your plans must change.

Fourth, people overestimate their ability to make estimates. As shown throughout this book, financial planning has multiple moving parts, and they're not always black and white. Successful planning requires you to make estimates that are much better suited for experienced financial planners. Do-it-yourselfers believe they can substitute rough guesses for that experience. People, however, are notoriously bad at making estimates, and when it comes to financial planning, they're even worse. Here's one to try for a test. Don't pull out a calculator, but instead, trust your intuition. How long is one million seconds? What about one billion seconds? What's your best estimate for both?

Before I give the answers, think about the question for a moment. Everyone's familiar with time, and everyone knows the concepts of one million and one billion. They're interesting questions because they require you to combine familiar concepts in unfamiliar ways. That's what happens when people try to estimate financial risks over long periods of time.

One million seconds is just under 12 days, but one billion seconds is nearly 32 years. If you were off in your estimates, you're in good company, as nearly everyone gets it wrong. The chances of individual investors accurately estimating the necessary number of dollars to invest, the effects of inflation and compounding, the amount of risk they're taking, or the right strategies for the right times are virtually zero. They're routine problems for good financial planners on one condition.

All must be on the same page. Their decisions must be based on the same estimates, same outlooks, and same risk tolerances. No matter how strong your planners' resumes may look, if they're not following the same plan, their skills are likely to do more harm than good.

OFF TO THE RACES

My daughter Maggie, the equestrian competitor, asked me to put this in since New Jersey's state animal is the horse and she helps out at our farm. During financial seminars, I often joke around to make a point by asking the audience a question or two. Which is more likely to win a race? A cart pulled by a single horse? Or one pulled by a team of six horses? The essence of teamwork proposes we're more powerful in groups, so the six-horse team will win the race. Well, hold on there, cowboy.

What if one horse was harnessed in backwards? You see, all benefits of strength, power, and speed are eliminated, so what sounded like a sure-fire winning team turns out to be a disaster. There is power in numbers, provided you include the most important word—*together*. As Henry Ford[154] said, "If everyone is moving forward together, then success takes care of itself."

When using separate advisors—three blind mice—there is no togeth-erness. Each operates under separate plans, estimates, and assessments of risk. Further, each has different incentives and is in competition for your business. It's in their best interest not to share their strategies with the others. Their actions center on doing what's best for their portion of your portfolio, not what's best for your overall financial picture.

Financial planning is necessary to accomplish life's bigger goals. A new car, home, wedding, children, and college, just to name a few. However, all plans must ultimately be tied to a retirement plan, as there's no sense in succeeding today at the expense of failing tomorrow. Retirement plan-ning, however, means you must plan to get to it and through it. Financial planners say the greatest paradox of retirement is that it takes work. If you're planning to retire, you must work on planning to change.

"Something tells me we are
NOT on the same page."

CHAPTER 11

TRAP #11:

Let's Get Together Your Team And Concerns

I t was my first bike, a 10-speed Flandria[155] I bought for $120. It was the best, at least for me. All my friends had fancy Schwinns, but my pocket wasn't that deep, and I had to pay for it myself. I went to the bank of DAD, so I could buy the bike, and he agreed to loan me $70. As we sat together at the kitchen table, he drew up an agreement showing the amount of each payment and when it was due. I was so excited because I knew I could mow one lawn a week and pay back the loan. So I signed the 10 percent interest loan, which was payable at $10 per week. Although my dad trusted me, he said the piece of paper was a reminder of what we agreed on; just in case either of us forgot, we could review the agreement. As Dad went over the terms of our agreement, I couldn't help but watch the clock. It was 5:45 p.m., and the bike shop closed in 15 minutes. It would have been traumatic for a child to be sitting in a parking lot holding a contract and no bike. Even though it was 50 years ago, that little lesson taught me so much.

At age 10 this was my first time dealing with a legal document. The best part—it was simple, clear cut, and without any room for misunderstandings. Dad was fair, tough, and always looked for teachable moments for me to grow.

Now, looking back, it's been a tremendous tool that I've tried to use all my life. A contract, like money, can be a clear and useful tool, or it can be a divider of families and friends. Money and misunderstandings can lead to turmoil.

Potentially overlooking some terms of a $70 bike contract is one thing, but when it comes to your estate, it's a much bigger deal. Families have been destroyed over it. So whether you have a small or large estate, it's important to have a clear plan in place. At some point in your life, you will become disabled, incapacitated, or pass away. Sorry for the gloom and doom, but estate planning is a large part of financial planning, and you don't want family rifts because your wishes weren't in writing and clearly defined. You know the old saying, "Where there's a will, there's family." Money separates the wheat from the chaff.

An attorney is a crucial part of your planning, because Mr. Chaos will arrive, and at the worst possible time. This is why advisors should read the legal documents and ask about your situation yearly. Why? Because life happens! The good, the bad, and the truly awful. One day you're on the golf course lining up your first eagle putt, and the next day you're in the hospital with no memory of whether you made it or not, and hours later you're seeing my mom and dad at the pearly gates. You'll love them, I promise. Sure, at that point, not much matters down here on earth, but it does matter to those still here.

Perhaps you're getting older and your lights are starting to dim. Or maybe they're on but no one's home. In other words, Alzheimer's, dementia, or stoke. Who is your advocate? There needs to be a proper legal document in place.

Do you have a backup plan? Who can help you during this chaotic time? Many types of legal documents, policies, and strategies can be used, but there are three documents at a minimum you must be familiar with. The power of attorney (POA) for financial and health-care matters, a will, and a living will. Should a good advisor have the most current copies of these three documents on file? YES! It reveals who the advisor can speak to in a time of need. Like the HIPPA privacy act for insurance policies, these documents are essential. Otherwise, your advisor may not even be allowed to speak with your children or heirs.

The reason my firm works with lawyers, accountants, and other advisors is simple. Everyone has their specialized niche. Everyone isn't in a cookie-cutter situation. So, make sure when you're drawing up the legal documents that you make your dreams, desires, and concerns clear. An advisor not knowing about the family dynamics can cause real unforeseen dilemmas that could have been avoided.

I've noticed that most families have legal documents such as power of attorney for financial and health-care matters, a will, and a living will but they never reviewed them to make sure their intentions or beneficiaries are still the same.[156] They're all essential, especially when you're older. I can't tell you how many families I've met with, whether rich or poor, who do not have the proper documents.

When Dad was passing away, my sister Sandy wanted to feed him to make him more comfortable as the inevitable was looming. Unbeknownst to me, she called the nurse in to feed him through a tube. Thank goodness I understood that her heart took over, not her head. We both knew Dad didn't want any heroics, just water and oxygen. As the nurse arrived, I simply handed her Dad's living will, and all was halted. This could have been an awful argument, but it was easily avoided. Frankly, the few drops of ink and the piece of paper kept our brittle emotions intact and avoided a battle neither of us wanted. I can assure you it wasn't over money. It was about Dad's written wishes. After Dad passed away, Mom and I went to the bank, and as I promised her, I would help with the bills, oversee the accounts, and keep it up to date. The banker prepared the paperwork and then asked me to sign. Voila! Another magician showed up to cause more problems. I told the banker I would not sign the paperwork. Mom looked at me with a deep concern, as I asked the banker to make the account a single account, not joint. I asked to be power of attorney on her account and not the joint owner. You see, Mom was getting older, and her driving was just OK, so if she caused an accident, I could be named in a lawsuit, and that would put my assets in jeopardy and vice versa for her. I see this problem in a majority of families I speak with and it's a recipe for disaster. With Mom opening an individual account but adding me as the POA,[157] this disastrous situation is eliminated. I can handle all of Mom's banking needs without the liability! This is one of many ways I help clients by working closely with all financial matters. If there is a death in the family, we can help guide them to make smart, informed decisions when emotions would otherwise take over. Everyone sleeps better at night because we've eliminated the trees where the vultures like to perch salivating to take advantage.

In recent surveys, it's been found that only 4 out of 10 people have a will or living trust. The top two reasons for not having either one is that they haven't gotten around to it (47 percent) or they didn't have enough assets to leave to anyone (29 percent).[158] These are crucial documents that everyone over 18 should have.

If advisors are responsible for the assets, wouldn't it make sense that they should have the supporting documents for review and clarity? Make sure your legal documents are up to date, signed, and there are no changes needed on them. Visit our website for more details on how to improve your estate no matter how big or small it may be.

I started the McLean Tax Advisory Group in 2008 for the sole purpose of doing taxes for clients. You see, tax returns reveal a ton of vital information that can assist your advisor in making financial decisions. Heck, they are like a good EKG or MRI to a doctor. They give advisors the heads-up on the best ways to take withdrawals. Should you convert your IRA to a Roth or contribute to a Roth IRA? In other words, the tax return is a historical storybook, which acts as a guide on how to prepare, reduce, or eliminate future taxes.

Bruce and Alyssa were brand-new clients—both age 70 ½—who came into my office to pick up their tax return. Thankfully, they liked my educational workshops where I teach many subjects, and this was one that they really needed—required minimum distributions, or RMDs. Since they both had birthdays a day apart, it required them to take their required minimum distributions.[159] Because that amount was so high, it triggered their Social Security to be taxed at the highest bracket—85 percent. Ouch! Had they been clients previously, I would have seen the pending RMDs and could have easily made adjustments to sharply reduce the taxes. Instead, they received a much smaller tax refund, but at least they know why. Not understanding how taxes work can really upset people, especially if they owe a ton of money and aren't aware of how it happened.

Now imagine you're married for 45 or more years, and your spouse does all the finances, taxes, and pays the bills. Suddenly their lights go dim, and you're left with making financial decisions. What a nightmare! It can be overwhelming, but it's an easy transition for our clients, as we know their history, and that means we can continue putting them on the best financial path. Decisions can be made more easily with all the facts at hand when your financial advisor seeks information from past history.

In the event a spouse passes away, the surviving spouse is now in the highest tax bracket: filing Single. Thus, one of the reasons I started the tax firm is to be the financial light in times of darkness and hopefully head off or alert our clients of potential problems.

REAL-LIFE SCENARIOS
LEGAL AND FINANCIAL

Wow, time flies. It seems like just yesterday, with anticipation and excitement, my daughter Meredith turned 16 years old—the dreaded driving age. I constantly heard, "Dad, can I drive? Let's go somewhere. I know Mom needs something at the store; let's go right now." This is what I call the 16-year-old pre–heart attack. You're excited for them because you know that thrill of getting behind the wheel for the first time, but it's also stressful. Teenagers and steering wheels don't always mix well. Potential heart attacks aside, we took off at dusk for the store. At one major intersection, she caught a red light, so she was anxiously waiting for the checkered flag to drop. As we were talking, the light turned green as I shouted, "Don't go—stop! Keep your foot on the brake!" Then we heard the sound of horns blasting and one finger waving, as if we were in New York City rush-hour traffic. I told her to ignore everything except my words. Thank goodness she listened to me, as a car barreled through the intersection at top speed. That would have hurt. Jokingly, I said to her, "It was my side, honey." What a great teachable moment.

1. Look both ways while crossing an intersection, whether the light is red or green.
2. Don't let distractions cause you to take your eyes off the road—not the phone, texts, or radio (boyfriends came later).
3. Driving too fast could cost someone their life.
4. Focus on the main thing—safety—then worry about driving.
5. When others are impatient, don't be pressured, especially if it means putting your life in jeopardy.

Where did those wise insights come from? Forty-four years of driving experience, which included learning from others, as well as Mom and Dad, and let's not forget Drivers Ed in high school. Okay, it also included a few prior accidents and tickets, but all experience counts, whether good or bad.

Like getting in a car accident, financial mistakes can be fatal, so I hope this section will help you take action and correct any wrongs, especially if you're working with three blind mice. Isn't this what you want in your advisor when it comes to your finances?

When I meet people for the first time, or meet for annual reviews, I ask a plethora of questions to make sure nothing has changed. I make it clear to clients the psychology behind my questions. I feel it's my fiduciary responsibility to ferret out previous, current, and potential future financial challenges in order to prevent a fatal financial crash. All too often, clients get impatient waiting for the financial light to turn green without considering what may happen if a car is coming the other way. Sound financial advice isn't just drawing from what's happened in the past. It also comes from what may happen in the future. Decades of experience can prevent these disasters, assuming you're not working with three blind mice.

Scenarios

Margaret, an 84-year-old widow, came to my office with her daughter, who had attended one of my Social Security workshops. Margaret wanted to know if she could increase her Social Security income from the current monthly $454 check she was collecting. After speaking with her for a while, I found there were many holes in her plan.

Did you know there are 567 different ways of collecting Social Security and if you picked the second-best option, it could cost as much as $100,000 or more in lifetime benefits? How anyone can make the right decision without the sophisticated software today is beyond me. I found out her husband was in the Army during WWII, stationed stateside and not in conflict. There was no power of attorney or living will. When I read her will, I noticed it was a copy and not the original. She had $40,000 in a CD and $20,000 in savings and checking.

I found out she was entitled to more money from Social Security. Then I explained she needed to update all her legal documents. Most courts desire original legal documents, not copies, and not marked or written on, as it may be voided. If Margaret became incapacitated, she did not have a power of attorney. Thus, nobody could help her with health care or financial matters. As HIPAA says, everyone over the age of 18 should have a POA. New legal documents are needed and provide beneficiaries on all investments and bank accounts to avoid probate. Make sure all legal documents are not marked on at all. Sometimes, I see parents making corrections when the daughters get married. NO! The courts want original legal documents.

Margaret was also unaware of her husband's free long-term-care coverage she was entitled to through the VA. **I can't tell** you how many spouses are not aware of this much-needed VA benefit and the fantastic medical facilities available to them. Margaret could have received approximately $1,100 per month and she was eligible to go to a VA facility for free.

In New Jersey, there are three great facilities I recommend my clients to visit to understand all the benefits. Why spend $3,000 to $9,000 a month if you're entitled to free VA[160] benefits? She was unaware of this amazing benefit, and no one told her until I met her. This one discovery was a real benefit for all.

Consider this scenario, too. Tim is 64 years old, divorced with no children. After nine years he got married to Barbara, who is 60 years old and also with no children. I met them after a financial educational seminar for a complimentary review. They were a lovely couple. Tim was looking for an advisor. Barbara mentioned a desire to keep her financial advisor, whom she had for over 14 years. I wished them the best and to please call if they needed help. Three years after our original meeting, Barbara came to the office and shared with me that Tim passed away from a massive heart attack. She wanted to know what to do, as I looked at her with a puzzled look. Didn't she already have an advisor? She went on to tell me that Tim's ex-wife received $245,000, of which $200,000 was from his life insurance policy and $45,000 from his three IRAs and one bank account. His children received $25,000 each, which left her with $5,000 in the joint savings account. Barbara mentioned she just cashed in her only asset—a $100,000 IRA. I asked why, over the 14 years of being with her financial advisor, hadn't he ever asked about the beneficiary arrangement. I wasn't surprised to hear her say that her advisor never asked because he assumed she had a will. She mentioned to me she felt uncomfortable talking about money since they were newly married and she didn't want Tim to feel like she was after his money.

Since Tim's will was never updated after their marriage, Tim's house was part of his estate and the will directed where the assets would go. Perhaps his ex-wife would receive them. When I asked her why she cashed in her entire IRA, she said she needed the money to live on so she called her advisor a few months after Tim's death and asked for the money. He sent it at once. No questions asked.

Good and bad news. The good news is she can collect the spousal Social Security benefit since it was higher than hers. The bad news was, because she took the $100,000 as a lump sum from her IRA and she was now at a single taxpayer rate, she would be taxed at the highest rate. I advised her to put it back into an IRA before the 60-day rollover period was over and only withdraw money as needed. She seemed concerned, as her advisors said she could have it. True, but that's not the full story, as the potential for a tax complication is always there and needs to be reviewed often. Remember, asking uncomfortable questions now may make you comfortable later, especially when you need it most.

Tonya, 26, passed away in a tragic car accident, with her 8-year-old daughter surviving the accident. Tonya did not have a will, power of attorney, living will, or any life insurance. Have you asked your adult children whether their legal documents and insurance policies are up to date? Remember the three critical legal documents: power of attorney for financial and health-care matters, will, and living will. You may end up raising your children's children or someone else's, as we did, though she is a real blessing to us. Remember the story of training my daughter to drive? We can learn from anyone's mistakes. The travesty comes from not learning from mistakes and repeating them. Did your advisor and lawyer ask detailed questions about your children and grandchildren such as their current health and other things that could affect your overall financial situation? Make sure they are aware. Three blind mice don't have the incentive to ask. Are they selling or serving you?

THREE BLIND MICE, ASLEEP

John is 69, and his wife, Kerri, is 62, with children Sarah, Alex, and Eric. Sarah is 37, divorced, and great with children, but terrible with money. For every dollar she receives, she spends $2. Alex is a 35-year-old autistic man, living with his parents, while 33-year-old Eric is married with five children.

As for John's 401(k), if he dies, his beneficiary is his wife. If Kerri dies, her 403(b) goes to John as the primary. Then if John dies, it will be equally divided among their three children.

The IRAs, investments, and bank accounts go to each other, but they don't stipulate any contingent beneficiaries. With total assets, including the house, approaching one million dollars, let's see how this potential train wreck can be mitigated.

DETAILS MATTER—VANISHING INHERITANCE

If the advisor asked more questions and read the will, he or she would have immediately known there's a problem. As you can see, there's a real need for a trust account to control Sarah's awful spending habits. Perhaps a spendthrift provision would be beneficial! It could be set up to provide a monthly allowance with annual increases for inflation. For Alex, once he receives his inheritance, his Medicaid benefits will cease until all the money he receives is spent. Then, once it's spent down, someone will have to reapply to Medicaid.[161] Oh joy, that will be fun. If the will was written correctly with a special-needs trust provision, none of Alex's inherited assets would be jeopardized.

Life, health, and wealth change, and questions about who the money goes to should be asked yearly, as well as any changes to one's health.

Fix all the beneficiary and legal wording in the will and all of the accounts individually. Anything going through the will goes through probate.

But wait, there's more now for John's 401(k) account. If John's wife were to predecease him, then his 401(k) would go to the children via the will because he did not fill out the beneficiary form for any contingent beneficiaries. Thus, probate will be involved. The will takes over, and since it's incorrectly based on what John and Kerri's desires are, the vanishing magic act begins. Let's see.

Now, before the money is divided among the children as per the will, the 401(k) account must be closed and distributed to the estate, which would cause a 100 percent taxable situation to the three children. Abracadabra, and the money's gone. Small oversights can mean your children get nothing, not even a thank-you card from the IRS. If John had simply put contingent beneficiaries after his wife on his 401(k) form, then the children could roll over the inheritance, and they could have taken small amounts over their lifetime to meet the Required Minimum Distribution rules.

OK, we bumped off Kerri. Now it's John's turn, so let's consider the final scenario. Kerri's 403(b) benefit will go to John, but since he's dead, it goes to the stated contingent beneficiaries, the children.

It's quite obvious the financial advisor and lawyer did not speak to one another, nor did either ask John or Kerri for detailed information about the children and their desires. Finally, John was a Vietnam veteran and was in Camp Lejeune for two years. After asking John detailed questions about Vietnam and where he was, it was evident he could have several health issues pending, as he drank the infected water while in Camp Lejeune, and served in Vietnam and the DMZ zone in Korea where Agent Orange was sprayed.[162] He already was showing symptoms, as I shared with both of them. I want them to take action on that front at once. Both of them may qualify for long-term care because of his service and perhaps a compensation benefit up to $3,300+ a month they were not aware of. Not to mention that they could apply to eliminate real estate taxes on their house. For more on veterans benefits, visit www.3blindmice.com.

All vets deserve the benefits they're entitled to, so I ask many questions of our veterans and spouses because it's a large part of the financial puzzle.

Let's dive a little deeper. This is an area almost all families and advisors never discuss because it hardly ever happens, but when it does, the crows and clowns show up at the funeral with their hand out, leaving beneficiaries baffled. And yes, sometimes even fights break out. John and Kerri mentioned that if their children Sarah or Eric were to pass away before they did, and later John and Kerri died, they wanted to make sure the children—not their spouses—got the money. Thus, Sarah's children would get her third and Eric's children would get his third of the estate—ensuring that the grandchildren would not be cut out and they would not have to change the will if a child did pass away. There's a simple but powerful phrase called "*per stirpes,*" which can easily be added to the beneficiary section, and most people never know to consider. *Per stirpes* is Latin for "roots" or "per branch," which means to pass the assets to the blood line. In other words, each "branch" of the family receives and equal share an estate.

Warning: If you're in a similar awkward situation, please seek proper advice. Don't delay. Check your will and make sure your assets go to the heirs you intend.

There are so many other scenarios I've encountered, but they share one thing in common. The solutions can be found by asking questions. If someone tries to sell without educating you, that's suspicious. Ask the advisor to call the lawyer to see how the beneficiaries should be set up.

Hopefully the advisor will ask for the legal and tax documents the very first time you meet! Kudos to the advisors who do this.

PORTFOLIO—TAXES AND THE WILL

I met 67-year-old Art from my Will and Trust seminar. I disclosed I was not an attorney but just a conduit to gather information to better understand his deepest desires. He said he heard me on the radio, as I was discussing the New Jersey Estate Inheritance Tax.[163] Art was married to the love of his life, Cindy, for 38 years before she died of cancer six months prior to our meeting. She had two children from her previous deceased husband. Art and Cindy married when the children were ages four and six at the time. Art practically raised the children. It was Art's goal to pass what he had acquired on to their two children. After asking a multitude of questions, I asked to see the will, power of attorney for financial and health-care matters, and living will, which were just 10 months old. After reading the documents, I was floored. I asked Chris, an attorney who happened to be in the office, to join me as I asked four final questions.

1. Did the attorney know the children were Cindy's from her previous marriage? Answer: Yes.
2. Did the attorney know you wanted to give your two children everything? Answer: Yes.

3. Do you want to make your New Jersey Estate and Federal Inheritance Tax as tax-free as possible? Answer: Yes.

4. Would you like to adopt the adult children? Answer: Yes.

I asked this because they were not his children—they would pay at the highest state tax bracket. So, based on New Jersey's estate tax, the children would have to pay approximately $330,000, but if he adopted them, they would pay nothing, zero, nada, zilch. The will gave everything to the two children.

I also pointed out to the lawyer that Cindy was on both his will as executor and acting as his power of attorney, but he had no contingents on either document. Thus, if he died, Mr. Chaos would arrive.

Now, as state and federal inheritance taxes change, so must the planning. If you do your taxes, you must ask the relevant questions and make your own changes. If you have any investment advisors, then you must make sure all your beneficiary paperwork is the same. If you have one advisor, then I hope you're discussing these matters yearly.

The Three Blind Mice are alive and well. Wake up and take action.

Visit me at www.3blindmice.com.

ENDNOTES

1. **Published By Frederick Warne & Co.:** An illustrated children's book by John W. Ivimey entitled *The Complete Version of Ye Three Blind Mice*, fleshes the mice out into mischievous characters who seek adventure, eventually being taken in by a farmer whose wife chases them from the house and into a bramble bush, which blinds them. Soon after, their tails are removed by "the butcher's wife" when the complete version incorporates the original verse—although the earliest version from 1609 does not mention tails being cut off. The story ends with them using a tonic to grow new tails and recover their eyesight, learning a trade (making wood chips, according to the accompanying illustration), buying a house and living happily ever after. Published perhaps in 1900, the book is now in the public domain.
    https://en.wikipedia.org/wiki/Three_Blind_Mice

2. **Stephen Edwin King, Born September 21, 1947:** Is an American author of horror, supernatural fiction, suspense, science fiction and fantasy. His books have sold more than 350 million copies, many of which have been adapted into feature films, miniseries, television series, and comic books.
    https://en.wikipedia.org/wiki/Stephen_King

3. **McLean Tax Advisory Group, LLC:** Is an independent, family-owned practice built on the core values of trust, integrity, competency, and service. Scott S. McLean, founder, has been navigating retirees through smooth and turbulent waters since 1983. McLean Tax Advisory Group offers simple financial solutions to the complex retirement challenges people can face. They develop tax and insurance strategies to address your personal needs and prevent future concerns, to ultimately cultivate lasting peace of mind.
    https://www.mcleantaxadvisory.com/

4. **Plato, Born 428/427 or 424/423BC (Died 348/347 BC):** Along with his teacher, Socrates, and his most famous student, Aristotle, Plato laid the foundations of Western philosophy and science. Alfred North Whitehead once noted: "the safest general characterization of the European philosophical tradition is that it consists of a series of footnotes to Plato." In addition to being a foundational figure for Western science, philosophy, and mathematics, Plato has also often been cited as one of the founders of Western religion and spirituality.
    https://en.wikipedia.org/wiki/Plato

5. **Health Insurance Portability And Accountability Act—HIPAA:** Is the acronym for the Health Insurance Portability and Accountability Act that was passed by Congress in 1996. HIPAA does the following:

- Provides the ability to transfer and continue health insurance coverage for millions of American workers and their families when they change or lose their jobs;

- Reduces health care fraud and abuse;

- Mandates industry-wide standards for health care information on electronic billing and other processes; and

- Requires the protection and confidential handling of protected health information.
https://www.dhcs.ca.gov/formsandpubs/laws/hipaa/
Pages/1.00WhatisHIPAA.aspx

6. **"Pass The Buck":** To blame someone or make them responsible for a problem that you should deal with. https://dictionary.cambridge.org/us/dictionary/english/pass-the-buck

7. *Back To The Future,* **Martin Seamus McFly:** Is a fictional character and the main protagonist of the *Back to the Future* trilogy. He is portrayed by actor Michael J. Fox. McFly also appears in the animated series, where he was voiced by David Kaufman. In the videogame by Telltale Games, he is voiced by A.J. Locascio; in addition, Fox voiced McFly's future counterparts at the end of the game. In 2008, McFly was selected by *Empire* magazine as the 12th Greatest Movie Character of All Time.
https://en.wikipedia.org/wiki/Marty_McFly

8. **John Francis "Jack" Welch Jr. Born (November 19, 1935):** Is an American business executive, author, and chemical engineer. He was chairman and CEO of General Electric between 1981 and 2001. During his tenure at GE, the company's value rose 4,000%. In 2006, Welch's net worth was estimated at $720 million. When he retired from GE he received a severance payment of $417 million, the largest such payment in history.
https://en.wikipedia.org/wiki/Jack_Welch

9. **Mark Elliot Zuckerberg (Born May 14, 1984):** Is an American technology entrepreneur and philanthropist. He is known for co-founding and leading Facebook as its chairman and chief executive officer. Born in White Plains, New York, Zuckerberg attended Harvard University, where he launched Facebook from his dormitory room on February 4, 2004, with college roommates Eduardo Saverin, Andrew McCollum, Dustin Moskovitz, and Chris Hughes. Originally launched to select college campuses, the site expanded rapidly and eventually beyond colleges, reaching one billion users by 2012. Zuckerberg took the company public in May 2012 with majority shares. His net worth is estimated to be US $61.4 billion as of October 19, 2018, declining over the last year with Facebook stock as a whole.
https://en.wikipedia.org/wiki/Mark_Zuckerberg

10. **Chipotle Mexican Grill, Inc.:** Is an American chain of fast casual restaurants in the United States, United Kingdom, Canada, Germany and France, specializing in tacos and Mission-style burritos. Its name derives from chipotle, the Nahuatl name for a smoked and dried jalapeño chili pepper. The company trades on the New York Stock Exchange under the ticker symbol CMG. Founded by Steve Ells on July 13, 1993, Chipotle had 16 restaurants (all in Colorado) when McDonald's Corporation became a major investor in 1998. By the time McDonald's fully divested itself from Chipotle in 2006, the chain had grown to over 500 locations.
https://en.wikipedia.org/wiki/Chipotle_Mexican_GrillChipotle Mexican Grill, Inc. NYSE: CMG https://www.google.com/search?client=firefox-b-1 -d&q=cmg+stock

11. **S&P 500 Index:** Is a basket of 500 of the largest U.S. stocks, weighted by market capitalization. The index is widely considered to be the best indicator of how large U.S. stocks are performing on a day-to-day basis. Composition of the S&P 500. As we mentioned, the S&P 500 consists of 500 large-cap U.S. stocks, which combine for about 80% of all U.S. market capitalization. For this reason, the S&P 500 is considered to be a good indicator of how the U.S. markets are doing. To be added to the S&P 500, the following criteria must be met:

   ■ It must be a U.S. company.

   ■ The market cap must be $5.3 billion or more.

   ■ The public float must consist of at least 50% of outstanding shares.

   ■ It must have positive reported earnings in the most recent quarter, as well as over the four most recent quarters.

   ■ The stock must have an active market and must trade for a reasonable share price.

   Meeting these criteria isn't a guarantee that a stock will join the S&P 500—these are just the minimum requirements.
   https://www.fool.com/knowledge-center/what-is-the-sp-500.aspx

12. **Mutual Fund:** Is a company that pools money from many investors and invests the money in securities such as stocks, bonds, and short-term debt. The combined holdings of the mutual fund are known as its portfolio. Investors buy shares in mutual funds. Each share represents an investor's part ownership in the fund and the income it generates.
   https://www.investor.gov/investing-basics/investment-products/mutual-funds

13. **Leveraged Funds:** Are mutual funds using aggressive investment techniques of financial leverage, such as buying on margin, short selling and option trading, to obtain maximum capital appreciation for investors in the fund. Leveraged funds use a variety of financial instruments from equity swaps to derivatives, such as futures contracts, to achieve their returns. Leveraged funds try to achieve returns that are more sensitive, by a specific magnitude, to market movements than non-leveraged funds. The returns for leveraged funds usually vary between two times and three times the movement in a given index or market sector.
   https://definitions.uslegal.com/l/leveraged-fund/

14. **Inverse Exchange-Traded Fund:** Is an exchange-traded fund (ETF), traded on a public stock market, which is designed to perform as the inverse of whatever index or benchmark it is designed to track. These funds work by using short selling, trading derivatives such as futures contracts, and other leveraged investment techniques. By providing, over short investing horizons and excluding the impact of fees and other costs, performance opposite to their benchmark, inverse ETFs give a result similar to short selling the stocks in the index. An inverse S&P 500 ETF, for example, seeks a daily percentage movement opposite that of the S&P. If the S&P 500 rises by 1%, the inverse ETF is designed to fall by 1%; and if the S&P falls by 1%, the inverse ETF should rise by 1%. Because their value rises in a declining market environment, they are popular investments in bear markets.

Short sales have the potential to expose an investor to unlimited losses, whether or not the sale involves a stock or ETF. An inverse ETF, on the other hand, provides many of the same benefits as shorting, yet it exposes an investor only to the loss of the purchase price. Another advantage of inverse ETFs is that they may be held in IRA accounts, while short sales are not permitted in these accounts.

https://en.wikipedia.org/wiki/Inverse_exchange-traded_fund

15. **Mutual Funds, Open-End And Closed-End:** While these two types of funds look similar, they are actually quite different. Both offer investors a low-cost way to pool their money so they can purchase shares in a diversified portfolio of stocks and/or bonds that is professionally managed and meets a particular objective. But a closer look reveals quite a few differences between these two types of mutual funds—mostly in the way they are structured and sold to investors.

https://www.americanfunds.com/individual/planning/mutual-fund-basics/closed-end-vs-open-end-funds.html

16. **Open-End Funds:** You invest your money in an open-end mutual fund by buying shares at the net asset value (NAV). Net asset value is the market value of the fund's assets at the end of each trading day minus any liabilities divided by the number of outstanding shares. Open-end funds determine the market value of their assets at the end of each trading day. For example, a balanced fund, which invests in both common stocks and bonds, uses the closing prices of the stock and bond holdings for the day to determine market value. The total number of shares of each of the stocks and bonds that the fund owns is multiplied by the closing prices. The resulting total of each investment is added together, and any liabilities associated with the fund (such as accrued expenses) are subtracted. The resulting total net assets are divided by the number of shares outstanding in the fund to equal the net asset value price per share. The NAV changes daily because of market fluctuations of the stock and bond prices in the fund. NAVs are important because:

1. The NAV is used to determine the value of your holdings in the mutual fund (the number of shares held multiplied by the NAV price per share).

2. The NAV is the price at which new shares are purchased or redeemed. https://www.merrilledge.com/article/whats-the-difference-between-open-and -closed-end-mutual-funds

17.   **Front Load And Back Load:** There are two types of load funds: front-end and back-end, which usually charge higher expenses. A front-end load means the fee (generally between 3 percent and 6 percent of the investment, or sometimes a flat fee, depending on the provider) is charged upon purchase of the mutual fund. A back-end load, also known as a contingent deferred sales charge, means the fee is charged when an investor redeems the mutual fund. The fee usually starts at 5 percent for investors who redeem shares within a year and declines by a percentage point each year after until the fee is eliminated. https://www.americanfunds.com/individual/planning/mutual-fund-basics/load- no-load-funds.html

18.   **Contingent Deferred Sales Charge:** The most common type of back-end sales load is the "contingent deferred sales load," also referred to as a "CDSC," or "CDSL." The amount of this type of load will depend on how long the investor holds his or her shares and typically decreases to zero if the investor holds his or her shares long enough. For example, a contingent deferred sales load might be 5% if an investor holds his or her shares for one year, 4% if the investor holds his or her shares for two years, and so on until the load goes away completely. The rate at which this fee will decline will be disclosed in the fund's prospectus. https://www.sec.gov/fast-answers/answersmffeeshtm.html

19.   **Closed-End Fund:** Is legally known as a closed-end investment company, is one of three basic types of investment companies. The two other types of investment companies are open-end funds (usually mutual funds) and unit investments trusts (UITs). Exchange-traded funds (ETFs) are generally also structured as open-end funds, but can be structured as UITs as well. A closed-end fund invests the money raised in its initial public offering in stocks, bonds, money market instruments and/or other securities. https://www.investor.gov/additional-resources/general-resources/glossary/closed- end-funds

20.   **Capital Gains:** Refers to profit that results from a sale of a capital asset, such as stock, bond or real estate, where the sale price exceeds the purchase price. The gain is the difference between a higher selling price and a lower purchase price. Conversely, a capital loss arises if the proceeds from the sale of a capital asset are less than the purchase price. Capital gains may also refer to a different form of profit received from an asset which refers to "investment income" in the form of cash flow or passive income that arises in relation to real assets, such as property; financial assets, such as shares/stocks or bonds; and intangible assets. https:// en.wikipedia.org/wiki/Capital_gain

21.   **Exchange-Traded Fund (ETF):** Is an investment fund traded on stock exchanges, much like stocks. An ETF holds assets such as stocks, commodities, or bonds and

generally operates with an arbitrage mechanism designed to keep it trading close to its net asset value, although deviations can occasionally occur. Most ETFs track an index, such as a stock index or bond index. ETFs may be attractive as investments because of their low costs, tax efficiency, and stock-like features. By 2013, ETFs had become the most popular type of exchange-traded product.
https://en.wikipedia.org/wiki/Exchange-traded_fund

22.   **Standard & Poor's Depositary Receipts:** On 29 January 1993 . . . Boston asset manager SSGA (State Street Global Advisors) launched as the first exchange-traded fund in the United States (preceded by the short-lived Index Participation Shares which had launched in 1989). The fund is part of the SPDRs ETF chain. Designed and developed by American Stock Exchange executives Nathan Most and Steven Bloom, the fund first traded on that market, but has since been listed elsewhere, including the New York Stock Exchange.
https://en.wikipedia.org/wiki/Standard_%26_Poor%27s_Depositary_Receipts

23.   **Standard & Poor's:** Is a business intelligence corporation. Its corporate name is S&P Global. It provides credit ratings on bonds, countries, and other investments. S&P Global also calculates more than 1 million stock market indices. The most well-known is the S&P 500. The company provides customized analyses using its data. Standard and Poor's are the names of the two financial companies that merged in 1941. It's ironic that a company that measures wealth has the word "poor" in its title. That name came from one of the company's founders, Henry Varnum Poor. In 1860, he published the "History of Railroads and Canals of the United States." Mr. Poor was concerned about the lack of quality information available to investors. His book began a campaign to publicize details of corporate operations.
https://www.thebalance.com/what-are-sandp-credit-ratings-and-scales-3305886

24.   **Moody's Investors Service:** Is a subsidiary of Moody's Corporation and provides credit ratings, research and risk analysis. The company was first called Moody's Analyses Publishing Company and was founded in 1909 by John Moody. The company originally produced statistics for stock and bonds along with bond ratings. John Moody is recognized as the inventor of modern bond credit ratings. In 1975, Moody's was recognized by the U.S. Securities and Exchange Commission as a Nationally Recognized Statistical Rating Organization. Moody's was originally owned by Dun & Bradstreet but became a separate entity in 2000. The headquarters is located at 7 World Trade Center, New York City. Moody's Investors Services has a presence in more than 115 countries worldwide.
https://www.thebalance.com/moodys-investors-service-4137213

25.   **Fitch Ratings:** Is part of the Fitch Group and is jointly owned by the Hearst Corporation and Fimalac, S.A. The company was founded by John Knowles Fitch in 1913 and is headquartered in New York City. Fitch Ratings holds the distinction of being the first rating company to develop the "AAA" to "D" financial rating scale. There are more than 50 offices worldwide with over 2,000 employees. In addition to providing credit ratings for insurance companies and

other financial organizations, it also conducts market research important to investors and other financial professionals.
https://www.thebalance.com/fitch-ratings-financial-reporting-you-can-trust-1969742

26. **Zero-Coupon Bond:** Also discount bond or deep discount bond. Is a bond where the face value is repaid at the time of maturity. Note that this definition assumes a positive time value of money. It does not make periodic interest payments, or have so-called coupons, hence the term zero-coupon bond. When the bond reaches maturity, its investor receives its par (or face) value. Examples of zero-coupon bonds include U.S. Treasury bills, U.S. savings bonds, long-term zero-coupon bonds, and any type of coupon bond that has been stripped of its coupons.
https://en.wikipedia.org/wiki/Zero-coupon_bond

27. **Preferred Stock:** Also called preferred shares, preference shares or simply preferreds. Is a type of stock which may have any combination of features not possessed by common stock including properties of both, equity and a debt instrument, and is generally considered a hybrid instrument. Preferred stocks are senior (i.e., higher ranking) to common stock, but subordinate to bonds in terms of claim (or rights to their share of the assets of the company) and may have priority over common stock (ordinary shares) in the payment of dividends and upon liquidation. Terms of the preferred stock are described in the articles of association.
https://en.wikipedia.org/wiki/Preferred_stock

28. **Convertible Preferred Stock:** That a stockholder may exchange, at any time after a waiting period, for common stock in the company issuing the bond. The number of shares one receives for each preferred share is determined when the convertible preferred stock is issued. A convertible preferred stock is a relatively low-risk investment because of the guaranteed dividends, but it affords the investor a great amount of leeway because he or she can exchange it for common shares, which have higher risk and higher returns. See also: Conversion ratio, Convertible bond.
https://financial-dictionary.thefreedictionary.com/Convertible+preferred+stock

29. **Real Estate Investment Trust (REIT):** Is a company that owns, and in most cases operates, income-producing real estate. REITs own many types of commercial real estate, ranging from office and apartment buildings to warehouses, hospitals, shopping centers, hotels and timberlands. Some REITs engage in financing real estate. REITs can be publicly traded on major exchanges, public but non-listed, or private. The two main types of REITs are equity REITs and mortgage REITs (m-REITs). In November 2014, equity REITs was recognized as a distinct asset class in the Global Industry Classification Standard by S&P Dow Jones Indices and MSCI. The key statistics to examine the financial position and operation of a REIT are net asset value (NAV), funds from operations (FFO), and adjusted funds from operations (AFFO).
https://en.wikipedia.org/wiki/Real_estate_investment_trust

30. **Assets Under Management (AUM):** Is very popular within the financial industry as a measure of size and success of an investment management firm, compared with its history of assets under management in previous periods, and compared with the firm's competitors. Methods of calculating AUM vary between firms. Investment management companies generally charge their clients fees as a proportion of assets under management, so assets under management, combined with the firm's average fee rate, are the key factors indicating an investment management company's top line revenue. The fee structure depends on the contract between each client and the firm or fund. Assets under management rise and fall. They may increase when investment performance is positive, or when new customers and new assets are brought into the firm. Rising AUM normally increases the fees which the firm generates. Conversely, AUM are reduced by negative investment performance, as well as redemptions or withdrawals, including fund closures, client defections and other generally adverse events. Lower AUM tends to result in lower fees generated. https://en.wikipedia.org/wiki/Assets_under_management

31. **Frank Scully (Born Francis Joseph Xavier Scully; 28 April 1892–23 June 1964):** Was an American journalist, author, humorist, and a regular columnist for the entertainment trade magazine *Variety*. https://en.wikipedia.org/wiki/Frank_Scully

32. **John Davison Rockefeller (Born July 8, 1839, Richford, New York, U.S.— died May 23, 1937, Ormond Beach, Florida):** American industrialist and philanthropist, founder of the Standard Oil Company, which dominated the oil industry and was the first great U.S. business trust. https://www.britannica.com/biography/John-D-Rockefeller

33. **Risk-To-Reward Ratio:** Is used to assess profit potential of a trade relative to its loss potential. In order to attain the risk/reward of a trade, both the risk and profit potential of a trade must be defined by the trader. Risk is determined using a stop loss order, where the risk is the price difference between the entry point of the trade and the stop loss order. A profit target is used to establish an exit point should the trade move favorably. The potential profit for the trade is the price difference between the profit target and the entry price. https://www.thebalance.com/risk-to-reward-ratio-1031350

34. **Artemus Ward, Pseudonym Of Charles Farrar Browne (Born April 26, 1834, Waterford, Maine, U.S.—died March 6, 1867, Southampton, Hampshire, Eng.):** One of the most popular 19th-century American humorists, whose lecture techniques exercised much influence on such humorists as Mark Twain. https://www.britannica.com/biography/Artemus-Ward

35. **Auction Rate Securities (ARS):** Are debt or preferred equity securities that have interest rates that are periodically re-set through auctions, typically every 7, 14, 28, or 35 days. ARS are generally structured as bonds with long-term maturities (20 to 30 years) or preferred shares (issued by closed-end funds). Municipalities and public authorities, student loan providers and other institutional borrowers first began using ARS to raise funds in the 1980s. ARS were marketed to retail

investors who were seeking a "cash-equivalent" investment that paid a higher yield than money market mutual funds or certificates of deposit, although ARS did not have the same level of liquidity as those other instruments. https://www.investor.gov/introduction-investing/basics/investment-products/auction-rate-securities

36. **Warren Buffett:** Known as the "Oracle of Omaha," is one of the most successful investors of all time.

   ■ Buffett runs Berkshire Hathaway, which owns more than 60 companies, including insurer Geico, battery maker Duracell and restaurant chain Dairy Queen.

   ■ The son of a U.S. congressman, he first bought stock at age 11 and first filed taxes at age 13.

   ■ He's promised to give away over 99% of his fortune. So far he's donated $35 billion, much of it to the foundation of friends Bill and Melinda Gates.

   ■ In 2010, he and Gates launched the Giving Pledge, asking billionaires to commit to donating half their wealth to charitable causes.

   https://www.forbes.com/profile/warren-buffett/#5be2ba284639

37. **Steven Alexander Wright (Born December 6, 1955):** Is an American stand-up comedian, actor, writer, and film producer. He is known for his distinctly lethargic voice and slow, deadpan delivery of ironic, philosophical and sometimes nonsensical jokes, paraprosdokians, non sequiturs, anti-humor, and one-liners with contrived situations. https://en.wikipedia.org/wiki/Steven_Wright

38. **Warren Buffett Quote:** "It isn't how many dollars you have, but how many cheeseburgers you can buy." In other words, if stocks double but so does the price of milk, gas and cornflakes, you haven't actually gained anything in real net worth. https://www.joshuakennon.com/the-money-illusion-why-thinking-about-things-in-nominal-currency-can-destroy-your-net-worth/

39. **Hamburgers Yesterday And Today:** Toppings may change, but the basic ingredients of a hamburger—and more importantly, each fast-food giant's special recipe—stay relatively constant over time. https://www.thisisinsider.com/fast-food-burgers-cost-every-year-2018-9#in-2013-your-burger-cost-an-average-of-220-24

40. **Ronald Reagan (Born February 6, 1911, Died June, 2004):** Was an American politician and film actor who served as the 40th president of the United States from 1981 to 1989. Prior to his presidency, he was a Hollywood actor and union leader before serving as the 33rd governor of California from 1967 to 1975. https://en.wikipedia.org/wiki/Ronald_Reagan Quotes: https://www.brainyquote.com/authors/ronald_reagan

41. **Venezuela:** Is a country on the northern coast of South America, consisting of a continental landmass and a large number of small islands and islets in the Caribbean Sea. The capital and largest urban agglomeration is the city of Caracas.
https://en.wikipedia.org/wiki/Venezuela

42. **Nicolas Maduro—Socialist President Of Venezuela:** Shortages in Venezuela and decreased living standards led to protests beginning in 2014 that escalated into daily marches nationwide, repression of dissent and a decline in Maduro's popularity. According to *The New York Times*, Maduro's administration was held "responsible for grossly mismanaging the economy and plunging the country into a deep humanitarian crisis" and attempting to "crush the opposition by jailing or exiling critics, and using lethal force against antigovernment protesters."
https://en.wikipedia.org/wiki/Nicol%C3%A1s_Maduro

43. **Yugoslavia Economic Collapse And The International Climate:** A major problem for Yugoslavia was the heavy debts incurred in the 1970s, which proved to be difficult to repay in the 1980s. Yugoslavia's debt load, initially estimated at a sum equal to $6 billion U.S dollars, instead turned to be equal to sum equivalent to $21 billion U.S. dollars, which was a colossal sum for a poor country. The Reagan administration in a Secret Sensitive 1984 National Security Decision Directive NSDD 133 expressed concern that Yugoslavia's debt load might cause the country to align with the Soviet bloc. The 1980s were a time of economic austerity as the International Monetary Fund (IMF) imposed stringent conditions on Yugoslavia, which caused much resentment at the Communist elites who had so mismanaged the economy by recklessly borrowing of money abroad. The policies of austerity also led to the uncovering of much corruption by the elites, most notably with the "Agrokomerc affair" of 1987, when the Agrokomerc enterprise of Bosnia turned out to the center of a vast nexus of corruption running all across Yugoslavia and that the managers of Agrokomerc had issued promissory notes equivalent to $500 US dollars without collateral, forcing the state to assume responsibility for their debts when Agrokomerc finally collapsed.
https://en.wikipedia.org/wiki/Breakup_of_Yugoslavia

44. **Hyperinflation:** Affected the German Papiermark, the currency of the Weimar Republic, between 1921 and 1923. It caused considerable internal political instability in the country, the occupation of the Ruhr by France and Belgium as well as misery for the general populace.
https://en.wikipedia.org/wiki/Hyperinflation_in_the_Weimar_Republic

45. **Hyperinflation In Zimbabwe:** Was a period of currency instability in Zimbabwe that began in the late 1990s shortly after the confiscation of private farms from landowners towards the end of Zimbabwean involvement in the Second Congo War. During the height of inflation from 2008 to 2009, it was difficult to measure Zimbabwe's hyperinflation because the government of Zimbabwe stopped filing official inflation statistics. However, Zimbabwe's

peak month of inflation is estimated at 79.6 billion percent in mid-November 2008. In 2009, Zimbabwe stopped printing its currency, with currencies from other countries being used. In mid-2015, Zimbabwe announced plans to have completely switched to the United States dollar by the end of 2015.
https://en.wikipedia.org/wiki/Hyperinflation_in_Zimbabwe

46. **The Consumer Price Index For All Urban Consumers:** All Items (CPIAUCSL) is a measure of the average monthly change in the price for goods and services paid by urban consumers between any two time periods. It can also represent the buying habits of urban consumers. This particular index includes roughly 88 percent of the total population, accounting for wage earners, clerical workers, technical workers, self-employed, short-term workers, unemployed, retirees, and those not in the labor force.
https://fred.stlouisfed.org/series/CPIAUCSL/

47. **Stock Portfolio Well Diversified:** With this said, if investors who are picking their own stocks find that their portfolios are similarly weighted across as many as 40 to 50 stocks, they may want to reconsider whether their research is thorough enough and if their standards for what constitutes a valuable investment are high enough. Even Buffett and his partner, Charlie Munger, have resorted to settling with just "one good idea a year."
https://www.fool.com/investing/2018/05/13/how-many-stocks-should-you-own-diversifying-your-p.aspx

48. **Standard & Poor's Depositary Receipts:** SPDRS, with symbol SPY commonly referred to as "Spiders," is the world's first and largest exchange traded fund (ETF), in terms of assets under management. As of January 2013, it also was the most traded US-listed equity. Created to track the value of the Standard & Poor's 500 Index, SPY was launched on the American Stock Exchange on January 29, 1993. The fund grew from $461.5 million assets under management in 1993 to more than $125 billion in January 2013, according to Index Universe, which tracks ETFs.
http://www.marketswiki.com/wiki/Standard_%26_Poor%27s_Depositary_Receipts

49. **General Electric Company (GE):** Is an American multinational conglomerate incorporated in New York and headquartered in Boston. As of 2018, the company operates through the following segments: aviation, healthcare, power, renewable energy, digital, additive manufacturing, venture capital and finance, lighting, transportation, and oil and gas. In 2017, GE ranked among the Fortune 500 as the 13th-largest firm in the U.S. by gross revenue. In 2011, GE ranked among the Fortune 20 as the 14th-most profitable company. As of 2012, the company was listed as the fourth-largest in the world among the Forbes Global 2000, further metrics being taken into account. Two employees of GE have been awarded the Nobel Prize: Irving Langmuir in 1932 and Ivar Giaever in 1973.
https://en.wikipedia.org/wiki/General_Electric

50. **International Business Machines Corporation (IBM):** Is an American multinational information technology company headquartered in Armonk, New York, United States, with operations in over 170 countries. The company began in 1911 as the Computing-Tabulating-Recording Company (CTR) and was renamed "International Business Machines" in 1924. IBM manufactures and markets computer hardware, middleware and software, and provides hosting and consulting services in areas ranging from mainframe computers to nanotechnology.
https://en.wikipedia.org/wiki/IBM

51. **Robert Burns Scottish Language Poem:** "To a Mouse, on Turning Her Up in Her Nest with the Plough, November, 1785." Was included in the Kilmarnock volume. According to legend, Burns was ploughing in the fields and accidentally destroyed a mouse's nest, which it needed to survive the winter. In fact, Burns's brother claimed that the poet composed the poem while still holding his plough.
https://en.wikipedia.org/wiki/To_a_Mouse

52. **Yogi Berra:** Said, "It's tough to make predictions, especially about the future."
https://www.goodreads.com/author/quotes/79014.Yogi_Berra

53. **Masters Tournament:** Winning score for 2019 by Tiger Woods was 275.
http://www.espn.com/golf/player/_/id/462/tiger-woods

54. **Calculating The Midpoint Between Two Numbers:** The midpoint between two numbers is the number exactly in the middle of the two numbers. Calculating the midpoint is the same thing as calculating the average of two numbers. Therefore, you can calculate the midpoint between any two numbers by adding them together and dividing by two.
https://sciencing.com/calculate-midpoint-between-two-numbers-2807.html

55. **Compounded Annual Growth Rate:** Compound annual growth rate (CAGR) is a business and investing specific term for the geometric progression ratio that provides a constant rate of return over the time period. CAGR is not an accounting term, but it is often used to describe some element of the business, for example revenue, units delivered, registered users, etc. CAGR dampens the effect of volatility of periodic returns that can render arithmetic means irrelevant. It is particularly useful to compare growth rates from various data sets of common domain such as revenue growth of companies in the same industry.
https://en.wikipedia.org/wiki/Compound_annual_growth_rate

56. **William Henry Gates III (Born October 28, 1955):** Is an American business magnate, investor, author, philanthropist, humanitarian, and principal founder of Microsoft Corporation. During his career at Microsoft, Gates held the positions of chairman, CEO and chief software architect, while also being the largest individual shareholder until May 2014.
https://en.wikipedia.org/wiki/Bill_Gates

57. **Jeffrey Preston Bezos Jorgensen (Born January 12, 1964):** Is an American technology entrepreneur, investor, and philanthropist. He is best known as the

founder, chairman, and CEO of Amazon. Bezos was born in Albuquerque, New Mexico and raised in Houston, Texas. He graduated from Princeton University in 1986 with degrees in electrical engineering and computer science. He worked on Wall Street in a variety of related fields from 1986 to early 1994. He founded Amazon in late 1994 on a cross-country road trip from New York City to Seattle. https://en.wikipedia.org/wiki/Jeff_Bezos

58.   **VIAVI Solutions:** Formerly part of JDS Uniphase (JDSU), is a San Jose, California-based network test, measurement and assurance technology company. The company manufactures testing and monitoring equipment for networks. It also develops optical technology used for a range of applications including material quality control, currency anti-counterfeiting and 3D motion sensing, including Microsoft's Kinect video game controller. The company was spun off from JDSU when the company divided itself up in August 2015. https://en.wikipedia.org/wiki/Viavi_Solutions

59.   **GIGO:** Garbage in, garbage out. Is a concept common to computer science and mathematics: the quality of output is determined by the quality of the input. So, for example, if a mathematical equation is improperly stated, the answer is unlikely to be correct. Similarly, if incorrect data is input to a program, the output is unlikely to be informative. https://searchsoftwarequality.techtarget.com/definition/garbage-in-garbage-out

60.   **Volatility Index, Or VIX:** The Chicago Board Options Exchange Volatility Index, or VIX, as it is better known, is used by stock and options traders to gauge the market's anxiety level. Put simply, it is a mathematical measure of how much the market thinks the S&P 500 Index option, or SPX, will fluctuate over the next 12 months, based upon an analysis of the difference between current SPX put and call option prices. Although the VIX isn't expressed as a percentage, it should be understood as one. A VIX of 22 translates to implied volatility of 22 percent on the SPX. This means that the index has a 66.7 percent probability (that being one standard deviation, statistically speaking) of trading within a range 22 percent higher than—or lower than—its current level, over the next year. The VIX rises when put option buying increases; and falls when call buying activity is more robust. (Note: A put option gives the purchaser the right—but not the obligation—to sell a security for a specified price at a certain time. A call option is a right to buy the same.) For contrarians, low readings on the VIX are bearish, while high readings are bullish. https://www.thestreet.com/topic/47306/vix.html

61.   **Time-Weighted Return:** In general, TWR is used by the investment industry to measure the performance of funds investing in publicly traded securities. By contrast, IRR is normally used to gauge the return of funds that invest in illiquid, non-marketable assets—such as buyout, venture or real estate funds. Investors want to know why public and private investment returns are reported differently and how the calculation methodologies differ. https://www.commonfund.org/news-research/article/time-weighted-return-and-internal-rates-of-return/

62. **Dollar-Weighted Returns:** IRR is the discount rate that equates the cost of an investment with the cash generated by that investment. IRR tracks the performance of actual dollars invested over time. Dollar-weighted returns do reflect cash inflows and outflows, as well as the investment performance of the funds chosen by the investor. Dollar-weighted returns can be heavily changed depending on if and when large cash flows in and/or out of an investment occur. http://www.dailyvest.com/prr/prr_TWRRvsDWRR.aspx

63. **Beardstown Ladies:** Is a group of older women who formed an investment club, formally known as the Beardstown Business and Professional Women's Investment Club, in Beardstown, Illinois, USA. Founded in 1983, the group achieved fame for their stock market acumen, claiming investment returns of more than 23.4% per year from their inception through 1994. They received considerable attention in national media outlets, and authored a best-selling book, *The Beardstown Ladies' Common-Sense Investment Guide*, following it up with four more books. https://en.wikipedia.org/wiki/Beardstown_Ladies

64. **Hyperion:** The Beardstown Ladies never recommended Enron stock. That foresight was not much consolation to the media conglomerate being punished for publishing their best-selling, and now famously misleading, books on investment advice. The women had claimed that their investment club had earned an average annual return of 23.4 percent and published five folksy books that mingled recipes like five-hour stew with investment tips. But in 1998, accountants announced that the authors had miscalculated and that their club had averaged 9.1 percent annual returns, far less than the Standard & Poor's 500. Buyers in California and New York sued. https://www.nytimes.com/2002/03/01/us/beardstown-ladies-case-ends-in-offer-to-trade.html

65. **Robert Burns:** No matter how carefully a project is planned, something may still go wrong with it. The saying is adapted from a line in "To a Mouse," "The best laid schemes o' mice an' men / Gang aft a-gley." https://www.dictionary.com/browse/the-best-laid-plans-of-mice-and-men-often-go-awry

66. **Annual Operating Expense Ratio:** An expense ratio is an annual fee expressed as a percentage of your investment—or, like the term implies, the ratio of your investment that goes toward the fund's expenses. If you invest in a mutual fund with a 1% expense ratio, you'll pay the fund $10 per year for every $1,000 invested. That money is swept out of your investment in the fund, meaning you won't get a bill for the charge. That's one reason why these fees are easy to miss. The other reason? They're not so easy to find. You have to dig into the fund's prospectus—available on the fund company's website, or you can look on the fund's information page on your online broker's or retirement plan provider's website. If you work with a financial advisor, he or she should also share information about these expenses with you. https://www.nerdwallet.com/blog/investing/typical-mutual-fund-expense-ratios/

67. **Charles Schwab Corporation:** Is a bank and brokerage firm, based in San Francisco, California. It was founded in 1971 by Charles R. Schwab and is one of the largest banks in the United States as well as one of the largest brokerage firms in the United States.
https://en.wikipedia.org/wiki/Charles_Schwab_Corporation

68. **State Street Global Advisors (SSGA):** Is the investment management division of State Street Corporation and the world's third largest asset manager, with nearly $2.8 trillion (USD) in assets under management as of 31 December 2017. The company services financial clients by creating and managing investment strategies for non-profit foundations, businesses, corporations, associations, governments, educational institutions, and religious organizations.
https://en.wikipedia.org/wiki/State_Street_Global_Advisors

69. **The United Services Automobile Association (USAA):** Is a Texas-based Fortune 500 diversified financial services group of companies including a Texas Department of Insurance-regulated reciprocal inter-insurance exchange and subsidiaries offering banking, investing, and insurance to people and families who serve, or served, in the United States military.
https://en.wikipedia.org/wiki/USAA

70. **FANG Stocks:** In early 2013, former money manager and CNBC personality Jim Cramer coined the FANG acronym. The whole idea was that investors should put their money to work in companies that represent the future. Between Facebook (NASDAQ:FB), Amazon (NASDAQ:AMZN), Netflix (NASDAQ:NFLX) and Google (NASDAQ:GOOG), FANG represented the future by being the internet's unchallenged behemoths.
https://investorplace.com/2018/09/the-5-new-fang-stocks-you-invest-in-for-long-term-gains/

71. **Style Drift:** A situation in which a mutual fund's investment strategies or goals change from what they were originally. Style drift can be explicit or implicit. For example, style drift may occur implicitly when a fund manager seeks ever larger returns for shareholders and tries out any number of investment strategies to achieve them. This is usually thought to be naive or even dangerous. Style drift can arise explicitly when a fund's situation has changed a significant amount; for example, a stock in the fund may grow to the point where it is advantageous for the fund to change its capitalization requirements. Style drift, if handled responsibly, can show flexibility on the part of the fund managers.
https://financial-dictionary.thefreedictionary.com/Style+drift

72. **Trust Fund:** There are many ways to set up a financially secure future for your loved ones. You could enlist the help of a financial advisor to come up with a comprehensive financial plan. Trust funds are another way to set your children or grandchildren up for future financial success. And they aren't just for the very wealthy. You can open a trust fund to ensure your loved ones manage and distribute your assets in a specific way, regardless of your net worth.
https://smartasset.com/retirement/what-is-a-trust-fund

73. **Peter John Gzowski (July 13, 1934–January 24, 2002):** Known colloquially as "Mr. Canada", or "Captain Canada", was a Canadian broadcaster, writer and reporter, most famous for his work on the CBC radio shows *This Country in the Morning* and then *Morningside*. His first biographer argued that Gzowski's contribution to Canadian media must be considered in the context of efforts by a generation of Canadian nationalists to understand and express Canada's cultural identity.
https://en.wikipedia.org/wiki/Peter_Gzowski

74. **Scientific Jury Selection, Often Abbreviated SJS:** Is the use of social science techniques and expertise to choose favorable juries during a criminal or civil trial. Scientific jury selection is used during the jury selection phase of the trial, during which lawyers have the opportunity to question jurors. It almost always entails an expert's assistance in the attorney's use of peremptory challenges— the right to reject a certain number of potential jurors without stating a reason—during jury selection. The practice is currently confined to the American legal system.
https://en.wikipedia.org/wiki/Scientific_jury_selection

75. **Cost Of Carry Or Carrying Charge:** Is the cost of storing a physical commodity, such as grain or metals, over a period of time. The carrying charge includes insurance, storage and interest on the invested funds as well as other incidental costs. In interest rate futures markets, it refers to the differential between the yield on a cash instrument and the cost of the funds necessary to buy the instrument.
https://en.wikipedia.org/wiki/Cost_of_carry

76. **Mobileye:** Is an Israeli subsidiary of the Intel Corporation that develops vision-based advanced driver-assistance systems (ADAS) providing warnings for collision prevention and mitigation. Mobileye headquarters and main R&D center is located in Jerusalem operating under the company name Mobileye Vision Technology Ltd. The company also has sales and marketing offices in Jericho, New York; Shanghai, China; Tokyo, Japan and Düsseldorf, Germany. In March 2017, Intel announced that they had agreed to a US $15.3 billion takeover of Mobileye. This is the largest acquisition of an Israeli company to date.
https://en.wikipedia.org/wiki/Mobileye

77. **Michael Monroe Lewis (Born October 15, 1960):** Is an American non-fiction author and financial journalist. Lewis described his experiences at Salomon and the evolution of the mortgage-backed bond in *Liar's Poker* (1989). In *The New, New Thing* (1999), he investigated the then-booming Silicon Valley and discussed obsession with innovation.
https://en.wikipedia.org/wiki/Michael_Lewis

78. **Spread Networks:** Is a company founded by Dan Spivey and backed by James L. Barksdale (former CEO of Netscape Communications Corporation) that claims to offer Internet connectivity between Chicago and New York City at ultra-low latency (i.e. speeds that are very close to the speed of light), high bandwidth, and high reliability, using dark fiber. Its customers are primarily

firms engaged in high-frequency trading, where small reductions in latency are important to the extent that they help one close trades before one's competitors. https://en.wikipedia.org/wiki/Spread_Networks

79. **Efficient Market Theory (EMT):** A market theory that evolved from a 1960's Ph.D. dissertation by Eugene Fama, the efficient market hypothesis states that at any given time and in a liquid market, security prices fully reflect all available information. The EMH exists in various degrees: weak, semi-strong and strong, which addresses the inclusion of non-public information in market prices. This theory contends that since markets are efficient and current prices reflect all information, attempts to outperform the market are essentially a game of chance rather than one of skill.
http://www.morningstar.com/InvGlossary/efficient_market_hypothesis_definition_what_is.aspx

80. **Goldman Sachs Group, Inc.:** Is an American multinational investment bank and financial services company headquartered in New York City. Apart from investment banking, it offers services in investment management, securities, asset management, prime brokerage, and securities underwriting.
https://en.wikipedia.org/wiki/Goldman_Sachs

81. **Best Buy Co., Inc.:** Is an American multinational consumer electronics retailer headquartered in Richfield, Minnesota. It was originally founded by Richard M. Schulze and James Wheeler in 1966, as an audio specialty store called Sound of Music. In 1983, it was rebranded under its current name with more emphasis placed on consumer electronics.
https://en.wikipedia.org/wiki/Best_Buy

82. **Cambridge Analytica Ltd (CA):** Was a British political consulting firm which combined data mining, data brokerage, and data analysis with strategic communication during the electoral processes. It was started in 2013 as an offshoot of the SCL Group. The company closed operations in 2018 in the course of the Facebook–Cambridge Analytica data scandal, although related firms still exist.
https://en.wikipedia.org/wiki/Cambridge_Analytica

83. **The Efficient-Market Hypothesis (EMH):** Is a theory in financial economics that states that asset prices fully reflect all available information. A direct implication is that it is impossible to "beat the market" consistently on a risk-adjusted basis since market prices should only react to new information.
https://en.wikipedia.org/wiki/Efficient-market_hypothesis

84. **Nicholas William "Nick" Leeson (Born 25 February 1967):** Is an English former derivatives broker famous for his time at Barings Bank, the United Kingdom's oldest merchant bank. A rogue trader who made fraudulent, unauthorized and speculative moves, his actions led directly to the 1995 collapse of Barings Bank, for which he was sentenced to prison.
https://en.wikipedia.org/wiki/Nick_Leeson

85. **Long-Term Capital Management, Or LTCM:** Was founded in 1994 by John W. Meriwether, the former vice-chairman and head of bond trading at Salomon Brothers. Members of LTCM's board of directors included Myron S. Scholes and Robert C. Merton, who shared the 1997 Nobel Memorial Prize in Economic Sciences for a "new method to determine the value of derivatives." Initially successful with annualized return of over 21% (after fees) in its first year, 43% in the second year and 41% in the third year, in 1998 it lost $4.6 billion in less than four months following the 1997 Asian financial crisis and 1998 Russian financial crisis, requiring financial intervention by the Federal Reserve, with the fund liquidating and dissolving in early 2000. https://en.wikipedia.org/wiki/Long-Term_Capital_Management

86. **Nobel Prize In Economic Sciences:** The prize was established in 1968 by a donation from Sweden's central bank the Riksbank to the Nobel Foundation to commemorate the bank's 300th anniversary. Nobel Prize in Economics, is an award for outstanding contributions to the field of economics, and generally regarded as the most prestigious award for that field. https://en.wikipedia.org/wiki/Nobel_Memorial_Prize_in_Economic_Sciences

87. **DALBAR, Inc.:** Is the financial community's leading independent expert for evaluating, auditing and rating business practices, customer performance, product quality and service. Launched in 1976. https://www.dalbar.com/

88. **Elaine Garzarelli:** Gained some notoriety on Wall Street back in 1987 when she predicted an imminent collapse of the U.S. stock market on October 12, just a week prior to the 22-percent Black Monday crash. Garzarelli founded her own business, Garzarelli Research, in 1995 and had been ranked as Wall Street's top quantitative analysts for 11 consecutive years in *Institutional Investor* magazine's poll. https://finance.yahoo.com/news/day-market-history-elaine-garzarellis-151101162.html

89. **Ronald Graham (Born in Taft, California):** In 1962, he received his Ph.D. in mathematics from the University of California, Berkeley and began working at Bell Labs and later AT&T Labs. He was director of information sciences in AT&T Labs, but retired from AT&T in 1999 after 37 years. https://en.wikipedia.org/wiki/Ronald_Graham

90. **Contrarian Investing:** Is an investment strategy that is characterized by purchasing and selling in contrast to the prevailing sentiment of the time. A contrarian believes that certain crowd behavior among investors can lead to exploitable miss-pricings in securities markets. For example, widespread pessimism about a stock can drive a price so low that it overstates the company's risks, and understates its prospects for returning to profitability. Identifying and purchasing such distressed stocks, and selling them after the company recovers, can lead to above-average gains. https://en.wikipedia.org/wiki/Contrarian_investing

91. **Momentum Investing:** Is a system of buying stocks or other securities that have had high returns over the past three to twelve months, and selling those that have had poor returns over the same period. While no consensus exists about the validity of this strategy, economists have trouble reconciling this phenomenon, using the efficient-market hypothesis. Two main hypotheses have been submitted to explain the effect in terms of an efficient market. In the first, it is assumed that momentum investors bear significant risk for assuming this strategy, and, therefore, the high returns are a compensation for the risk.
https://en.wikipedia.org/wiki/Momentum_investing

92. **George Douglas Sanders (Born July 24, 1933):** Is a retired American professional golfer who won 20 events on the PGA Tour and had four runner-up finishes at major championships.
https://en.wikipedia.org/wiki/Doug_Sanders

93. **Willis Towers Watson—Arlington, VA, June 2, 2016:** Despite an improvement in their financial situation and retirement confidence, roughly one in four U.S. employees believe they won't be able to retire until after age 70, if at all, according to a survey by Willis Towers Watson (NASDAQ: WLTW), a leading global advisory, broking and solutions company. Additionally, nearly one-third (32%) anticipate retiring later than previously planned. The Global Benefits Attitudes Survey of nearly 5,100 U.S. employees found 23% believe they'll have to work past age 70 to live comfortably in retirement; another 5% don't think they'll ever be able to retire. According to the survey, while the average U.S. employee expects to retire at age 65, they admit there is a 50% chance of working to age 70.
https://www.willistowerswatson.com/en-US/press/2016/06/one-in-four-us-employees-expect-to-work-beyond-age-70

94. **Federal Reserve Bank Of New York's Center For Microeconomic Data:** [Today, February 12, 2019] Issued its Quarterly Report on Household Debt and Credit, which shows that total household debt increased by $32 billion (0.2%) to $13.54 trillion in the fourth quarter of 2018. It was the 18th consecutive quarter with an increase and the total is now $869 billion higher than the previous peak of $12.68 trillion in the third quarter of 2008. Furthermore, overall household debt is now 21.4% above the post-financial-crisis trough reached during the second quarter of 2013.
https://www.newyorkfed.org/newsevents/news/research/2019/20190212

95. **Eight Fun Facts About Credit Cards:** Laid end-to-end, all the credit cards on earth would circle the globe 3.5 times. As of 2013, there were over 1.635 billion credit cards in circulation around the world, according to Super Money. If all of those cards were laid end-to-end, they would stretch over 86,981 miles, which would circle the earth three and a half times.
https://www.wisebread.com/8-fun-facts-about-credit-cards

96. **Bankrate:** Credit Card Debt Calculator.
https://www.bankrate.com/calculators/credit-cards/credit-card-payoff-calculator
.aspx
Credit Karma: Debt Repayment Calculator.
https://www.creditkarma.com/calculators/debtrepayment

97. **The Equal Credit Opportunity Act:** 15 U.S.C. 1691 et seq. prohibits creditors
from discriminating against credit applicants on the basis of race, color, religion,
national origin, sex, marital status, age, because an applicant receives income
from a public assistance program, or because an applicant has in good faith
exercised any right under the Consumer Credit Protection Act.
https://www.justice.gov/crt/equal-credit-opportunity-act-3

98. **A New Survey From Bankrate:** Found that only 29 percent of Americans have
enough emergency savings to last more than six months and just 18 percent
have sufficient savings to cover three to five months, meaning only 47 percent of
Americans—less than half—are truly prepared for an emergency.
https://www.cnbc.com/2018/06/22/how-much-money-you-should-put-in-
your-emergency-fund.html

99. **Immediate Annuity—Deferred Annuity:** An annuity is a contract you make
with an insurance company that requires it to make payments to you. When
you sign an annuity contract, you can choose either an immediate or a deferred
annuity. With an immediate annuity, you'll annuitize your investment at once—
meaning you'll convert that lump sum of money into a stream of future payments.
https://www.fool.com/retirement/2018/01/04/immediate-vs-deferred-annuity-
which-is-best-for-yo.aspx

100. **Deferred Annuity:** Deferred annuities allow you to leave your invested funds
sitting with the insurance company for years or even decades, which gives
the money a chance to grow before you lock in your payment amount by
annuitizing the investment (indeed, many holders of deferred annuities never do
annuitize their contracts).
https://www.fool.com/retirement/2018/01/04/immediate-vs-deferred-annuity-
which-is-best-for-yo.aspx

101. **The Employee Retirement Income Security Act Of 1974 (ERISA):** Is a federal
law that sets minimum standards for most voluntarily established retirement
and health plans in private industry to provide protection for individuals in
these plans.
https://www.dol.gov/general/topic/retirement/erisa

102. **IRS:** Are you self-employed? Did you know you have many of the same options
to save for retirement on a tax-deferred basis as employees participating in
company plans?
https://www.irs.gov/retirement-plans/retirement-plans-for-self-employed-people

103. **Variable Annuity:** A variable annuity is a contract between you and an
insurance company, under which the insurer agrees to make periodic payments
to you, beginning either immediately or at some future date. You purchase a

variable annuity contract by making either a single purchase payment or a series of purchase payments.
https://www.sec.gov/investor/pubs/sec-guide-to-variable-annuities.pdf

104. **Lou Gehrig's Disease:** ALS, or amyotrophic lateral sclerosis, is a progressive neurodegenerative disease that affects nerve cells in the brain and the spinal cord. A-myo-trophic comes from the Greek language. "A" means no. "Myo" refers to muscle, and "Trophic" means nourishment—"No muscle nourishment." When a muscle has no nourishment, it "atrophies" or wastes away. "Lateral" identifies the areas in a person's spinal cord where portions of the nerve cells that signal and control the muscles are located. As this area degenerates, it leads to scarring or hardening ("sclerosis") in the region.
http://www.alsa.org/about-als/what-is-als.html

105. **Medicare Parts A & B Premiums And Deductibles:** The standard monthly premium for Medicare Part B enrollees will be $135.50 for 2019, an increase of $1.50 from $134 in 2018. An estimated 2 million Medicare beneficiaries (about 3.5%) will pay less than the full Part B standard monthly premium amount in 2019 due to the statutory hold harmless provision, which limits certain beneficiaries' increase in their Part B premium to be no greater than the increase in their Social Security benefits. The annual deductible for all Medicare Part B beneficiaries is $185 in 2019, an increase of $2 from the annual deductible $183 in 2018.
https://www.cms.gov/newsroom/fact-sheets/2019-medicare-parts-b-premiums-and-deductibles

106. **Balanced Budget Act Of 1997:** The Balanced Budget Act signed into law by the President on August 5, 1997 contains the largest reductions in federal Medicaid spending in Medicaid since 1981. The legislation is projected to achieve gross federal Medicaid savings of $17 billion over the next five years and $61.4 billion over the next ten years. After the legislation's offsetting increases in Medicaid spending are accounted for, the legislation is estimated to achieve net federal Medicaid savings of $7.3 billion over the next five years and $36.9 billion over the next ten years.
https://www.cbpp.org/archives/908mcaid.htm

107. **HMO, PPO:** The healthcare industry is stuffed to the gills with meaningless acronyms and complicated jargon that convolute what should be a straightforward industry. This idea is especially prominent when discussing the different types of health insurance plans (HMO vs PPO).
https://theolsongroup.com/hmo-vs-ppo/

108. **2020 Medicare Advantage And Part D Flexibility Final Rule (CMS-4185-F):** On April 5, 2019, the Centers for Medicare & Medicaid Services (CMS) issued a final rule that updates the Medicare Advantage (MA or Part C) and Medicare Prescription Drug Benefit (Part D) programs by promoting innovative plan designs, improved quality, and choices for patients.
https://www.cms.gov/newsroom/fact-sheets/contract-year-2020-medicare-advantage-and-part-d-flexibility-final-rule-cms-4185-f

109. **Medicare Depletion In 2029:** Page 7 (13 of 263) paragraph 3, Short-Range Results: The estimated depletion date for the Federal Hospital Insurance trust fund is 2029, one year later than in last year's report. As in past years, the Trustees have determined that the fund is not adequately financed over the next 10 years.
https://www.cms.gov/Research-Statistics-Data-and-Systems/Statistics-Trends-and-Reports/ReportsTrustFunds/Downloads/TR2017.pdf

110. **Medigap:** A Medicare Supplement Insurance (Medigap) policy helps pay some of the health care costs that Original Medicare doesn't cover, like:

   ■ Copayments

   ■ Coinsurance

   ■ Deductibles

   Medigap policies are sold by private companies. Some Medigap policies also cover services that Original Medicare doesn't cover, like medical care when you travel outside the U.S. If you have Original Medicare and you buy a Medigap policy, here's what happens:

   ■ Medicare will pay its share of the Medicare-approved amount for covered health care costs.

   ■ Then, your Medigap policy pays its share.

   https://www.medicare.gov/supplements-other-insurance/whats-medicare-supplement-insurance-medigap

111. **S&P Mutual Funds:** Picking a fund that tracks the S&P 500 Index may seem like a simple task. After all, an index fund is designed to mirror an index's holdings, so issues such as a manager's quality or investment style don't come into play. But it's actually harder than you might expect. There are more than 50 S&P 500 Index funds to choose from.
https://www.consumerreports.org/personal-investing/how-to-choose-an-index-fund/

112. **The Personal Finances Of Professional American Athletes:** Is a subject of widespread discussion due to the often high salaries of such athletes and the high rates of personal bankruptcy and other financial distress. As of 1911 the average salary for the about 500 players in Major League Baseball was slightly more than $2,000 a season ($53,800 today). The star hitter Ty Cobb received $9,000 a season ($242,000 today), and sold automobiles in the off season. While Cobb encouraged young men to play professionally, top pitcher Christy Mathewson—who had made more money as a player than Cobb—warned, "Keep out of baseball unless you are sure of being a star." He stated that the average player did not make enough over a ten-year career to justify devoting those years to the sport.
https://en.wikipedia.org/wiki/Personal_finances_of_professional_American_athletes

113. **The National Whistleblower Center (NWC):** A non-profit, tax-exempt, non-partisan organization is the leading whistleblower legal advocacy organization with an almost 30-year history of protecting the right of individuals to report wrongdoing without fear of retaliation.
https://www.whistleblowers.org/

114. **Latin Definition:** Fido, fidere, fisus Definitions: trust (in), have confidence (in) (w/DAT or ABL).
https://latindictionary.net/definition/20608/fido-fidere-fisus

115. **SEC (Securities And Exchange Commission):** Investment advisor firms registered with the SEC may be required to provide to state securities authorities a copy of their Form ADV and any accompanying amendments filed with the SEC. These filings are called "notice filings."
https://secsearch.sec.gov/search?utf8=%3F&affiliate=secsearch&query=fiduciary

116. **The Securities And Exchange Commission (SEC):** Regulates investment advisors, primarily under the Investment Advisors Act of 1940 (the "Advisors Act"), and the rules adopted under that statute (the "rules"). One of the central elements of the regulatory program is the requirement that a person or firm meeting the definition of "investment advisor" under the Advisors Act register with the Commission, unless exempt or prohibited from registration.
https://www.sec.gov/divisions/investment/iaregulation/memoia.htm

117. **The Department Of Labor:** Administers federal labor laws to guarantee workers' rights to fair, safe, and healthy working conditions, including minimum hourly wage and overtime pay, protection against employment discrimination, and unemployment insurance.
https://www.usa.gov/federal-agencies/u-s-department-of-labor

118. **Certified Financial Planner:** The mission of Certified Financial Planner Board of Standards, Inc. is to benefit the public by granting the CFP® certification and upholding it as the recognized standard of excellence for competent and ethical personal financial planning.
https://www.cfp.net/

119. **Why Is Financial Planning Important? Consider The Following:**

      ■ 60 percent of U.S. adults lack a budget. This number has grown by more than 8 percent just since 2011.

      ■ Less than half of Americans have a savings plan with associated goals.

      ■ 34 percent of U.S. adults have zero non-retirement savings.

      ■ 29 percent of adults save none of their annual income for retirement.

      ■ 33 percent of U.S. households carry credit card debt from month to month.

      ■ 30 percent of workers say that they worry about their personal finances while at work.

      ■ 44 percent of adults age 50-64 do not have a will.

- Nearly 1 in 4 Americans admits to paying bills late.

- 30 percent of Americans are not at all confident about their retirement savings.

- 37 percent of workers expect to retire after age 65.

After reading the above statistics, the need for financial planning becomes clear. Seeking the counsel of an independent, qualified financial planner who has the education, experience, knowledge and character to guide your personal financial needs can help you plan for both short and long-term goals.
https://www.napfa.org/financial-planning

120. **CEFEX:** Certified firms adhere to a standard representing the best practices in their industry. The standards include specific criteria which have been substantiated by regulation or written in consultation with leading firms.
https://www.cefex.org/

121. **Psalm 23:** The theme of God as a shepherd was common in ancient Israel and Mesopotamia. For example, King Hammurabi, in the conclusion to his famous legal code, wrote: "I am the shepherd who brings well-being and abundant prosperity; my rule is just . . . so that the strong might not oppress the weak, and that even the orphan and the widow might be treated with justice." This imagery and language was well known to the community that created the Psalm, and was easily imported into its worship.
https://en.wikipedia.org/wiki/Psalm_23

122. **Assets Under Management (AUM):** Is very popular within the financial industry as a measure of size and success of an investment management firm, compared with its history of assets under management in previous periods, and compared with the firm's competitors. Methods of calculating AUM vary between firms. Investment management companies generally charge their clients fees as a proportion of assets under management, so assets under management, combined with the firm's average fee rate, are the key factors indicating an investment management company's top line revenue. The fee structure depends on the contract between each client and the firm or fund.
https://en.wikipedia.org/wiki/Assets_under_management

123. **Definition Of Caveat Emptor:** A principle in commerce: without a warranty the buyer takes the risk. Caveat emptor is a reasonable approach for many consumer products.
https://www.merriam-webster.com/dictionary/caveat%20emptor

124. **In The United States, The Financial Industry Regulatory Authority, Inc. (FINRA):** Is a private corporation that acts as a self-regulatory organization (SRO). FINRA is the successor to the National Association of Securities Dealers, Inc. (NASD) and the member regulation, enforcement, and arbitration operations of the New York Stock Exchange. It is a non-governmental organization that regulates member brokerage firms and exchange markets. The government agency which acts as the ultimate regulator of the securities industry, including FINRA, is the Securities and Exchange Commission.
https://en.wikipedia.org/wiki/Financial_Industry_Regulatory_Authority

125. **SRO:** A professional organization, unaffiliated with a government, has certain, limited regulatory authority over members. An example is the American Dental Association, which has the ability to set standards and enforce discipline over dentists in the United States. In trading, most exchanges are self-regulatory organizations, as are trading-related professional organizations. SROs assist the SEC and government regulators in the maintenance of operating standards and the arbitration of disputes.
https://financialdictionary.thefreedictionary.com/Self-Regulating+Organization

126. **FINRA Rule 2111:** Suitability obligations are critical to ensuring investor protection and promoting fair dealings with customers and ethical sales practices. FINRA Rule 2111 governs general suitability obligations, while certain securities are covered under other rules that may contain additional requirements. FINRA Rule 2111 requires that a firm or associated person have a reasonable basis to believe a recommended transaction or investment strategy involving a security or securities is suitable for the customer. This is based on the information obtained through reasonable diligence of the firm or associated person to ascertain the customer's investment profile.
http://www.finra.org/industry/suitability

127. **Bitcoin:** Is a cryptocurrency, a form of electronic cash. It is a decentralized digital currency without a central bank or single administrator that can be sent from user-to-user on the peer-to-peer bitcoin network without the need for intermediaries. Transactions are verified by network nodes through cryptography and recorded in a public distributed ledger called a blockchain. Bitcoin was invented by an unknown person or group of people using the name Satoshi Nakamoto and released as open-source software in 2009. Bitcoins are created as a reward for a process known as mining.
https://en.wikipedia.org/wiki/Bitcoin

128. **Silk Road:** Was an online black market and the first modern dark-net market, best known as a platform for selling illegal drugs. As part of the dark web, it was operated as a Tor hidden service, such that online users were able to browse it anonymously and securely without potential traffic monitoring.
https://en.wikipedia.org/wiki/Silk_Road_(marketplace)

129. **FBI:** Who owns the single largest Bitcoin wallet on the internet? The U.S. government. In September, 2013 the FBI shut down the Silk Road online drug marketplace, and it started seizing bitcoins belonging to the Dread Pirate Roberts—the operator of the illicit online marketplace, who they say is an American man named Ross Ulbricht.
https://www.wired.com/2013/12/fbi-wallet/

130. **Satoshi Nakamoto:** Is the name used by the unknown person or group of people who developed bitcoin, authored the bitcoin white paper, and created and deployed bitcoin's original reference implementation. As part of the implementation, they also devised the first blockchain database. In the process, they were the first to solve the double-spending problem for digital currency using a peer-to-peer network. They were active in the development of bitcoin up until December 2010.
https://en.wikipedia.org/wiki/Satoshi_Nakamoto

131. **A Negative Correlation:** Is a relationship between two variables such that as the value of one variable increases, the other decreases.

     Examples of negatively correlated variables include:

     ■ Yellow cars and accident rates.

     ■ Commodity supply and demand.

     ■ Pages printed and printer ink supply.

     ■ Education and religiosity.

     ■ Conservativism and cognitive ability.

     https://whatis.techtarget.com/definition/negative-correlation

132. **Financial Technology:** Nowadays better known under the term 'fintech'. Describes a business that aims at providing financial services by making use of software and modern technology. Today, fintech companies directly compete with banks in most areas of the financial sector to sell financial services and solutions to customers. Mostly due to regulatory reasons and their internal structures, banks still struggle to keep up with fintech startups in terms of innovation speed. Fintechs have realized early that financial services of all kinds—including money transfer, lending, investing, payments,—need to seamlessly integrate in the lives of the tech-savvy and sophisticated customers of today to stay relevant in a world where business and private life become increasingly digitalized.
     https://www.fintechweekly.com/fintech-definition

133. **The Price/Earnings Ratio:** (Often shortened to the P/E ratio or the PER) Is the ratio of a company's stock price to the company's earnings per share. The ratio is used in valuing companies.
     https://en.wikipedia.org/wiki/Price%E2%80%93earnings_ratio

134. **Dynamical Bias In The Coin Toss:** (Persi Diaconis, Susan Holmes, Richard Montgomery) We analyze the natural process of flipping a coin which is caught in the hand. We show that vigorously flipped coins tend to come up the same way they started. The limiting chance of coming up this way depends on a single parameter, the angle between the normal to the coin and the angular momentum vector. Measurements of this parameter based on high-speed photography are reported.
     https://statweb.stanford.edu/~cgates/PERSI/papers/dyn_coin_07.pdf

135. **Incubator:** Business Definition Facility established to nurture young (startup) firms during their early months or years. It usually provides affordable space, shared offices and services, hand-on management training, marketing support and, often, access to some form of financing.
     http://www.businessdictionary.com/definition/business-incubator.html

136. **S&P 500 Inverse ETF, "Short ETF":** Is an exchange-traded fund designed to return the exact opposite performance of a certain index or benchmark. Companies such as ProShares and Direxion offer a variety of inverse

ETFs. Here are some things to consider before investing in one.
https://www.fool.com/knowledge-center/heres-how-inverse-etfs-work.aspx

137. **The Bubble Popping In 2000:** Was a lot like an avalanche. It wasn't clear exactly which snowflake was the one that put it over the tipping point, but once confidence was lost, it went very quickly.
https://www.quora.com/What-was-the-trigger-for-the-tech-bubble-to-burst-in-2000

138. **Disposition Effect:** The disposition effect is an anomaly discovered in behavioral finance. It relates to the tendency of investors to sell assets that have increased in value, while keeping assets that have dropped in value. Hersh Shefrin and Meir Statman identified and named the effect in their 1985 paper, which found that people dislike losing significantly more than they enjoy winning. The disposition effect has been described as "one of the most robust facts about the trading of individual investors" because investors will hold stocks that have lost value yet sell stocks that have gained value. In 1979, Daniel Kahneman and Amos Tversky traced the cause of the disposition effect to the so-called "prospect theory." The prospect theory proposes that when an individual is presented with two equal choices, one having possible gains and the other with possible losses, the individual is more likely to opt for the former choice even though both would yield the same economic result. The disposition effect can be minimized by a mental approach called "hedonic framing."
https://en.wikipedia.org/wiki/Disposition_effect

139. **Risk Capacity:** Risk capacity, unlike tolerance, is the amount of risk that the investor "must" take in order to reach financial goals. The rate of return necessary to reach these goals can be estimated by examining time frames and income requirements. Then, the rate of return information can be used to help the investor decide upon the types of investments to engage in and the level of risk to take on.
https://www.investopedia.com/ask/answers/08/difference-between-risk-tolerance-and-risk-capacity.asp

140. **Natixis Global Asset Management Survey, 2018:** Financial Advice in Volatile Markets Advisor success hinges on fusing empirical data with personal empathy: **Many individual investors aren't thinking about risk at all.** That may be because they don't really understand it. More than 8 in 10 say that investors are too focused on short-term performance, and 79% said clients don't recognize risk until it's been realized in their investments.
https://www.im.natixis.com/us/research/financial-professional-survey-2018

141. **CNBC November 2015 Survey:** About 20 percent of registered investment advisor representatives have some sort of disclosure document on file, and about 2 percent have reported criminal charges like a felony conviction or investment-related misdemeanor, according to a Big Crunch analysis of the data. To be fair, financial advisors are also a rather law-abiding group. Even if every financial

advisor charged with a felony was convicted, that would still only be 1 percent of the group. Compare that to the average adult American—almost 9 percent of them have a felony conviction.
https://www.cnbc.com/2015/11/09/is-your-financial-advisor-a-criminal-stats-say.html

142. **The Madoff Investment Scandal:** Was a major case of stock and securities fraud discovered in late 2008. In December of that year, Bernard Madoff, the former NASDAQ Chairman and founder of the Wall Street firm Bernard L. Madoff Investment Securities LLC, admitted that the wealth management arm of his business was an elaborate Ponzi scheme.
https://en.wikipedia.org/wiki/Madoff_investment_scandal

143. **The Bayou Hedge Fund Group:** Was a group of companies and hedge funds founded by Samuel Israel III in 1996. Approximately $450m was raised by the group from investors. Its investors were defrauded from the start with funds being misappropriated for personal use. After poor returns in 1998, the investors were lied to about the fund's returns and a fake accounting firm was set up to provide misleading audited results. In 2005, Samuel Israel III and CFO Daniel Marino pleaded guilty to multiple charges including conspiracy and fraud. Marino was convicted of fraud and sentenced to 20 years in prison. Israel was sentenced to 20 years prison and ordered to forfeit $300 million.
https://en.wikipedia.org/wiki/Bayou_Hedge_Fund_Group

144. *America's Most Wanted:* Is an American television program that was produced by 20th Television.
https://en.wikipedia.org/wiki/America%27s_Most_Wanted

145. **Bank-Robbing Broker, Stephen Trantel:** A successful oil commodities futures trader on the New York Mercantile Exchange. **The Broker** A New York commodities broker goes on a losing streak. Stephen Trantel is out of a job and hundreds of thousands of dollars in debt. Broke and desperate, he makes an unthinkable decision. The broker turns to bank robbery.
https://www.cnbc.com/id/100000046

146. **NYMEX Holdings, Inc.:** The former parent company of the New York Mercantile Exchange and COMEX, became listed on the New York Stock Exchange on November 17, 2006, under the ticker symbol NMX. On March 17, 2008, Chicago based CME Group signed a definitive agreement to acquire NYMEX Holdings, Inc. for $11.2 billion in cash and stock and the takeover was completed in August 2008.
https://en.wikipedia.org/wiki/New_York_Mercantile_Exchange

147. **Marcus Schrenker (Born 1971):** Is a former financial advisor from Indiana. He is best known for attempting to fake his own death due to personal, financial, and legal trouble and for the multi-state, three-day manhunt that followed in January 2009.
https://en.wikipedia.org/wiki/Marcus_Schrenker

148. **Ponzi Scheme:** Is an investment fraud that pays existing investors with funds collected from new investors. Ponzi scheme organizers often promise to invest your money and generate high returns with little or no risk. But in many Ponzi schemes, the fraudsters do not invest the money. Instead, they use it to pay those who invested earlier and may keep some for themselves.
https://en.wikipedia.org/wiki/Marcus_Schrenker

149. **FAANG:** Is an acronym for the market's five most popular and best-performing tech stocks, namely Facebook, Apple, Amazon, Netflix and Alphabet's Google. FAANG was born out of the original acronym, FANG, which did not have Apple included when CNBC's Jim Cramer coined the term.
https://www.investopedia.com/terms/f/faang-stocks.asp

150. **Lynda Gratton:** The 100-Year Life: Living and Working in an Age of Longevity.
http://www.100yearlife.com/

151. **Demography:** (From prefix demo- from Ancient Greek δῆμος, *dēmos* meaning "the people," and -*graphy* from γράφω, *graphō*, implies "writing, description or measurement" is the statistical study of populations, especially human beings. As a very general science, it can analyze any kind of dynamic living population, i.e., one that changes over time or space.
https://en.wikipedia.org/wiki/Demography

152. **International Association For Financial Counseling:** Saturday, December 12, 1969, was a day that will live forever in the financial planning movement. On that day, the first discussions about forming a professional organization for those providing financial services took place. That first organization, the International Association for Financial Counseling, provided the foundation for other organizations that followed.
https://www.onefpa.org/business-success/newtotheprofession/Pages/History-of-the-Profession.aspx

153. **Retirement Options:** Opinion, "How to plan for retirement when you don't want to retire." More frequently, I am meeting with new clients that have no interest in retiring at all. These are people who genuinely enjoy their careers, make a strong wage and for some, their career may even be part of their identity. This brings up some crucial questions: If you don't plan to retire, how differently would you save? How differently would you spend? How differently would you invest? Even those who find themselves in this enviable position still need to have a retirement game plan.
https://www.marketwatch.com/story/how-to-plan-for-retirement-when-you-dont-have-any-plan-to-retire-2019-06-12

154. **Henry Ford (July 30, 1863–April 7, 1947):** Was an American captain of industry and a business magnate, the founder of the Ford Motor Company, and the sponsor of the development of the assembly line technique of mass production. Although Ford did not invent the automobile or the assembly line, he developed and manufactured the first automobile that many middle-class Americans could afford.
https://en.wikipedia.org/wiki/Henry_Ford

155. **Flandria 10 Speed Bicycle:** Is from Belgium and one of the most successful cycling teams worldwide! With legendary status and its instantly recognizable red frames with white badge. Flandria bicycles were ridden by great cycling champions like Freddy Maertens, Herman Van Springel, Jan Janssen, Erik De Vlaeminck and so many more! Our vintage Flandria road racer from the 1970s is fully equipped with the first generation Shimano Dura Ace group from that time. It is an ideal bicycle for a vintage cycling race like L'Eroica or La Mitica. https://www.steel-vintage.com/flandria-legendary-vintage-road-bike-1970s-detail/ Also see: https://flandriabikes.com/

156. **Living Wills:** The first document you need to create to ensure that your medical wishes are honored is usually called a living will. This written document sets out how you should be cared for in an emergency or if you are otherwise incapacitated. Your living will sets forth your wishes on topics such as resuscitation, desired quality of life and end of life treatments including treatments you don't want to receive. This document is primarily between you and your doctor, and it advises them how to approach your treatment. Try to be as specific as possible in this document, realizing that you can't account for every possibility, which is where the durable power of attorney for health care comes in. https://estate.findlaw.com/living-will/the-definition-of-power-of-attorney-living-will-and-advance.html

157. **Powers Of Attorney:** Do not survive death. After death, the executor of the estate handles all financial and legal matters, according to the provisions of the will. An individual can designate power of attorney to his attorney, family member or friend and also name that same person as executor of the estate. When an individual assigns power of attorney to an agent, that agent represents him in life. When the individual names an executor of his estate in his will, that agent represents him in death. A durable power of attorney with broad authority and specific prohibitions helps protect the individual's estate during his lifetime. https://info.legalzoom.com/still-power-attorney-someone-dies-24156.html

158. **Wills And Living Trusts:** Age and assets are the greatest barriers. As one might expect, older Americans are the most likely demographic to have an estate plan in place. According to the survey, 81 percent of those aged 72 or older have a will or living trust. However, that percentage declines significantly with younger people. A staggering 78 percent of millennials (ages 18-36) do not have a will. Even more surprising is that 64 percent of Generation X (ages 37 to 52) doesn't have a will, and nearly half of respondents in the 53 to 71-year-old age group (40 percent) said they don't have one. https://www.caring.com/caregivers/estate-planning/wills-survey/2017-survey/

159. **Required Minimum Distributions:** You cannot keep retirement funds in your account indefinitely. You generally have to start taking withdrawals from your IRA, SIMPLE IRA, SEP IRA, or retirement plan account when you reach age 72. Roth IRAs do not require withdrawals until after the death of the owner. Your required minimum distribution is the minimum amount you must withdraw from your account each year. You can withdraw more than

the minimum required amount. Your withdrawals will be included in your taxable income except for any part that was taxed before (your basis) or that can be received tax-free (such as qualified distributions from designated Roth accounts).
https://www.irs.gov/retirement-plans/plan-participant-employee/retirement-topics-required-minimum-distributions-rmds

160. **Veterans Benefits, Official Explains Federal Tax Changes For Military And Spouses:** A number of pieces of legislation affect military taxpayers, he said: The Tax Cuts and Jobs Act, the Veterans Benefits and Transition Act and the Combat-Injured Veterans Tax Fairness Act are just a few.
https://www.defense.gov/Newsroom/News/Article/Article/1740689/official-explains-federal-tax-changes-for-military-spouses/

161. **Medicaid:** In the United States is a federal and state program that helps with medical costs for some people with limited income and resources. Medicaid also offers benefits not normally covered by Medicare, including nursing home care and personal care services. The Health Insurance Association of America describes Medicaid as "a government insurance program for persons of all ages whose income and resources are insufficient to pay for health care."
https://en.wikipedia.org/wiki/Medicaid

162. **Agent Orange:** Is a herbicide and defoliant chemical, one of the "tactical use" Rainbow Herbicides. It is widely known for its use by the U.S. military as part of its herbicidal warfare program, Operation Ranch Hand, during the Vietnam War from 1961 to 1971. It is a mixture of equal parts of two herbicides, 2,4,5-T and 2,4-D. In addition to its damaging environmental effects, traces of dioxin (mainly TCDD, the most toxic of its type) found in the mixture have caused major health problems for many individuals who were exposed.
https://en.wikipedia.org/wiki/Agent_Orange

163. **New Jersey Estate Inheritance Tax:** On October 14, 2016, Governor Christie signed into law a transportation funding bill that included the repeal of the New Jersey Estate Tax.

   ■ The New Jersey Estate Tax repeal was to be effective as of January 1, 2018. The current $675,000 exemption was scheduled to increase to a $2 million exemption on January 1, 2017. The Estate Tax was to be eliminated as of January 1, 2018. (The New Jersey Inheritance Tax is still in effect. This is a tax imposed on transfers to beneficiaries who are not spouses, parents, children or grandchildren [i.e., nieces, nephews, siblings, friends, etc.] New Jersey Inheritance Tax rates start at 11 percent and go as high as 16 percent.)

   ■ As part of the new law, there is a tax break for retirees. There will be an increase in the New Jersey gross income tax exclusion on pension or retirement income over four years (in 2020) to $100,000 for couples, $75,000 for individuals, and $50,000 for married taxpayers who file separately.

- On January 1, 2017, the sales tax was to be reduced from 7 percent to 6.875 percent and will be further reduced to 6.625 percent on January 1, 2018.

- Gas tax will increase by 23 cents a gallon.

https://www.tiaa.org/public/offer/services/individual . . . /repeal-of-the-nj -estate-tax

CHARTS

Chart A – Source - Chipotle Mexican Grill, Inc.: Founder Steve Ells attended the Culinary Institute of America in Hyde Park, New York. Afterward, he became a line cook for Jeremiah Tower at Stars in San Francisco. There, Ells observed the popularity of the taquerías and San Francisco burritos in the Mission District. In 1993, Ells took what he learned in San Francisco and opened the first Chipotle Mexican Grill in Denver, Colorado, in a former Dolly Madison Ice Cream store at 1644 East Evans Avenue, near the University of Denver campus, using an $85,000 loan from his father. Ells and his father calculated that the store would need to sell 107 burritos per day to be profitable. After one month, the original restaurant was selling over 1,000 burritos a day.
https://en.wikipedia.org/wiki/Chipotle_Mexican_Grill
https://finance.yahoo.com/quote/CMG/history?period1=1494561600&period2=1503633600&interval=1d&filter=history&frequency=1d

Chart B – Source – Bond Prices: Bond prices and yields move in opposite directions, which you may find confusing if you're new to bond investing. Bond prices and yields act like a seesaw: when bond yields go up, prices go down, and when bond yields go down, prices go up. In other words, an upward change in the 10-year Treasury bond's yield from 2.2 percent to 2.6 percent is a sign of negative market conditions, because the bond's interest rate moves up when the market trends down. Conversely, a downward move in the bond's interest rate from 2.6 percent down to 2.2 percent actually indicates positive market performance. You may ask why the relationship works this way, and there's a simple answer: There is no free lunch in investing.
https://www.thebalance.com/why-do-bond-prices-and-yields-move-in-opposite-directions-417082

Chart C – Source – One Toss: If you toss a coin one time, you'll either get "heads" or "tails." It's not possible to reach your $1,000 target. Instead, you're subjecting your investments to extreme outcomes: You'll either double the amount you were aiming for—or lose it all.

Chart D – Source – Two Tosses: By flipping a coin two times, you have two chances to be right. While no single coin flip can earn $1,000, by using two, your average winnings are $1,000, and that will happen half the time. More importantly, the chances for the extreme outcomes of $0 and $2,000 have been cut in half from 50 percent to 25 percent. By adding an additional toss, you've sharply reduced the chances of an extreme outcome—and greatly increased the chances for meeting your goal.

Chart E – Source – Eight Tosses: Flipping a coin eight times increases the benefits further. No single toss could meet your goal, but by giving yourself eight chances, you have a 64 percent chance for winning at least $1,000 and an 86 percent chance for winning at least $750. The chances for extreme outcomes have nearly been eliminated.

Chart F – Source – Probability: Is a measure quantifying the likelihood that events will occur. See glossary of probability and statistics. Probability is expressed as a number between 0 and 1, where, 0 indicates impossibility and 1 indicates certainty. The higher the probability of an event, the more likely it is that the event will occur. A simple example is the tossing of a fair (unbiased) coin. Since the coin is fair, the two outcomes ("heads" and "tails") are both equally probable; the probability of "heads" equals the probability of "tails"; and since no other outcomes are possible, the probability of either "heads" or "tails" is 1/2 (which could also be written as 0.5 or 50%).
https://en.wikipedia.org/wiki/Probability

Chart G – Source – Viavi Solutions: Formerly part of JDS Uniphase (JDSU), is a San Jose, California-based network test, measurement and assurance technology company. The company manufactures testing and monitoring equipment for networks. It also develops optical technology used for a range of applications including material quality control, currency anti-counterfeiting and 3D motion sensing, including Microsoft's Kinect video game controller. The company was spun off from JDSU when the company divided itself up in August 2015.
https://en.wikipedia.org/wiki/Viavi_Solutions

Chart H – Source – S&P 500 January To October 2019: Blackstone's Byron Wien. Beyond 2019, forget about 15% yearly gains on S&P 500 for a while. The S&P 500 may be on a roll this year, but don't expect it to make double-digit percentage gains in 2020 and beyond, longtime market strategist Byron Wien told CNBC on Thursday. However, Wien added on "Squawk on the Street" that investors should not expect that type of annual gain past the end of the year.
https://www.cnbc.com/2019/09/19/blackstone-byron-wien-15-percent-annual-gains-on-s-and-p-500-over-for-a-while.html

Chart I – Source – S&P 500 January 2018 To October 2019: Is this record-setting stock market setting up investors for a fall? By Ray Martin April 30, 2019. With the stock market now up more than 25 percent since its late 2018 low point, many investors are wondering what's next. Is this as good as it will get, and will the coming move be downward? Some even worry that a bear market—a 20 percent drop from the recent highs, which the S&P 500 came close to in December—will shortly follow, taking down 401(k) accounts and hard-earned savings. There's good reason to worry, too. While the U.S. has remained a global bright spot (posting a 3.2 percent annualized growth rate in the last quarter), economies in other countries remain sluggish or are slowing. Diminishing global growth could drag down the U.S. also. Plus, although the Federal Reserve is now signaling a halt in its rate hiking, it has raised interest rates nine times since December 2015. At some point, those higher rates become the gravitational force that pulls down stock prices.
https://www.cbsnews.com/news/is-record-setting-stock-market-setting-up-investors-for-a-fall/

Chart J – Source – S&P 500 January 2000 To October 2019: The recent S&P rebound looks a lot like 2000 and 2007 — but that's not a bad thing, says JP Morgan Published Sun, Feb 3 2019. Article by Nia Warfield. The markets have surged into the new year with the Index posting its best January in more than three decades. Investor optimism of late has been fueled by a stronger-than-expected earnings season, and a Federal Reserve that is expected to pull back on plans to hike interest rates. The S&P 500 is now up more than 15 percent from its December 24 closing low. Jason Hunter, technical strategist at JPMorgan, told CNBC recently that new highs could be on the way. Given the recent rebound, Hunter noted that the S&P 500 is "right back into the underside of what potentially is viewed as a distribution pattern," which is giving him flashbacks to 2000 and 2007.
https://www.cnbc.com/2019/02/03/the-recent-sp-rebound-looks-a-lot-like-2000-and-2007.html

Chart K – Source – Computer-Simulated Stock – 20 Percent Volatility: The chart shows hundreds of computer-generated stocks trading at 20 percent volatility for one year. All stocks begin with a $100 price, but after a full year of trading, very different outcomes can result. At the end of the year, the average price will be $100—the same as the starting price—but you could see some as low as $40 and others as high as $160. Stock price randomness can create vastly different outcomes.

Chart L – Source – CBOE Volatility Index (VIX): Introduced in 2004 on Cboe Futures Exchange (CFE), VIX futures provide market participants with the ability to trade a liquid volatility product based on the VIX Index methodology. VIX futures reflect the market's estimate of the value of the VIX Index on various expiration dates in the future. Monthly and weekly expirations are available and trade nearly 24 hours a day, five days a week. VIX futures provide market participants with a variety of opportunities to implement their view using volatility trading strategies, including risk management, alpha generation and portfolio diversification. http://www.cboe.com/vix The CBOE Volatility Index, known by its ticker symbol VIX, is a popular measure of the stock market's expectation of volatility implied by S&P 500 index options. It is calculated and disseminated on a real-time basis by the Chicago Board Options Exchange (CBOE), and is commonly referred to as the fear index or the "fear gauge." As stock prices fall, the VIX index tends to spike.
https://en.wikipedia.org/wiki/VIX

Chart M – Source – S&P 500 Index 1927 To 2019: Comparison to S&P 500 Index. The average inflation rate of 2.97% has a compounding effect between 1927 and 2019. As noted above, this yearly inflation rate compounds to produce an overall price difference of 1,375.63% over 92 years. To help put this inflation into perspective, if we had invested $980,000 in the S&P 500 index in 1927, our investment would be nominally worth approximately $6,723,008,507.61 in 2019. This is a return on investment of 685,921.28%, with an absolute return of $6,722,028,507.61. These numbers are not inflation adjusted, so they are considered nominal. In order to evaluate the real return on our investment, we must calculate the return with inflation taken into account. The compounding effect of inflation would account for 93.22% of returns ($6,266,491,229.34) during this period. This means the inflation-adjusted real return of our $980,000 investment is $455,537,278.27.
https://www.officialdata.org/us/inflation/1927?amount=980000

Chart N – Source – Compounding: What Is Compound Interest? It's simply the ability to earn "interest on interest." If you deposit $1,000 into a bank account that pays 10 percent, you'll earn $100 interest, for a total of $1,100. However, the following year, the bank pays interest on the full $1,100 balance. Not only did you earn 10 percent on your initial $1,000, but you also earned 10% on the $100 in interest. It doesn't sound like a big difference, but eventually, the interest you'd earn on interest becomes far greater than the interest you'd earn on the initial $1,000 deposit. That's the power of compounding.

Chart O – Source – Percent of Loss: If your investment increases from $100 to $150, it's a 50 percent increase. However, if it falls from $150 back to $100, it's a 33 percent decrease. Even though the increase and decreases were exactly $50, the percentages are different because you're comparing them to different starting points. The chart shows two investors, one who buys the S&P 500 with a .09 percent fee, and another who buys a fund with a 2 percent fee. The differences are small in the early years, but they compound over time. After 40 years, the first investor has nearly twice the amount of money. Mutual fund fees add up.

Chart P – Source – S&P 500 SPDR (SPY): The S&P 500® Index is composed of five hundred (500) selected stocks, all of which are listed on national stock exchanges and spans over approximately 24 separate industry group.

- The SPDR® S&P 500® ETF Trust seeks to provide investment results that, before expenses, correspond generally to the price and yield performance of the S&P 500® Index

- The S&P 500 Index is a diversified large cap U.S. index that holds companies across all eleven GICS sectors

- Launched in January 1993, SPY was the very first exchange traded fund listed in the United States

https://us.spdrs.com/en/etf/spdr-sp-500-etf-trust-SPY?mrkgcl=1238& mrkgadid=3334218697&WT.mc_id=ps_spy_us_ssga_text_apr19&utm _source=google&utm_edium=cpc&adpos=1t2&creative=345660186219 &device=c&matchtype=e&network=g&gclid=EAIaIQobChMIw6X CoKvR5QIVmoVaBR0uWQ1VEAAYAiAAEgLmfvD_BwE

Chart Q – Source – Mobileye: Is a global leader in the development of computer vision and machine learning, localization and mapping, and driving policy for advanced driver assistance systems (ADAS), autonomous driving, and big data insights to empower smarter cities. Mobileye was launched in 1999 with the belief that vision-safety technology will make our roads safer, reduce traffic congestion and save lives. With a cutting edge team of more than 1,700 employees, Mobileye has developed a range of software products that is deployed on a proprietary family of computer chips named EyeQ®.
https://www.crunchbase.com/organization/mobileye-vision-technologies

Chart R – Source – Computer Simulation: The four charts above were all created by flipping coins to determine whether the price would rise or fall, and by rolling dice to determine by how much. Complete randomness can produce charts indistinguishable from actual stock price charts. When looking at stock charts, avoid the temptation of thinking the patterns are predictable – even though they may appear to tell a viable story. It could just as easily be noise. "Best Stock Market Simulators Quick Look, Best Stock Market Simulators To Use Right Now".

- Thinkorswim by TD Ameritrade
- Bear Bull Traders Simulator
- TradeStation
- Warrior Trading
- NinjaTrader Free Trading Simulator
- MarketWatch
- Stock Trainer
- Wall Street Survivor

https://www.benzinga.com/money/best-stock-market-simulator/

Monte Carlo methods, or Monte Carlo experiments, are a broad class of computational algorithms that rely on repeated random sampling to obtain numerical results. The underlying concept is to use randomness to solve problems that might be deterministic in principle. They are often used in physical and mathematical problems and are most useful when it is difficult or impossible to use other approaches. Monte Carlo methods are mainly used in three problem classes: optimization, numerical integration, and generating draws from a probability distribution.
https://en.wikipedia.org/wiki/Monte_Carlo_method

Chart S – Source – Mortgage Amount: Chart S – Source – Mortgage Amount: Paying additional money each month on your mortgage greatly reduces the time to pay off the home – and the interest you'd owe. With a 30-year mortgage, if you send a one-time additional $300 payment for your first month, it reduces that amount from the loan for the next 30 years. Even though $300 doesn't sound like much, you're eliminating the compounding effect. By sending an extra $300 each month, you're compounding the benefits, and that's why it greatly reduces the required time to pay off the loan.
https://www.interest.com/mortgage/

Chart T – Source – S&P 500 Index 1996 To 2014: Is a stock market index that measures the stock performance of 500 large companies listed on stock exchanges in the United States. It is one of the most commonly followed equity indices, and many consider it to be one of the best representations of the U.S. stock market. The average annual total return of the index, including dividends, since inception in 1926 has been 9.8%; however, there were several years where the index declined over 30%. The index has posted annual increases 70% of the time. For a list of the components of the index, see List of S&P 500 companies. The components that have increased their dividends in 25 consecutive years are known as the S&P 500 Dividend Aristocrats. The S&P 500 is a capitalization-weighted index and the performance of the 10 largest companies in the index account for 21.8% of the performance of the index.
https://en.wikipedia.org/wiki/S%26P_500_

TABLES

Table A – Source: In 2018 and 2019 the capital gains tax rates are either, 0%, 15% or 20% for most assets held for more than a year. Capital gains tax rates on most assets held for less than a year correspond to ordinary income tax brackets (10%, 12%, 22%, 24%, 32%, 35% or 37%). Capital gains are the profits from the sale of an asset — shares of stock, a piece of land, a business — and generally are considered taxable income. A lot depends on how long you held the asset before selling. https://www.nerdwallet.com/blog/taxes/capital-gains-tax-rates/

Table B – Source: Viavi Solutions (stylized VIAVI Solutions), formerly part of JDS Uniphase (JDSU), is a San Jose, California-based network test, measurement and assurance technology company. The company manufactures testing and monitoring equipment for networks. It also develops optical technology used for a range of applications including material quality control, currency anti-counterfeiting and 3D motion sensing, including Microsoft's Kinect video game controller. The company was spun off from JDSU when the company divided itself up in August 2015. https://finance.yahoo.com/quote/VIAV/history?period1=852354000& period2=1167541200&interval=1mo&filter=history&frequency=1mo

Table C – Source: Compound Annual Growth Rate (Annualized Return): A problem with talking about average investment returns is that there is real ambiguity about what people mean by "average". For example, if you had an investment that went up 100% one year and then came down 50% the next, you certainly wouldn't say that you had an average return of 25% = (100% - 50%)/2, because your principal is back where it started: your real annualized gain is zero. In this example, the 25% is the simple average, or "arithmetic mean". The zero percent that you really got is the "geometric mean", also called the "annualized return", or the CAGR for Compound Annual Growth Rate. Volatile investments are frequently stated in terms of the simple average, rather than the CAGR that you actually get. (Bad news: the CAGR is smaller.) http://www.moneychimp.com/features/market_cagr.htm

Table D – Source: Compound Annual Growth Rate (Annualized Return): A problem with talking about average investment returns is that there is real ambiguity about what people mean by "average". For example, if you had an investment that went up 100% one year and then came down 50% the next, you certainly wouldn't say that you had an average return of 25% = (100% - 50%)/2, because your principal

is back where it started: your real annualized gain is zero. In this example, the 25% is the simple average, or "arithmetic mean". The zero percent that you really got is the "geometric mean", also called the "annualized return", or the CAGR for Compound Annual Growth Rate. Volatile investments are frequently stated in terms of the simple average, rather than the CAGR that you actually get. (Bad news: the CAGR is smaller.) This calculator lets you find the annualized growth rate of the S&P 500 over the date range you specify; you'll find that the CAGR is usually about a percent or two less than the simple average.
http://www.moneychimp.com/features/market_cagr.htm

Table E – Source: The Expansion of the U.S. Stock Market, 1885 – 1930 - Historical Facts and Theoretical Fashions:
https://www.jstor.org/stable/23700715?seq=1#page_scan_tab_contents

The Hard Lessons of Stock Market History:
http://www.summitgp.com/wp-content/uploads/2018/01/Caicedo.Hard-Lessons-of-Stock-Market-History.01.08.18.pdf

1928–1954 Stock Chart Pre-Through-Post Great Depression Era: You can see by looking at this 1929-1954 stock chart, that once the bottom was finally in place in late 1932, the market gradually rose over the next two decades. Notice that it took just about 25 years from the peak in the stock market in 1929 for it to reach this level again.
http://www.online-stock-trading-guide.com/1928-1954-stock-chart.html

Eleven Historic Bear Markets: By one common definition, a bear market occurs when stock prices fall for a sustained period, dropping at least 20 percent from their peak. The Great Recession was accompanied by a painful bear market that lasted nearly a year and a half. Here is a look at some notable bear markets of the past 80 years, with the crash of 1929 shown for comparison.
http://www.nbcnews.com/id/37740147/ns/business-stocks_and_economy/t/historic-bear-markets/#.XMsYWNh7lD0

Table F – Source: A dividend yield tells you how much income you receive in relation to the price of the stock. Buying stocks with a high dividend yield can provide a good source of income, but if you are not careful, it can also get you in trouble. Companies do not have to pay dividends. Trouble comes when a company lowers its dividend. The market will often anticipate this move, and the stock price will drop before the company announces its plans to lower the dividend.
https://www.thebalance.com/understanding-the-dividend-yield-on-a-stock-2388525

Hi-Crush Partners LP (HCLP): Ex-Dividend Date Scheduled for October 31, 2018.
https://www.nasdaq.com/article/hi-crush-partners-lp-hclp-ex-dividend-date-scheduled-for-october-31-2018-cm1045804

SandRidge Permian Trust (PER): Ex-Dividend Date Scheduled for November 8, 2018.
https://www.nasdaq.com/article/sandridge-permian-trust-per-ex-dividend-date-scheduled-for-november-08-2018-cm1051558

Mobile Telesystems (MBT): Ex-Dividend Date Scheduled for October 5, 2018.
https://marketchameleon.com/Overview/MBT/Dividends/

Pacific Coast Oil Trust (ROYT): Ex-Dividend Date Scheduled for December 7, 2018.
https://www.nasdaq.com/article/pacific-coast-oil-trust-royt-ex-dividend-date-scheduled-for-december-07-2018-cm1065207

Norbord, Inc. (OSB): Ex-Dividend Yield, History & Payout Ratio Ex-Dividend Date
Scheduled for November 1, 2018.
https://www.marketbeat.com/stocks/tse/osb/dividends

BP Prudhoe Bay Royalty Trust (BPT): Ex-Dividend Date Scheduled for October 15,
2018.
https://www.dividend.com/dividend-stocks/basic-materials/oil-and-gas-refining-and-marketing/bpt-bp-prudhoe-bay-royalty-trust/#dividend-yield-history

AT&T (T): Ex-Dividend Date Scheduled for December 14, 2018.
https://www.fool.com/investing/2018/12/14/atts-dividend-yield-inches-toward-7.aspx

ILLUSTRATIONS

Based in the city of Bath in the west of England, CartoonStock was founded in early 1997 as a stock house through which quality cartoonists could sell unpublished work or work in which they had retained the copyright. We sell to large and small publishers, advertising, design and PR agencies, and countless corporate purchasers and private individuals worldwide. As well as selling stock, we can also arrange the commissioning of artwork from almost all of our artists through our Hire an Artist service. Our close-knit team has a wealth of knowledge of the cartooning industry, and we can provide assistance with almost all cartoon sourcing issues.
https://www.cartoonstock.com/about.asp

Page 8—Mice building a huge trap.
Cartoonist: Kinsella, Paul
Search ID: pknn936
High-Res: 1659 x 1950 px

Page 42—Time and money on a seesaw are equals.
Cartoonist: Carter, Jon
Search ID: jcen1975
High-Res: 5643 x 1800 px

Page 109—"Just remember, if you give a hundred and ten per cent, I get twenty per cent of that."
Cartoonist: Eckstein, Bob
Search ID: CC141749
High-Res: 3088 x 2271 px

Page 123—"We have three confirmations, the crystal ball, the magic 8-ball and the coin flip, all say to buy."
Cartoonist: Carpenter, Dave
Search ID: dcrn1314
High-Res: 1920 x 1804 px

Page 145—Why we always fail.
Cartoonist: Fran
Search ID: forn5486
High-Res: 3304 x 2166 px

Page 158—"Bad news—that's just for the lawn."
Cartoonist: Mankoff, Bob
Search ID: CX300509
High-Res: 2509 x 1807 px

Pages 176—All-way stops.
Cartoonist: O'Brien, John
Search ID: CX304793
High-Res: 2431 x 1957 px

Page 204—"Something tells me we are NOT on the same page."
Cartoonist: Wildt, Chris
Search ID: cwln2152
High-Res: 1800 x 1887 px

INDEX